TELL THE BOSSES WE'RE COMING

TELL THE BOSSES WE'RE COMING

A New Action Plan for Workers
in the Twenty-first Century

SHAUN RICHMAN

MONTHLY REVIEW PRESS

New York

Library of Congress Cataloging-in-Publication data
available from the publisher.

ISBN 978-158367-8565 cloth

MONTHLY REVIEW PRESS, NEW YORK
www.monthlyreview.org

5 4 3 2 1

Contents

For my wife, Kate,
and my daughters, Audrey and Bernadette

Preface

YOU'RE READING THIS BOOK. I'm going to assume that, like me, you take it as an article of faith that we need to restore the power of unions and protect workers' rights. I'm not here to convince you that unions are good for our democracy and our economic well-being.

There are plenty of good books on why we need more—and more powerful—unions. If you haven't read them, I would recommend Jake Rosenfeld's *What Unions No Longer Do,* Michael D. Yates's *Why Unions Matter,* or Thomas Geoghegan's *Only One Thing Can Save Us.*

This book aims to get past abstraction. "What a union is" is a combination of legal and political structures that are not consistent across history, across industries, and across the globe. The details matter. Bringing unions back from the edge of institutional annihilation where they currently find themselves is no simple proposition. It is complicated by the law, but also by union structure and strategy, along with comfort with what is known and familiar. It is complicated by a sort of historical amnesia about how our country's system of labor relations developed. It is complicated by a whole zoo's worth of elephants in the room, sacred cows roaming free, and chickens coming home to roost.

Specifically, we will first break down "what a union is" into its constituent parts. Exclusive representation, for instance, was not written into our nation's main labor law, the National Labor Relations Act (NLRA), when it was passed in 1935. It was simply not the explicit intent of the Act at a time when many unions did actually compete for members and workplace leadership on the shop floor. Unions competing in the workplace is a perfectly normal part of many other countries' labor relations systems.

We need to have a much more informed conversation about what parts of the system are worth preserving—and possibly reforming— and which we should seek to get rid of. This book represents my attempt to aid that conversation.

Happily, there are some changes that are completely within union activists' power to change that don't require legislative reform. I've sketched out some thoughts about the changes we can and should make in how we organize, how we protest, and how we engage with the National Labor Relations Board and the courts.

Finally, fixing the system so that workers can get the representation they want and deserve and restoring our power will require new laws. I will explore some thoughts about the principles we should be applying when we think about labor law reform.

I don't pretend to have all the answers. But I do hope that I'm asking the right questions, and that this facilitates more dialogue and a deeper searching for breakthrough strategies and reform.

THERE ARE MANY PEOPLE to thank for this book.

I'd like to thank Sarah Jaffe for giving me early advice on how to start and finish writing a whole damn book while we sat on Jesse Sharkey's lawn and ate his delicious barbecue. I'd like to thank Sharkey for being one of the first people to really push me to write this book, and I'd like to thank both of them for giving me the opening to write such an insufferably name-droppy paragraph.

On more than one occasion, Nick Unger read a new draft of this manuscript and got me on the phone for an hour or two to pick the whole thing apart and force me to sharpen my arguments. Over many years of teaching and conversation, Kate Bronfenbrenner, Joshua Freeman, and Ed Ott have helped me analyze the labor movement with clarity, specificity, and nuance. (If you disagree that my writing has any of those qualities, the blame falls squarely on me.)

Whether by phone, DM's, or over whisky or wine, I'd like to thank Chris Aikin, Brett Banditelli, Sharon Block, Valerie Braman, Chris Brooks, Leo Casey, Peter Cole, Bryan Conlon, Daniel Gross, Steve Lawton, Elana Levin, Erik Loomis, Stephen Lerner, Moshe Marvit, Jim Pope, Micah Uetricht, and Douglas Williams for spit-balling and shit-talking with me while I drafted this manuscript. Moshe probably deserves a co-author credit for a chunk of this book.

Equally influential were the many good organizers and campaign strategists that I've worked with over the years. This is hardly an exhaustive list (and some names don't appear here because they show up in other parts of this Venn Diagram of thanks), but I thought about each of these comrades at least once while writing this book: Alisha Ashley, Mark Bostic, Alan Cage, Yonna Carroll, Liz Chimienti, Jim Donovan, Carlos Fernandez, Otoniel Figueroa Duran, Richelle Fiore, Jessica Foster, Audra George, Carrie Gleason, Glenn Goldstein, Jacob Lieberman, Sam Luebke, Evan Lundeen, Matthew Luskin, Rich Maroko, Victoria Miller, Jackson Potter, Richard O'Brien, Leah Raffanti, Leigh Shapiro, Casey Sweeney, Nate Walker, and Jesse Zeigler.

Thank you also to Jeremy Brecher, Edmund Bruno, Joe Burns, Lynne Dodson, Michael B. Fabricant, Bill Fletcher Jr., Harris Freeman, Charlotte Garden, Julius Getman, William A. Herbert, Phil Kugler, Sam Lieberman, Mariah Montgomery, Bradford Murray, Ed Ott, Paul Secunda, Shayna Strom, and Andrew Stettner for reviewing drafts and providing helpful feedback on sections of this book.

I'd like to thank my colleagues at the Harry Van Arsdale Jr. School of Labor Studies at SUNY Empire State College for their continued support and friendship.

Writing is often a lonely process (at least until one starts working with an editor). I'd like to thank my fellow writers for encouragement and community, particularly Chris Brooks, Rachel Cohen, Rebecca Givan, Hamilton Nolan, Dania Rajendra, and Jessica Stites.

I'm greatly appreciative of my editors, Michael Yates and Erin Clermont, as well as Martin Paddio, Susie Day, and all the comrades at Monthly Review who helped get this over the finish line.

Finally, I want to thank my family. I began writing this book at my in-laws Jim and Kathy's kitchen table, and my own parents, Bob and Margaret, helped watch the kids while I continued to work on it in the home office. This book simply would not exist if it weren't for the support and patience of my wife, Kate.

ONE

The System Is a Trap

WHY CAN'T UNIONS GROW?

In an age of rampant inequality, at a time of increasing social protest, including a notable uptick in workers' strikes, and when a majority of workers say they want to be union members, why does union density continue to decline?

The reason is that we have structural problems, lots of them, one piled on top of another. The system of labor relations that came out of the New Deal and matured in the post–Second World War era has evolved into a complex and insidious trap. This trap prevents workers who want to join unions from doing so. It legally restricts workers' rights to protest our routine use and abuse by rich and powerful corporations. It confines unions to sectors of the economy that are not growing. It gives bosses veto power over whether a new union can even be formed in a workplace. It sharply narrows the scope of issues that unions can even put on the bargaining table.

The combination of exclusive union representation, mandatory agency fees, no-strike clauses, and "management rights" are the foundation of our peculiar "union shop." No other country structures its labor relations system quite like this. Our labor system didn't always look like this. It developed through a series of historical accidents. It has been made unworkable by a dogged anti-union legal campaign run by the vast right-wing conspiracy of think tanks, industry lobbyists, and bloodthirsty billionaires.

The system has become a trap.

Part of the trap, however, is in our own heads. Too many union activists and allies take for granted what a union is—how it should be organized, what collective bargaining looks like.

There's an analogy that makes the rounds in Cornell University's labor extension programs. It involves a man sharing his grandma's pot roast recipe with a friend. The first step of the recipe calls for cutting the ends off the raw rump, which prompts the friend to ask, "Really? Does that, like, make the roast more tender—or what?"

The man sharing the recipe, who had never questioned why it called for the ends to be cut off, calls his mom to ask why the recipe calls for the ends of the rump roast to be cut off. She confesses that she never thought about it either and suggests that her older sister might know. So the man proceeds to call his aunt who is similarly thrown off by the simple question. She had never questioned why the recipe called for this bit of home butchery. All she knew is that the dish she made when following the recipe tasted good; it tasted *familiar*.

And so on and so forth as this man called through the family historians and home cooks until he finally visits his grandma at the nursing home. And she dismissively explains, "Oh, it's because the grocer only sold rump roasts that were too big for our roast pan."

This is the most devastatingly on-the-nose analogy for how unions engage in long-term strategy. We hope and assume that sometime in the past, someone smarter than we are considered all the possible options and settled on what we are currently doing as the best possible choice.

We want there to be more unions and assume that means more unions that are just like our current unions. And so we get excited for silver bullet solutions like forgoing NLRB elections in favor of majority sign-up (or "card check") certifications or overturning right-to-work that seem like they would help unions grow.

Even when we argue among ourselves about how unions need to change to win more, we nibble around the edges of what the problem is. More robust union organizing departments running comprehensive organizing campaigns would be good and valuable, just as more face-to-face organizing conversations in existing union shops and networks of trained workplace leaders would revitalize many unions. But these won't grow the labor movement in any appreciable way, because we're still trapped in a rotten anti-union system.

Organizing Won't Save Us

How can I so casually and confidently assert that more organizing won't significantly add to the ranks of union membership? Because it hasn't.

We are nearly a quarter-century into what I call the "organize or die" push by unions to significantly increase the amount of money and energy they spend on new union organizing. Of course, when it comes to organizing many unions talk the talk but fail to walk the walk. I'll discuss some of the reasons why in chapter 4.

However, there are unions that have developed and actually maintained fidelity to organizing model strategies, putting hundreds of organizers in the field and successfully organizing thousands of bargaining units and new union members. These unions have survived, but they have not thrived. They have not greatly increased their density or their power. And the millions of workers who want to be union members remain outside the labor movement's ranks.

When most of us speak of the "organizing model," we are talking about methods of organizing within our broken system that may vary from each other slightly but are all informed by the research of Dr. Kate Bronfenbrenner at Cornell. Dr. Bronfenbrenner identified ten "comprehensive organizing tactics" from her own previous organizing experience. These include:

1. **Adequate and appropriate staff and financial resources**. This means not just putting enough staff organizers on the ground—Bronfenbrenner recommends a ratio of one staffer for every one hundred workers—but also research and communications support and enough money to take out ads, hold rallies, get buttons and T-shirts for the activists.

2. **Strategic targeting**. Organizing employees in the same or related industries so that both the workers you are seeking to organize and the members you are asking to help see this as a reasonable plan to gain power.

3. **Active representative rank-and-file committee**. That is, an organizing committee made up of leaders in the workplace, reflective of the racial and gender makeup of the workforce and the diversity of jobs and shifts.

4. **Effectively utilized member volunteer organizers**. Getting existing members at other shops to take part in the organizing campaign.

5. **Person-to-person contact inside and outside the workplace**. Rank-and-file committee members talking to potential supporters on the job and staff, member volunteers, and organizing committee members doing house visits.

6 **Benchmarks and assessments**. Testing and measuring your support through public actions in which workers are called upon to participate.

7. **Issues that resonate in the workplace and community**. Respect, dignity, voice in decision-making. Not just problems that the boss can throw money at or "fix" without a union.

8. **Escalating pressure tactics in the workplace**. Start with buttons. Build toward a march on the boss.

9. **Escalating pressure outside the workplace**. Start with handbills. Build toward rallies.

10. **Building for the first contract before the election**. Surveying all the workers—not just supporters—on issues of importance. Working on contract language. This way, collective bargaining isn't an abstract concept and the debate isn't "should there be a union" but "what do we want to do when we get our union."

Bronfenbrenner then surveyed 442 NLRB union representation elections between 1998 and 1999 to find out what if any of these ten comprehensive tactics were utilized. She found that "union win rates increase dramatically as the number of comprehensive organizing

tactics increase, ranging from 32 percent for no comprehensive organizing tactics, to 44 percent for one to five tactics, to 68 percent for
more than five tactics, and 100 percent for the 1 percent of the campaigns where unions used eight tactics."[1]

So we know from such a study what it takes to win. As frustrating
as it is that many unions have not taken Bronfenbrenner's lessons to
heart and adopted an organizing model, it's worth considering the
unions that have embraced the organizing model and haven't set the
world on fire.

The Hotel and Restaurant Employees' union (HERE) went through
a process of developing an organizing model in the 1980s and '90s.
Part of this came by learning from frustrating losses like a failed card
check at the massive Marriott Marquis hotel in New York. Part of it
came by the successful organizing drive for clerical and food service
workers at Yale University, which evolved into a dramatic community
campaign and which brought forth many of the union's leadership.
Julius Getman wrote a compelling book on HERE's evolution into an
effective organizing operation titled *Restoring the Power of Unions*.[2] It's
worth reading in light of the question of why unions aren't growing.

HERE organizing drives have real organizing committees (OC) that
move the campaign forward. Organizers target respected workplace
leaders to join the OC because campaigns don't move forward if they
can't convince those leaders to support the union effort. They train
their leaders to be bona fide organizers who can hold effective one-
on-one conversations, call the question, and challenge a co-worker to
rise to action. As they continue to organize new shops in a local, they
quickly build up a small army of member volunteer organizers who
can talk not just of the union difference but from experience of the
organizing process.

Everyday is a button day, and supporters are asked to be public.
They march on the boss and escalate from there. They mostly eschew
NLRB elections and instead press inside the shop and outside for vol-
untary recognition while they build toward a strike.

As a small illustration, I spoke with a longtime organizer at the
international union about the legal campaign that I think unions

should lead to put an end to captive audience meetings (see "Labor's Bill of Rights" in the Appendix). He was slightly dismissive of the value of that. "We just train the workers to shut those meetings down," he said. "They come away much more powerful from the experience."

Which, of course, they do. It's a great organizing model that empowers workers and doesn't just seek to increase numbers. And UNITE HERE has grown, somewhat. But that's what we have to grapple with. The union spends millions on intensive, slow-building campaigns to organize shop-by-shop in a handful of markets. But most hotel workers remain non-union and will continue to remain so absent some profound change.

Let's take the American Federation of Teachers (AFT), where I was a deputy director of organizing for several years. The AFT's organizing model is, literally, a book. If you took the AFT's logo off the cover and replaced it with *Labor Notes*, it would be right at home at one of their Troublemakers School organizer trainings.

Given that the union's organizing staff was strongly attuned to numerical analysis, we were unbelievably persnickety about the numbers. You simply had to have at least 10 percent of the bargaining unit on the organizing committee or the campaign would not be permitted to move forward.

Milestones were measurable "go/no-go" points in a campaign's development. Have you assessed a majority of the workers in the bargaining unit? Good. Are they above 50 percent in support? Okay. Now, have you got a majority of the workers publicly supporting the union effort?

There simply had to be public tests of support. It could be a signed "I'm voting yes" public poster after at least 65 percent of the workers in the unit have signed cards, or it could be a public petition in place of union authorization cards. A campaign director working with a rank-and-file organizing committee had some leeway to decide the actual instrument and order of these tests, but there had to be public tests and they had to clear specific, measurable thresholds.

How was it measurable? Through testing, rank-and-file worker observation, and numerical assessments. Now, organizers can generally have one hell of a bar fight about the relative merits of a 4-point assessment scale, a 5-point one, or an A/B or A, B, C test. We went for the 4-point scale to remove as much potential as possible for organizers—both staff and rank and file—to give into the squishy notion of "fence-sitters," while still allowing for nuance. Because, as Howard Zinn famously said, "*You can't be neutral on a moving train.*"

So, roughly speaking, a worker assessed as a "1" was an activist, a leader, someone who was doing the heavy lifting of making a union happen at her workplace. A "2" was a reliable, tested supporter. A "4" was a "no." This is not to say that a "4" was a scab, mind you. It's not what's in your heart, but where you stood on the last test of support. If you refused to sign a union card today—because you were scared, because you didn't respect the co-worker making the ask, because you were too distracted to really have much of a conversation about it— you're a "4." If you sign tomorrow, you passed the latest test and so you're now a "2" or maybe a "3."

And what's a "3"? Ah, well, this is where we get past the squishi-ness of "undecided." A "3" is an unreliable supporter, someone about whom there are conflicting observations or a mixed track record of standing with her co-workers on the most recent test.

Personally, I found this to be very important, particularly when asking rank-and-file activists to soberly assess whether their co-work-ers are really willing to stand with them or not. People hate to think the worst of their co-workers and will naturally make excuses for someone being evasive or, as the Bubs character on *The Wire* put it, "equivocat-ing like a motherfucker." So, if you're not careful, you can wind up with your organizing committee begging you to move ahead with an elec-tion because co-workers who were too scared to sign a public petition or even a private union authorization card were nevertheless promising that they would vote yes for the union when the time came.

They won't. There's too much experience and statistical evidence here. If they couldn't get over the psychological challenge of risking the boss's ire with a public demonstration of union support, they're going to chicken out—or worse—when the most crucial test comes along.

Meanwhile, if your rank-and-file activists are trained on a 4-point assessment scale that includes an "unreliable supporter" option, you wind up with funny debriefs:

"She signed the card but it took five minutes to convince her to wear the button. She's a 4." "All right. Good observation. But, since today's test was signing the card *and* wearing the union button, she has passed the most recent test, so that makes her a "2" tonight. But check back tomorrow and make sure she's still wearing the button and we can revisit the assessment."

In the AFT charter school organizing division, which I headed, we imported a number of the Hotel and Restaurant Employees' tactics that I learned from my time working for its New York local. We also marched on the boss to announce that we had formed a union. This always meant negotiating with the organizing committee about what it would look like for their particular school. Sometimes the committee wanted to politely schedule a meeting with the principal or board chair and have a small elected delegation present their petition and explain why they'd chosen to organize. Other times, the committee wanted all union supporters to corner the principal at the start of the day to do the same. I had no particular religion on the question except that there must be some kind of march on the boss.

We also had all the supporters we could muster write a short testimonial about why they were forming a union. This turned our "beautiful people" lit piece—for most unions, pictures and names of union supporters designed to give them some legal protection and to signal to the boss that the workers are not afraid—into a brochure, if not a book.

We demanded voluntary recognition, rarely ran NLRB elections, and filed tons of unfair labor practice (ULP) charges. Escalating actions could be basically shutting down school board meetings with parents and community allies and eventually preparing for strikes.

We won most of the campaigns we took on. But we walked away from many times more schools because we couldn't get the workers to the high level of support necessary to win in a union recognition process that is rigged in favor of recalcitrant employers.

And overall, the AFT did not grow. In fact, we lost density. State takeovers of urban districts like New Orleans and Detroit resulted in the legal fiction of "new" school districts that were carved out of the union contracts. The proliferation of charter schools is little more than the educational equivalent of "offshoring" to avoid the reach of the union. In higher education, colleges and universities used their "managements rights" to shift most of the workforce to part-time instructors, who have little or no job security or benefits, to erode union power. The AFT's strong commitment to an organizing model did help the union preserve much of its membership and relative power, particularly in the face of a coordinated corporate attack under the guise of "education reform."

Finally, let's look at the Service Employees International Union (SEIU). Probably more than any other union, SEIU devoted substantial resources to organizing. It's fashionable on the left to take swipes at their more staff-driven model, and perhaps a tendency to cut corners on the organizing model in some campaigns. However, unlike many other unions, they organize on a much larger scale, chasing units of thousands of workers at a time. And they actually grew! SEIU gained at least one million members in the twenty year period leading up to 2010.[3] But then the Supreme Court aimed directly at knocking out their public sector bargaining unions. The *Harris v. Quinn* and *Janus v. AFSCME* decisions cost the union a lot of the membership gains they had managed to eke out in a decade of organizing.

Rethinking the System

Don't get me wrong. I'm not trying to make some kind of "why bother?" argument. The unions that are using the organizing model should continue to do so and certainly be willing to make room for improvement. And the unions that have not embraced an organizing model like Bronfenbrenner has laid out should do so and commit serious resources to running strategic comprehensive campaigns.

But if every union was spending down their treasuries on organizing model comprehensive campaigns, we wouldn't grow on the scale or at the speed that we need. Because the system makes us organize shop by shop, company by company, and industry by industry and gives employers every opportunity to delay, to impede, and to refuse, we just wouldn't get to the kind of union density levels that are needed for the system to actually work the way it was once intended by its New Deal architects as a federally enforced check on rampant inequality and an impediment to periodic economic depressions. When unions represented one in every three jobs in the economy, collective bargaining was the rising tide that lifted all boats.[4] And because unions organize from positions of strength—that is, within industries in which we already have a toe-hold or in ancillary or related industries—the long decline in union density means that we would be hard-pressed to expand into the essential areas of the economy in which unions are all but locked out, such as information technology and financial services.

The breathless focus that many on the left have on the organizing model often carries with it an implied oppositionalism. Sometimes it comes with an explicit challenge against union leadership. Maybe here and there a union's leadership is an impediment to change, and fresh blood and a new approach to the work would be helpful. But, in general, I don't think pushing out one set of leaders for another is much of a solution.

I'm of a similar mind as the character President Roslin in the television series *Battlestar Galactica* who kept a running tally on her whiteboard of surviving humans following a robot holocaust. There are so few of us left doing this very hard work of trying to keep the labor movement going that it takes a lot for me to conclude that someone needs to get pushed out the airlock. All leaders would be trapped by the same system. I'm much more interested in education with a line of critical inquiry that has little patience for easy answers or sacred cows.

One of the shibboleths among leftists in the labor movement is to bemoan the Cold War purge of Communist activists as a singular tragedy and a key turning point for the labor movement. With the bravest leaders and organizers gone, the thinking goes, unions slid into business unionism and stopped organizing.

That's just a bunch of romantic hooey. It's a close cousin to the idea that some sort of wholesale leadership change is the magic solution to our problems. What the purging of the Communists did that actually was and continues to be detrimental to union strategy is that it purged the last bulwark of *disagreement* from the labor movement. I don't even necessarily mean good, wise, or principled disagreement. Just simple disagreement: looking at a challenge or opportunity and proposing an alternative plan. With the Communists dispatched, the AFL and the CIO merged, and a broad consensus developed that our peculiar union shop is simply what unions are, and what they should be.

For example, as states went "Right to Work," unions all basically accepted the rottenness of the free rider problem. There was no serious debate, at least not until recently, about whether to continue to accept the burdens of exclusive representation. As the courts proved to be incredibly hostile to workers' rights and NLRB decision-making, unions mostly accepted that the courts suck and should be avoided. There's been remarkably little debate about developing our own proactive legal strategies for winning a stronger constitutional basis for workers' rights.

There's been a remarkably broad acceptance of the rigged rules of the system. And organizers are actually some of the worst about this. There's this macho culture of telling workers, "Well, the boss is allowed to do that; he's allowed to fire you. That's why you need a union." As if the idea that the default status of workers (at least, of non-union workers) is at-will and the ever-present threat of termination shouldn't at least be debated and possibly challenged.

There actually are socialists in the labor movement today. Tons of them. The Cold War ended, of course, and the AFL-CIO elected new leadership in 1995 that embraced the hiring of more movement-based staff, many of them veterans of the 1960s New Left. As Joe Burns notes in his book *Reviving the Strike*, "Despite their background as part of the political and ideological left, the views pushed by many ex-1960s activists today demonstrate a remarkable pragmatism."[5]

That pragmatism consists of largely accepting the rigged rules of the system as a given and pushing against the boundaries of the law rather than challenging or outright breaking the law. There is a pervasive tendency in our movement to accept that when it comes to labor structure, strategy, and law, "It is what it is." The horrible structures of American collective bargaining rules are a given, and we don't have much opportunity to change them.

My generation was trained by that generation, and we largely respected the experience and expertise of those who came before us and mostly accepted this structural trap. Because we hammered out strategy in airless rooms where leaving with a consensus plan was a valued goal. Because Grandma's pot roast tasted like home.

I had to get out of the room. Toward the end of my tenure at the AFT, I read Stanley Aronowitz's *The Death and Life of American Labor*,[6] in which he names the trap that unions find themselves in "contract unionism." He argues that the scope of bargaining and the drudgery of contract bargaining and grievance handling, combined with no-strike clauses, structurally limits the vision of what unions are or can be and saps us of our potential for militancy. His experience in union leadership, as part of a successful opposition movement in his faculty union after a career spent criticizing bad leadership, drew him to the conclusion that the system is a trap no matter how well-intentioned the leadership is.

I couldn't unread it. His arguments gnawed at my sureness in what we were doing as organizers and as a left within labor. As soon as I found myself not working for a union for the first time in my adult life, I started playing with some of his ideas as I began to write for *In These Times*. Frankly, I think my writing made me unemployable for a while. I know that it's pissed off some of my friends. Stanley Aronowitz pisses people off way more. I mentioned the book to a friend, a union staffer in New York who is one of the labor movement's more prominent and thoughtful public intellectuals, and he instantly became agitated about Aronowitz's radical proposal that unions abandon contract bargaining entirely.

But at least he read it and thought about it. I'm often disappointed that my former colleagues at AFT don't read, or at least don't read anything that's critical about union strategy. It's not because, as they claim, that they don't have the time to read. It's that nobody who works their ass off for a union wants to let a nagging thought in that their hard work, combined with everyone else's at all the other unions, isn't going to restore the labor movement.

We need those nagging thoughts. We need questions that agitate and annoy. We need to critically reevaluate structure, strategy, and history. We need to read more, and talk more across unions, across generations, and across disciplines. We need to get out of those airless rooms. We need to cook that pot roast dozens of different ways.

Using the Crisis

Finally, another shibboleth is that there will be no labor law reform until we create a crisis through militant demonstrations of worker power—like sit-down strikes. These are particularly unhelpful when paired with a macho pose, so it's pointless to even think about or discuss labor law reform until that wave of sit-down strikes is in process.

In broad strokes, this is not wrong. But it misses some crucial nuance because there are really two kinds of crisis that can influence labor law. One is the crisis of capitalism, when the system, left to its own devices with no effective checks on its power, leads to political and economic turmoil that frightens a faction of the capitalist class into loosening some of the restrictions on unions in the hopes of stabilizing the economy and body politic. The other crisis occurs when we workers use the limited opening we've been provided to demonstrate our collective power—to ourselves and the bosses—to win a more accepted representational role in the workplace and in government.

The Great Depression of the 1930s was the first kind of crisis, and the Roosevelt administration provided an unanticipated opportunity. When Franklin Roosevelt was elected in 1932, unions were at one of their weakest points in history. Membership levels had declined from postwar highs, and strikes were uncommon. The American Federation of Labor did not endorse in the election, and there was no reason to expect the Democrats to do anything for labor.

And yet, one of the first acts of the New Deal administration, the

1933 National Industrial Recovery Act, guaranteed in Section 7a that "employees shall have the right to organize and bargain collectively through representatives of their own choosing, and shall be free from the interference, restraint, or coercion of employers of labor, or their agents, in the designation of such representatives or in self-organization or in other concerted activities for the purpose of collective bargaining or other mutual aid or protection."

Now, the main purpose of the law was to get competing firms to engage in price collusion to stabilize big business. The sad reality is that the weak nod to labor in the NIRA was merely a sweetener to help get a few extra votes for its passage. But its tripartite industrial boards, consisting of one representative each from companies, unions, and "the public" for each major industry, did have the power to establish minimum wages and work rules. Strong unions like the Amalgamated Clothing Workers and United Mine Workers were able to press the boards to raise wages and spread union standards across non-union firms in their industries. Elsewhere, the boards gave little thought to working conditions except for their dogged determination to keep on union-busting.

This gets lost in a popular understanding of labor history. First of all, Section 7a's "right to organize" had no enforcement mechanism, yet workers nevertheless took it as a signal that the government would have their backs. John L. Lewis famously sent organizers into the coal fields with the message, "*The President wants you to join the union!*" and restored the United Mine Workers sagging membership and power before similarly turning his attention to the steel industry.[7]

There's a lesson in this, in knowing what we have the power to change, and in being smart enough to recognize that the political environment has changed enough that our own approaches to the work should change too. Section 7a wasn't worth the paper it was printed on but to just enough workers in 1933 it meant something. The sit-down strikes that started in 1934 and the Wagner Act (NLRA) of 1935 might not have happened without that earlier signal.

Today, capitalism is in a crisis that exceeds the Great Depression as an existential threat to our democratic institutions. It's not just the rampant poverty and massive inequality but the resurgence of racist authoritarian violence. The decades-long attack on unions is a large contributor to these problems, a political reality that has not gone unnoticed among liberals and a large section of the centrist establishment.

The Democratic primaries saw almost all of the candidates, even those who were boosters of charter schools and other assaults on public education, fall all over themselves to endorse and support teachers strikes.[8] And, prodded by SEIU, every candidate who remained in the race long enough put out detailed and robust labor platforms endorsing the union's demand of "unions for all."[9] Even centrists like Beto O'Rourke[10] and Jay Inslee[11] endorsed some version of proposals I will outline in this book. This is different from the usual vague platitudes that Democrats are expected to spout in order to vie for union endorsements. This is an opportunity. Now, I'm not holding out any Democratic president as labor's savior, but what I am saying is that we'd be fools not to be debating legal reforms *now* that might be in consideration in the near future. What do we gain by abstaining?

Moreover, we must be much more strategically deft than we have historically been. The next few years are pregnant with possibilities. We should pursue reform as a dialectic. There are the changes that we have the power to make ourselves, and those that will be granted or imposed by the system itself. But every change—no matter how minor, no matter if it comes from above or below or if it's imposed on us by our enemies—creates the possibilities for more change. We should be constantly debating strategy and reexamining the political environment and workers' attitudes. We must be ready.

TWO

Our Peculiar Union Shop

IF THE SYSTEM IS A TRAP, then we need to understand what that system is and how it developed. Let's start with the framework under which most union leaders and activists would consider a workplace "unionized." It is a peculiar thing, from a historical and global standpoint. In the United States, a union shop is one in which one union, among many possible alternatives, serves as the exclusive representative of *all* employees within a legally defined bargaining unit based upon the majority of the affected workers' preference. And all workers in a union shop are expected to join the union or pay an agency fee.

To union members, leaders, and staff this feels totally normal and desirable. It is what a union is. Even as the "Right to Work" laws passed now by a majority of the states and the *Janus v. AFSCME* Supreme Court decision have made this arrangement illegal in many workplaces, we still strive to turn as many workplaces into union shops as we possibly can, even if that means changing the law where we must. But the fact is that this is a totally unusual structure. Unions in other countries do not look like this! This isn't even how unions have always been structured in this country.

We tend to assume that the collective bargaining framework was the product of active strategic choices. Surely Walter Reuther, Sidney Hillman, John L. Lewis and other leaders of labor's great upsurge in the 1930s sat around a table, debated all the possible alternatives, and decided that this framework is what we should pursue. However, the reality is that much of our system was produced by accident, the result of differing and conflicting strategies.

The Closed Shop and the Roots of the Labor Movement

The idea that everyone in a workplace should belong to a union is in the DNA of the U.S. labor movement, like the vestigial tailbone is part of the genetic code in human DNA. It's largely a holdover from a time we don't remember. It's rooted in the craft unions and the building trades that formed the first permanent worker organizations in this country.

Although unions have been around since the earliest days of the Republic, they were usually short-lived and inchoate efforts. Often, the focus was more on passing wage and hours legislation on a city or state basis, and so labor unions looked more like labor parties.[12] As modern capitalism and large corporations took shape and the world of work was restructured, unions' definition of who was a worker and who was a boss evolved slowly. The most prominent union of the 1870s and 80s, the Knights of Labor, extended membership to "all who labor." For the Knights, this included small business owners and supervisors (but excluded saloonkeepers and lawyers!).

This was a boom-and-bust era of labor organizing. Union ranks would swell during good economic times as worker demands for a fairer share of corporate profits frequently led to substantial strike waves. When the economy crashed, as it did about once a decade, employers would target the loudest union activists for layoffs and blacklisting, and the unions would be smashed.

The craft unions were able to form more permanent organizations by being deliberately smaller. The carpenters' union, for example, didn't want "all who labor" to join the union. They wanted all who labor as carpenters. They wanted to define the skills of the carpentry trade, control the training of new apprentice carpenters, and force employers to come to them when they needed skilled workers on a job site.

And employers needed the crafts. During economic downturns, they had little ability to fire union activists or recruit scabs because the craft unions functionally controlled the jobs. So, while less construction might mean fewer carpenters working, those who were working were doing so on a union basis. And when construction picked up during the next economic recovery, it too would be done on a union basis.

These unions would survive. The United Brotherhood of Carpenters and Joiners was formed in 1881. It still exists today. It was one of the unions that formed the American Federation of Labor (AFL) as an umbrella organization of all the various craft unions. For decades, these craft unions *were* the labor movement. It shouldn't be surprising that the industrial unions and public sector unions that eventually followed longed to emulate the model in which everyone on the job site has to belong to the union as a defining characteristic of a union shop.

But a craft union shop is actually a closed shop, and it is a model that is very difficult to emulate. Union membership in a craft or trade union precedes the job. You join the union. The union trains you in the craft. The union gets you hired on a job site where a contractor has signed a collective bargaining agreement with the unions for the duration of the construction. Of course, it's reasonable that the building trades unions demand that only union members get hired for the job and that everybody on the job is fully paid up in their union dues.

But that's not how most of the economy is structured. Consider the fate of one of the other founding affiliates of the AFL. The Amalgamated Association of Iron and Steel Workers was a craft union that functionally controlled steel production for a brief time in the 1880s. They defined the smelting process for making iron and steel. They controlled the training and supply of workers. They controlled the quality of the product. They controlled the pace of work, they controlled who worked, and they controlled prices.

This amount of worker control was unacceptable to the new captains of industry. Andrew Carnegie, who was buying up major steel mills and metal works factories in order to gain monopoly control of the industry, forced a confrontation at the Homestead Steel Works in 1892. He locked out the union and hired a private army of Pinkertons to wage armed warfare against the union men. In the entire bloody, violent, and murderous history of American class warfare, the Homestead strike still stands out for its barbarism.[13]

Bosses gave Carnegie's new economic model the ironically blood-less name "the open shop," and later and more sinisterly, "The American Plan." What this meant was that union members were not welcome. The company would choose who gets hired, take control of training, and de-skill the jobs to the greatest extent possible.

At the dawn of the twentieth century, the new methods of mass production that would come to define the "American Century" were designed to thwart the craft model of worker organization. It would not be the last time that corporations restructured the economy to counter the way that unions are organized and, in the process, avoid unions altogether.

Exclusive Representation and the Modern Labor Movement

The model of one union exclusively representing and bargaining on behalf of all the workers in a bargaining unit is a product of the law, but it was probably an unintentional development.

With bosses that would literally rather wage armed warfare on their workers than deal with a union, it became clear to the Roosevelt administration that crawling out of the Great Depression would require government intervention to legally force employers to recog-nize and bargain with unions. The National Labor Relations Act of 1935 had bare-bones procedural requirements. A union proves that it has members in a shop. The National Labor Relations Board (NLRB) then directs the employer to meet with union representatives and bargain "in good faith." The Act was much more focused on prevent-ing and forbidding common union-busting tactics called unfair labor practices.

In his book *The Blue Eagle at Work*, Charles J. Morris argues that there was never an intention that a union would have to win a major-ity of votes in a certification election. There was a clear understand-ing by the Act's authors and the early administrators of the National Labor Relations Board that in so-called open shops, there would be, at best, a militant minority of union activists but more likely a few scared and secret members of a union.[14] The purpose of the Act was to force employers to deal with these incipient unions, and the legitimacy that the union would achieve by actually meeting with management and negotiating over workplace issues might help the union attract more members and grow in power.

There were at the time also multiple unions in a lot of shops, competing for workers' loyalty, activism, and dues money. The nature of their competition, however, would ultimately result in the exclusive representation framework, particularly once the Congress of Industrial Organizations split from and began competing with the American Federation of Labor.

The CIO began as a committee of unions within the AFL that advocated for new unions to organize workers on the basis of the industry they worked in instead of by job classification. They wanted the Federation to charter a new union of autoworkers to represent all of the workers at Ford and GM, regardless of whether they welded the frame, installed a fuse, or swept the floor.

The craft unions of the AFL entered the 1930s still trying to make organizational sense of the mass production industries. They saw each of the tiny, timed movements on the assembly line as devalued crafts that they should represent individually and re-skill. The AFL granted a temporary charter for autoworkers only while the crafts debated how to divvy up the members.[15]

The decisive split between the CIO and the AFL arose over the question of what the unions' strategic orientation should be regarding the new labor law and the Roosevelt administration that signed it.[16] The craft unions were wary of involving the government in collective bargaining and inclined to stick with their traditional "reward your friends and punish your enemies" approach to electoral politics.

The CIO unions, led by the legendary Mineworkers president John L. Lewis, saw the labor board as essential to organizing auto, steel, and the steel industry's non-union "captive" mines. They feared losing the opportunity of the moment if Roosevelt did not win reelection, and they wanted labor to be a full-throated member of the New Deal coalition.

Once independent, the CIO began creating new unions for the auto factories, steel mills, textiles mills, and a host of other mass production industries. Thanks to a lot of brave organizers, creative job actions, and an interventionist federal government that forced employers to deal with unions, the CIO grew rapidly. Faced with the threat of political irrelevance, the AFL began organizing in earnest, forcing the NLRB to conduct elections to determine which union the workers preferred.[17]

The last thing the CIO wanted was to see its powerful new unions carved apart by craft unions, each claiming their couple dozen members. The CIO would file to represent broad categories of job titles and duties and bargain as a unit. And they filed to be the exclusive representative of those bargaining units. This is when the NLRB decisively shifted away from certifying the desire of any group of workers to be represented by a union to conducting elections to certify unions by majority vote.

There are two plainly political reasons why the CIO's vision of union certifications won out. First, the CIO was an ally of the administration and increasingly important to the New Deal electoral coalition, whereas the AFL's election activity was more muted. Second, employers preferred not to deal with multiple unions, particularly if they would be competing over who can make bigger demands and wage more militant job actions. Of course, a boss's preferred number of unions to deal with is almost always zero. But one is their second favorite number.

The Political Costs of Exclusive Representation

Unions that win certification as the exclusive representative of a bargaining unit do not automatically win dues-paying members. They win the right to bargain on behalf of the workers, and with that the legal and political obligations that have built up over time. Today, where they are strong enough to do so, unions negotiate "union shop" clauses into collective bargaining agreements, which demand that workers hired into bargaining unit jobs join the union.

The prewar industrial unions were voluntary membership groups. They certainly aimed to get every member of the bargaining unit to join the union. (Again, that notion was simply in the DNA of American unions.) And they were mostly successful. Unions were winning. Every new agreement brought substantial improvements in wages and working conditions. Workers were still moved by the spirit of solidarity that came from supporting each other in job actions. A worker who didn't join the union was a scab, a pariah, a social leper.

The Second World War changed everything. After the bombing of Pearl Harbor, the leadership of both labor federations immediately pledged not to strike for the duration of the war. Those newly organized steel mills and auto factories were converted into wartime production. America's factories were the home front. The union leaders were being patriotic. It may be ironic to some, but the Communists, who led some unions and were on staff at many more, were the most militant enforcers of tamping down worker militancy. After all, this was a war to fight the fascists in alliance with the Soviet Union!

The NLRB was temporarily supplanted by a War Labor Board that had the authority to approve or disapprove tentative agreements negotiated between unions and their employers. That this had been the fear of the AFL craft unions in 1935 and that they were now okay with it was another little irony.[18]

Less than one year later, Roosevelt issued an executive order for a wage freeze to combat wartime inflation. This put union leaders in a real bind. Most union members shared the patriotic impulse of their leaders and wanted to aid the war effort at home. But they were also workers who were dealing with faster and more intense demands on the job and a rapidly rising cost of living. Now they were told they could not get a raise and that their union leaders and staff were legally compelled to stop them from engaging in any protest activity that could slow down production.

So, many workers stopped paying their union dues. This wasn't scabbing. This was protest! Unions that had to expend significant resources maintaining labor peace and aiding the government and their employers in increasing productivity simultaneously faced the threat of a precipitous drop in their dues revenue.

In response, the industrial unions pushed hard in 1942–43 for closed-shop arrangements like the craft unions had long enjoyed. Employers resisted, and the resulting bargaining impasses wound up before the War Labor Board for arbitration. The government was keenly aware that without some guarantee that dues revenue would not continue to decline, there was a significant risk that some unions would abandon labor peace to win back lost members, imperiling wartime production.

The War Labor Board dictated a compromise that nevertheless set the stage for the union shop. "Maintenance of membership" provisions were inserted into collective bargaining agreements, thereby ensuring that anyone who was a member at the time the contract was signed had to remain a member for the duration of the agreement. With this endorsement of the union security principle from the federal government, most employers soon relented and agreed to "union shop" clauses in successor agreements.

This is a crucial point and a little understood distinction. From their inception, mandatory union fees were not intended to compensate unions for the *financial* costs they bear for bargaining and filing grievances. Mandatory union fees are the compensation for the *political* costs of representing all the workers in a shop and maintaining labor peace.

This remains true today. It is the combination of exclusive representation and the union shop that enables unions to agree to "shared sacrifice" or just plain old concessions and do the heavy lifting of selling them to the workers as being for the "good of the company" or the long-term viability of jobs. Unions wind up taking the heat for employers' bad business decisions and their demands that workers pay for them.

In the 1980s, the United Autoworkers agreed to the first contracts that contained rollbacks of compensation and work rules, ostensibly to help the "Big 3" auto companies stay competitive with foreign imports. Workers in the Canadian shops responded by bolting to form a new Canadian Autoworkers union. They were taking advantage of the fact that there's a separate body of Canadian labor law, and that protectionist trade policies and the difference in currency values gave them a better ability to resist the concessions.

Canadian workers dropped the UAW because they could. Imagine if the CIO had lost its push for the principle of exclusive representation. Imagine if American workplaces still had multiple competing unions. We'll play with this thought some more later in this book. For now, let's just say that the Big 3's push for concessions would have been messier and more chaotic and that the bosses would certainly have taken more heat and more of the blame for the situation from the workers.

The Duty of Fair Representation and the Workplace Constitution

Unions have a legal obligation to represent all members of a bargaining unit. That doesn't just mean bargain a contract that applies for everyone. It means that if a member of the bargaining unit comes to the union with a problem, the union must investigate and must expend resources on filing a grievance if the case has merit. And the union must do this regardless of whether or not the worker is paying dues.

This is called the duty of fair representation. It has the effect of bureaucratizing unions, to some extent, converting fighting organizations of workers into quasi-governmental workplace court systems. Workplaces need this kind of representation, but the way that we do this in the United States is unusual and, like so much of our labor relations system, was not entirely intentional.

The duty of fair representation developed partly in response to the shameful racism of some unions. In particular, the old railroad brotherhoods used their collective bargaining to try to maintain the workplace segregation that the bosses had fomented long before the unions came on the scene.[19] They barred black workers from membership and then tried to negotiate closed shops, which would have totally barred blacks from employment. Later, when black workers managed to get jobs on the railroads, the brotherhoods negotiated racially stratified job categories and pay scales and tried to keep blacks out of the better jobs. Other unions, particularly in the South, attempted to maintain segregated locals and bargaining units by jointly petitioning the NLRB to represent workers on a kind of "separate but equal" basis.

This is all ugly stuff and naturally aroused the NAACP to launch legal campaigns to prevent it. Led by Herbert Hill, NAACP lawyers soon moved beyond merely trying to prevent union discrimination and began trying to use labor law to advance a broader civil rights agenda.[20]

The period that I'm talking about here is the 1940s and '50s, when the idea of getting civil rights legislation passed was a very long term proposition (bordering on fantasy). But Hill and his allies saw the National Labor Relations Act as a pathway for getting constitutional rights into the workplace. Sophia Z. Lee has shone new light on this theory and the legal campaign that pursued it in her excellent book *The Workplace Constitution*.[21]

Now, in the twenty-first century, I know that it's fashionable for people to snark in the comments section that "freedom of speech is not freedom from the repercussions of speech." And union organizers tend to disabuse people of the notion that they have many enforceable rights at work (without a union contract, that is). But, stretch your mind a little bit and try to see what Herbert Hill saw.

The Bill of Rights and the Reconstruction Amendments (Thirteen, Fourteen, and Fifteen) are the best things in the U.S. Constitution. They clearly articulate human rights that people understand and believe in. The only problem with them is that, with the crucial exception of the Thirteenth Amendment, they only restrict the government from violating your rights. On a day-to-day basis, however, your boss has way more power over your life and liberty.

The NAACP looked at the NLRB and saw an arm of the federal government that was certifying that workers—Taxpayers! Citizens!—had democratically chosen an organization to represent them. This arm of the government, with the threat of a court injunction, had directed those workers' employer to meet with their representative and bargain in good faith. That arm of the government would also step in if any party claimed that the other side's behavior was unfair and would issue a decision that is binding.

This, Herbert Hill argued, was state action. Whatever the NLRB signed off on, whatever the NLRB blocked, was bringing the

government in as a party. If it was an action that would violate constitutional rights if the government were to do it *directly*, it would also
be a violation in government-regulated labor relations.

That was their argument anyway. In particular, they saw the NLRB
as a strategy for getting free speech, due process, and equal protection into workplaces. And those principles are respected in the duty
of fair representation, which they did win. But those principles still
don't apply to employer behaviors, largely because Hill's workplace
constitution approach was abandoned.

Congress did finally pass civil rights legislation in 1964, and many
activists found those laws a preferable way to address workplace discrimination. Plus, unions chafed at increased governmental regulation of their constitutions and collective bargaining, even if it was for
a righteous cause. Finally, Ronald Reagan's court appointments ushered in a new era of conservative jurisprudence that prioritized the
literal words written by long-dead white male slaveholders over novel
constitutional interpretations like Hill's.[22]

But the results of these efforts further solidified the legal preference
for exclusive representation and forced unions into the role of quasi-
governmental representative in the workplace. The responsibilities of
behaving as a workplace government can get particularly problematic when unions are prevented from collecting their "union shop"
equivalent of taxes, as "right to work" laws aim to do.

The "Right to Work" and the Dismantling of the Postwar Labor Movement

The maintenance of membership clauses of the Second World War
period, the closed shop agreements that the craft unions enjoyed
before them, and the union shop/union security provisions that were
bargained in the immediate postwar era drove captains of industry,
right-wing ideologues, and rabid racists out of their bloody minds.
Anti-labor propaganda and political pressures ensued.

Between 1944 and 1946, five states (Florida, Arkansas, South
Dakota, Nebraska, and Arizona) passed laws that were given the

confusing but populist-sounding name "Right to Work." Some of these laws aimed to make illegal the closed shop, which made union membership a precondition for getting hired on a job. Others aimed to outlaw any rule whereby a worker could lose his job for refusing to join or pay any kind of fee to a union after he was hired. All of the bills appealed to that peculiarly macho American notion of rugged individualism.

Unions initially responded with technical legal appeals. Their argument: the National Labor Relations Act was the nation's labor law. It allowed and indeed encouraged union-shop and closed-shop clauses as a subject of bargaining. Federal law is supreme and preempts state law; therefore these "right to work" laws were unconstitutional attempts by states to overrule the federal government.

The 1946 midterm elections saw the New Deal Democrats turned out of office for the first time. One of the factors in the Republicans' victory was the public's mixed opinion on the postwar strike wave. The strike wave was a result of workers' pent-up frustrations with wartime inflation and wage freezes compounded with long-simmering resentments from Depression-era privations. The strike wave resulted in greatly increased wages and a new private welfare state of employer-paid benefits. But it was also incredibly disruptive and convinced many politicians that labor had somehow become "too powerful."

The Taft-Hartley Act that the Republican Congress passed in 1947 was a series of amendments to the NLRA that aimed to blunt the power of unions and give bosses more legal tools to fight them. Its "right to work" section devolved the issue to the states, thereby killing the legal challenges that unions were pursuing.

Union leaders threatened hellfire and damnation for any politician that voted for Taft-Hartley. They increased their political fundraising and campaigning, and they made legislative repeal their number one priority. This was not a particularly effective strategy (so says this writer who has the benefit of seventy years of hindsight).

First, the obvious: Congress never repealed Taft-Hartley or meaningfully reformed labor law. This was despite tremendous efforts by unions to elect Democrats over the decades. There were substantial Democratic majorities in 1949, 1965, and 1977 and repealing Taft-Hartley was simply not prioritized by Presidents Truman, Johnson, and Carter.

The phrase "right to work" is a cynical manipulation by right-wingers, but it does have some support. Compelling workers to join a union or face termination is not the most popular thing in the world. As we have seen, union-shop clauses are compensation for the workplace governance functions that unions are legally compelled to provide. They could be seen as a tax. But unions are not just a neutral workplace government, a labor-management committee, or a works council. They are political organizations, with social views, and they work toward civil rights, openly allied with a political party.

This system is a bit of a muddle, but exclusive representation, the duty of fair representation, and the union shop are all essential components of what made it work. "Right to work" attacks put unions and their allies in the untenable position of having to defend the system solely based on its least popular component. This is not unlike forcing defenders of the Affordable Care Act to justify it solely because of the individual mandate. Both systems fall apart without forcing individuals to pay their fair share, but the individual mandate is the most divisive component of the system.

By focusing solely on legislative lobbying, unions engaged the issue as a special interest. For the remainder of the twentieth century, labor, where labor was strong, was able to prevent passage of state "right to work" bills. Where it was weak—the South and Southwest—states fell like dominoes.

Without the ability to negotiate union shops, unions have largely avoided new organizing in "right to work" states. As we'll see in the next chapter, this left labor regionally isolated and encouraged capital flight and union avoidance.

THREE

The Routine of Collective Bargaining

Management has no divine rights.
—WALTER REUTHER, 1948

A HUGE PART OF THE SYSTEM in which we are trapped is the routine of collective bargaining.[23] In contracts that last anywhere from three to seven years, unions trade preservation of wages, pensions, and health insurance for significant concessions on workplace protest and the boss's ability to run his business as he damn well pleases. The result is cutbacks in pay and benefits for which unions bear most of the blame, a decline in our power, and the perception by workers, inside and outside the labor movement, that unions can't be the change agents that workers want them to be.

Much of this is reinforced by our lousy labor law regime. But this is not an area where we are helplessly shackled to an out-of-date model. No, we're still following Grandma's pot roast recipe even though our kitchen looks nothing like hers.

The Treaty of Detroit

Unions bargain like it's still 1950. That's the year the United Autoworkers settled a landmark collective bargaining agreement with General Motors that set the postwar pattern for labor relations. It's often called the "Treaty of Detroit."[24] The agreement covered an unprecedented five-year period. It guaranteed there would be no work stoppages during that time. It gave wide latitude to management's rights to direct its business, setting product prices, for example. It guaranteed workers' wages that would keep pace with the cost of living and rise with productivity. It included a private welfare system of employer-paid pensions, health insurance, and other fringe benefits. This probably sounds awesome to a modern reader. But it involved significant trade-offs that have only worsened with time, and it was not the goal with which the union started.

The union began the postwar period with an audacious demand: a 30 percent wage increase accompanied by no rise in the price of cars.[25] This demand was put forth by Walter Reuther, then a vice president of the union, a few weeks after the Japanese surrender that ended the Second World War. At the time, people were understandably worried that the country would return to an economic depression once wartime spending on production was phased out. Reuther was convinced that the key to staying out of a Depression was to put more money in workers' pockets so that their rising living standards would drive the demand for consumer goods and keep the factories humming.

This was a demand for income redistribution. It's the demand that earned Reuther the sobriquet "the most dangerous man in Detroit." He was so christened by George Romney (father of Mitt), who headed the auto industry association, because "no one is more skillful in bringing about the revolution without seeming to disturb the existing forms of society."[26]

Workers who had long experienced price increases in food, shelter, and consumer goods that eroded whatever wage gains they were able to win rallied to the cause. The strike, which began on November 21, 1945, was the first time that the UAW completely shut down production at all of GM's facilities. Workers at Ford and Chrysler stayed on the job, so that GM would lose business to its competitors and be more likely to settle what the union hoped would be a pattern for the other car companies.

But the UAW was not the only union on strike. The bitter winter of 1945–46 saw a strike wave that put two million workers on picket lines. All the strikes were motivated by the same kind of worker demands for a bigger slice of the pie.

When the Steelworkers signed a deal with U.S. Steel that gave its members an 18½ cents an hour raise, with a corresponding rise in the price of steel, a pattern was set. Most strikes came to an end within a few weeks of the steel settlement, with similar raises. The GM strike lasted 133 days, the longest of all the strikes that winter. For their efforts, the GM workers got a penny more an hour than the Steelworkers, but GM still raised the price of its cars.[27]

That was a one-year contract. Most collective bargaining agreements were one-year deals back then, and they were fairly bare bones. They were basically an agreement over what that year's wage rates would be, with a dispute resolution process spelled out for the period of a truce in which the union promised not to strike.

For every year that followed, the UAW would single out one of the Big 3 auto companies for strike preparation and wage and benefit demands that aimed for significant, permanent improvements in workers' standard of living. In 1949, Chrysler bore the brunt of a 104-day strike after refusing to match Ford's fully paid pension. Out of this annual turmoil came the Treaty of Detroit. General Motors wanted five years of labor peace, and the UAW made them pay for it with pensions and health insurance.

Unions had begun to negotiate fringe benefits during the Second World War. After the War Labor Board froze wages to combat inflation, it exempted fringe benefits from the restrictions. This "Little Steel Formula" gave unions wiggle room to make some material gains for their restive members.[28] Many unions emerged from the war years with employer-sponsored health insurance and other benefits.

But not so much the CIO unions. Union leaders like Walter Reuther, who were more social democratic in their outlook, viewed health care and enhanced retirement benefits as the purview of the federal government. They wanted to win these things as universal rights for all Americans, as a part of a renewed New Deal.

This vision was frustrated by the Republican congressional victories in the 1946 midterms, but even congressional Democrats didn't

feel the same urgency of the Depression years to put money in workers' pockets even at the risk of incurring the wrath of the ruling class.
At their 1946 convention, CIO leaders vowed not to wait "for perhaps another ten years until the Social Security laws are amended
adequately" and to use their collective bargaining power to address
their members' health and retirement security.[29] The UAW believed
that by forcing all the auto companies to pay for the same benefits for
their employees, these benefits would be taken out of competition.
Reuther's hope was that by loading these additional payroll costs onto
the auto companies' bottom line, it would give them a financial incentive to lobby the government to assume these responsibilities.

Think about that. The celebrated Treaty of Detroit was a five-year
deal to make progress on a ten-year problem. And yet the private welfare system it built up has been a source of pride for union leaders
and members for generations. Pensions and "Cadillac" health care
plans and a host of other fringe benefits are the "union difference."
Bargaining for them is for many the sine qua non of what unions do.

Today, many unions face round after round of concessionary
demands to cut back member benefits. The "union difference" of substantially higher payroll costs gives employers a strong incentive to
offshore, outsource, and fiercely resist union organizing efforts. And
we're stuck with the trade-off to win that private welfare system: long-
term contracts that give management wide leeway to do what they
want while we are saddled with severe restrictions on protest activity.

Most union activists view our job as organizing as many new members and new shops as we can to increase density and get back to an
era where the Treaty of Detroit framework still works. I say that the
framework has become a trap, that we should critically evaluate it and
be willing to blow it up.

Mandatory Subjects of Bargaining

The corporate executives at General Motors fiercely resisted the
union's attempt to have a say on its business decisions, and they won.
Today, there are few unions that would even dare to offer an opinion

on how their employer profits or how they should bill the public, and fewer still that view co-determinism or joint decision-making as a legal right or even an achievable goal.

Labor law hasn't helped. The National Labor Relations Act's directive to employers to bargain with certified union representatives "in good faith" over "wages, hours and other terms and conditions of employment" is as broad as it is vague. There is no statutory requirement to actually reach an agreement, only to meet and respond to proposals.

The benefit of the NLRA is in restraining and enjoining Unfair Labor Practices (ULPs). Bargaining in bad faith only occurs when one party refuses to meet or refuses to respond to a so-called mandatory bargaining proposal. ULPs over the failure to bargain in good faith can bring significant leverage as remedies include orders to meet more frequently, the furnishing of budgetary and other documentation to justify a bargaining position, and orders to cease, or even reverse, any changes made prior to reaching agreement or impasse.

Unfortunately, the obligation to bargain in good faith has been drastically narrowed by the Supreme Court's artificial invention of "mandatory" and "permissive" subjects of bargaining. "Permissive" subjects are those that either party can simply refuse to discuss with no legal repercussions. Of course, the Court has privileged "managerial decisions, which lie at the core of entrepreneurial control" in this way.[30]

The road to this dichotomy also came through auto negotiations, albeit in a much more obscure event. Just three years after the Treaty, a UAW local in a contentious round of bargaining with an auto parts supplier rejected management's wage offer. The company refused to make another offer unless and until the union put the company's last offer up for a secret ballot vote by its membership. They refused to budge from this position. The union, eager to be done with the negotiations, put the offer up for a vote. It was swiftly rejected and management was compelled to improve on their last wage offer.

The union filed an unfair labor practice charge over management's intransigence in order to discourage such behavior in the future.

Today, one of the five broad categories of ULPs by employers that the law spells out is "to dominate or interfere with the formation or administration of any labor organization or contribute financial or other support to it."

This is the provision that bans company unions, and an employer dictating how the UAW should conduct its internal decision-making would seem to be a clear violation. But the years following the Treaty of Detroit were much more about managing and restraining union demands and protest activity than they were about reining in bad behavior by employers.

Instead, in the 1958 decision *NLRB v. Wooster Division of Borg-Warner*, the Court decided to tinker with bargaining rights. Once judges get in the business of weighing which demands are fair and which are foul, they almost inevitably privilege business. As legal scholar James B. Atleson has observed, courts make "the assumption that certain rights are necessarily vested exclusively in management or are based upon an economic value judgment about the necessary locus of certain power."[31]

So what kind of managerial decisions has the Court decided employers have no obligation to negotiate? Only the small matter of whether a union can protect members' jobs from subcontracting and outsourcing! An employer can hire another company or staffing agency to employ workers side-by-side with bargaining unit members, doing work that the now laid-off co-workers of union members used to do, but now at lower pay and little or no benefits. The employer has no legal obligation to negotiate with the union over the decision. The only right that the union has is to bargain over the impact of the decision that's been made.

So the union can propose how and in what order union members are laid off. They can ask that the laid-off workers get retrained and placed on a priority recall list for other jobs in the bargaining unit or for their old jobs with the new subcontractor. They can bargain for severance and COBRA health insurance payments. What they can't do is force the employer to bargain over the decision itself. They can't use the bargaining process to slow down the decision. They can't force the employer to open its books and justify the economic need for the decision.

Many unions, however, do have language in their collective bargaining agreements to prevent subcontracting. But keeping that language in their contracts has all too often turned into another way that union negotiations are done on a concessionary basis, as most employers would dearly love to be free of such "restrictions."

A union that doesn't have a contract, one where the workers have just organized, is particularly vulnerable. I'd say that every fourth organizing campaign I ever worked on involved the boss simply subcontracting a chunk of the bargaining unit, just to shake things up a little. It's a great way to drag out negotiations and make the workers question whether organizing was worth it. Worse, I can't think of a single campaign I've ever worked on where at least one worker didn't have a story about how she or a family relation lost a previous job and the union couldn't do anything to stop it.

A Temporary Truce That Became a Permanent Surrender

The five-year duration of the UAW's 1950 GM contract was unprecedented. It was a product of the union's annual threat to strike and its proven track record of being able to do so effectively. And, crucially, management *paid* for it with a very pricey wage and benefit package. Today, unions routinely bargain for long-term contracts. Almost all of them contain incredibly restrictive "no strike" clauses. This routine of collective bargaining has become a part of the system that traps us.

The most effective unions actually build strike preparation into those long contract cycles. The entire last two years before expiration are marked by escalating tensions and actions both inside the workplace and outside that measure and demonstrate members' readiness to strike if necessary. The long duration of these agreements is often a reflection of management's exhaustion and desire to delay the next dance for as long as possible. But other unions bargain for long contracts because they fear a strike. Every expiration date represents a potential drive by the employer to bust the union or take away benefits. Long contracts represent the union's desire for a truce in a one-sided class war.

What has changed is that, since the 1980s, employers have been exercising their legal right to permanently replace strikers. The law smiles on a boss who demands unacceptable cuts to wages, health insurance, and pensions. He can force a union to bargain over these mandatory subjects, hold firm to his demands and impose his "last, best" offer after the union has exhausted its legal strategies. Backed against the wall like this, the union members who choose to strike face the very real threat of losing their jobs to the scabs the boss has been busy recruiting to replace them.

Is it any wonder that strikes in this country have been so rare in recent decades?

And that is a huge problem, because our power as workers is still rooted in the work we do and our occasional refusal to do it. But how do we get workers to contemplate their power if they never see other workers exercising that power? How do you get eggs from chickens that have never seen an egg get laid?

This is where the no-strike clause becomes a straitjacket. Strike preparations by established unions have become a routinized kabuki theater. It's only once a half-decade that a union puts the question of striking to its membership. The unions that can strike, ironically, don't have to. The unions that can't strike either don't or do and get crushed.

So there's very little in formal training or leading by example when it comes to teaching workers to go on strike. What that leaves is workers figuring it out for themselves. Workers take it upon themselves to engage in some kind of collective protest over an unpopular decision by their boss. This could be anything from deciding everyone's going to go to lunch at the same time, or all clock out together at exactly 6 p.m., leaving the boss short-staffed and flat-footed.

This kind of spontaneous job action happens all the time, far more than anyone has measured or quantified. The problem is that if there is a union contract with a no-strike clause, the union is legally compelled to send a representative down to denounce the action, to tell the workers they must stop it or they will be fired. The union representative is pressed into service as the boss's cop, telling the workers that they must obey the boss's law!

Among the many anti-union Taft-Hartley amendments to the National Labor Relations Act act is Section 301, which lays out punishments for unions that strike "illegally." A union that strikes in violation of its contractual commitment can be ordered to pay back three times the amount of money that the employer claims it lost during the protest. If a union alleges that an employer committed an unfair labor practice—by, say, firing a union leader—it must work its way through the NLRB investigatory process for perhaps a year or more before the NLRB issues a ruling and then takes an intransigent employer to court. But if an employer complains that a union is striking during the terms of a contract, they get to go straight to court and ask a judge to make the union pay them millions of dollars.

Remember when the Rockettes were signed up to be one of the few entertainment acts at the pathetic presidential inauguration festivities of the pussy-grabbing reality television personality? Many dancers in the troupe publicly declared they would refuse to dance for the serial sexual predator. Their union leadership had to rush to put out a press release stressing their legal obligations to dance on command.

This was an incredibly dispiriting moment, one that likely caused allies to ask, "Why even bother having a union?" But if the union hadn't swiftly denounced the protest its members had declared, they likely would have been sued for millions. And a nod and a wink with a "We really think you should reconsider this" would not have been sufficient legal protection for the union. Work like hell to shut down the protest or pay through the nose is essentially the legal standard here.

Now contrast that with the New York Taxi Workers Alliance, whose members were able to swiftly declare and organize a spontaneous work stoppage at JFK airport on the night that the Trump administration rolled out its initial ban on refugees from seven majority-Muslim nations. The NYTWA doesn't have a no-strike clause. They don't even have a contract, or any collective bargaining rights at all as the National Labor Relations Board deems them to be self-employed independent contractors.

There are clearly benefits to being free of the restrictions of a no-strike clause. But getting free of the tyranny of no-strike clauses is no easy feat for unions that are regulated by the post–Taft-Hartley labor law regime. Courts have actually ruled that unions that have somehow managed to resist signing away their protest rights by agreeing to a no-strike clause have nevertheless surrendered them by agreeing to grievance procedures that include the recourse to neutral third-party arbitration.[32]

Management's Rights

Union contracts cede tremendous decision-making power to bosses. A typical "Management's Rights" clause goes something like this:

> All of the rights, powers, prerogatives, and authority of the management of the Employer's operations are retained by the Employer and remain exclusively within the rights of management. These include, but are not limited to, the right to direct, transfer, hire, discipline and discharge employees as well as determine the objectives and priorities of the company.
>
> It is understood and agreed that the rights of management shall be deemed only limited by the express provisions of the Agreement and not by implication or construction. The failure of the Employer to exercise its full rights of management or discretion on any manner or occasion shall not be a precedent or binding on the Employer, nor the subject or basis of any grievance nor admissible in any grievance proceeding.
>
> Any of the rights, powers, or authority that the Employer has prior to the signing of this Agreement are retained by the Employer, except those specifically abridged, delegated, granted to others, or modified by this Agreement or by any supplementary agreements that may hereafter be made.

Language like this was a reasonable concession when collective bargaining agreements were one-year truces that settled a few grievances and set the wages for the year. It's still sometimes reasonable in those rare bargaining relationships where the concept of "labor-management partnership" isn't a joke, where management accepts the presence of a union as a reality of life and tries to get along for the sake of maintaining a smooth operation. But when most employers are engaging in a one-sided class war, this sort of broad management's rights clause should not be treated as a routine of bargaining. It certainly should not be allowed to limit a union's vision of what workers want, or to lower members' expectations of what's winnable or to limit our power.

Today, it is common for union negotiators bargaining a first contract to actually *propose* the management's rights clause! The routine logic for this is that, of course, there's going to be a management's rights clause, so we might as well propose one that doesn't give away the shop. But I've also seen these union negotiators sign off on the management's rights clause long before the rest of the contract is settled. Historically, signing away the boss's duty to bargain over changes was the last item on the table until all grievances were settled and the money was good enough.

Moreover, the suggestion that a union bargaining a successor agreement (binding a successor employer) should start from the position that having a management's rights clause was okay for the last contract but not this contract would be greeted by negotiators on both sides of the table as stark raving lunacy.

But here's the crazy thing about that. A union with its back against the wall, bargaining for a successor agreement against an employer that's clearly aiming to gut the contract or bust the union, can find it very advantageous to continue to bargain after the contract's expiration and continue to stay on the job.

I mean, there are entire strategy manuals on working without a contract. It's a critical escalation of what are called "work to rule" or "inside" campaigns. When a collective bargaining agreement expires, the terms of the agreement don't automatically go away—just the management's rights clause. As a movement, we know there is power in this.

I run the risk here of oversimplifying, or having the NLRB change the rules two months after this book is published, but the basic rules of bargaining go like this: A non-union employer gets to make all the decisions. Once a union has been recognized as the representative, a kind of status quo is established. Oh, the employer can make changes, but if those changes affect those pesky "mandatory" subjects of bargaining (wages, hours, and working conditions), they must first be proposed to the union that represents the workers. The boss can only make the change if the union agrees, or if he can bargain the union to what's called "impasse." Impasse essentially means, "We don't agree." However, a union can drag out the process of not agreeing by pushing paper back and forth with minor changes to the boss's demands, or by requesting detailed, onerous, and relevant information requests.

Even where there's a well-established collective bargaining agreement, when it expires the workplace returns to the status quo of a newly organized shop. It is perhaps more disruptive in a workplace where management has been used to the routine of having the broad powers of a management's rights clause.

What's a mandatory subject of bargaining in this scenario? New uniforms for the workers, moving the start of the a.m. shift from 7:00 to 7:30, switching up the menu in the employee cafeteria, lowering the thermostat by one degree. Sometimes it takes a keen eye and creative mind. In contract fights at the Hotel Employees union, we would demand to bargain over new carpets and coffeepots in the guest rooms. Even the threat of us filing an unfair labor practice charge, seeking a remedy that the new carpeting should be removed until the hotel bargains in good faith over the change, was enough to provoke some movement by the other side.

Such a charge is obviously unlikely to be successful under a Republican majority NLRB. Nevertheless, we clearly understand that there's power in denying the boss his management's rights, but we don't pursue the strategy of denying management its unfettered right to run the enterprise as a matter of course.

Instead, we have capitulated to the notion that the boss gets to run his business, and we just get to ask for more money. This is, literally, not what workers want. Researchers Richard B. Freeman and Joel Rodgers have conducted deep surveys of workers' desires regarding workplace representation. Their book *What Workers Want* concluded that workers want "more" from workplace representation: "More say in the workplace decisions that affect their lives, more employee involvement in their firms, more legal protection at the workplace, and more union representation."

But "most workers do not believe that, under current U.S. policies, they can get the additional input into workplace decisions that they want."[33] Workers have very limited influence over the state of labor law, but we do control what we demand and fight for.

I want to take the briefest of respites from this fairly pessimistic narrative to acknowledge that most union members really value their collective bargaining agreements. Collective bargaining has improved the pay and working conditions of millions of workers, and most union members shudder at the thought of losing the protections of their CBAs.

But, that said, we have allowed a moral and strategic rot to set in. I can't tell you how many times I've overheard a union representative respond to a member's complaint with a gruff, "They're allowed to do that. It's management's rights." Look, I get it. Most union representatives work very hard; they're overwhelmed with how many grievances and negotiations they're juggling; and this is an easy way to make one more problem go away. Plus, whatever training they've received has probably emphasized the strict boundaries of management's rights, and for them to "tell the difference" between a grievance and a "gripe."

But what, exactly, do we expect a union member who's been told, "There's nothing we can do" to tell a friend or family member about their experience of being in a union? And why are we surprised that more workers aren't organizing?

"The Union Can't Protect Your Job"

So, finally, this is the trap in which we find ourselves caught. Unions can only represent us on a workplace-by-workplace basis, and only if a majority of eligible voters in a bargaining unit vote for union representation. When we represent a workplace, we must do so on an exclusive basis that forces us to take both the credit and blame for the pay, benefits, and work rules that everyone must labor under. We are also responsible for ensuring that all members of the bargaining unit do not protest, except under incredibly proscribed limits and during a small window of time. And if we're in a "right to work" state—or, thanks to the Supreme Court's *Janus* decision—in the public sector, unions have to expend significant financial resources representing workers who refuse to pay for them.

We're expected to deliver big wages and generous benefits for our members, but that only worked when we represented all the companies in the major industries and were able to make employers bear the costs equally, thereby taking wages (and benefits) out of competition. Once that became the framework, any foreign competitor or start-up could be instantly competitive by dint of their lower payroll costs. Our existing unionized employers had a financial incentive, and legal protections, for outsourcing and subcontracting jobs to remain "competitive." And all bosses have an economic drive to bust their unions or remain union-free.

Our "right" to strike, which would only be meaningful if it included the right to return to the job, has been severely curtailed. As a result—even with the recent uptick in strike activity—industrial actions are at a historical low ebb and very few workers understand their power and how to exercise it. One reasonable pathway to reviving the strike could be the spontaneous protest activity of union members, but the no-strike clauses in most collective bargaining agreements legally bind union representatives to clamp down on such job actions.

Meanwhile, management's rights and our restricted scope of bargaining give bosses near-dictatorial control over daily decision-making, and whether union members can even have reasonable job security.

Finally, when a group of workers gets brave enough to join together, when they have a union certification election scheduled, and when their employer exercises his right to force them to attend mandatory captive audience meetings to campaign against the union vote, what are the devastatingly effective statements he'll make?

- A union could make our company less competitive, and we might have to lay some people off.
- Unions only get what they want by going on strike, but if you go on strike you could lose your job.
- The union can't protect your job.

There is truth in all those statements. We let this happen. This is our trap.

FOUR

Two Reasons Why Most Unions Don't Do Large-Scale Organizing

IN 2005, THE LABOR MOVEMENT split, ostensibly over a disagreement about the institutional priority of organizing for membership growth. A number of unions seceded from the AFL-CIO to form a rival federation, Change to Win, only to (mostly) return quietly to the fold. Other unions merged, only to attempt to divorce shortly thereafter. There have been trusteeships[34] and membership raids, and some very good comprehensive campaigns for new members and new bargaining units. But, as the dust settles from this period of union conflict, the decline in union density has not been arrested. Moreover, significantly fewer unions seem to be engaged in large-scale organizing, and the broad consensus within labor on the need to prioritize organizing has faded.

The story of labor's wars could be thought of as a tug of war between competing institutional interests within the existing union framework—actually, a twin set of tensions. The first is between keeping decision-making and financial resources at the local union level and pooling resources and concentrating power in the international union. The other tension is between devoting resources to organizing the unorganized and focusing on winning better pay, working conditions, and rights for existing union members. These twin tensions are closely related but worth evaluating separately.

The Local vs. the International

The concept of Change to Win was inspired by Stephen Lerner's "Immodest Proposal: A New Architecture for the House of Labor," that unions should merge into ten to fifteen sector-focused international unions.[35] Lerner's thesis was that diluting labor's resources among sixty-six international unions (particularly when fifty-one of them accounted for less than a quarter of AFL-CIO membership) was untenable if unions were to grow. That dilution of resources gets even more hair-raising when one considers that international unions are divided into anywhere from a couple dozen to a couple thousand local unions, and that most union dues remain at the local level. Many locals barely have enough money to properly serve their existing members, let alone organize new members.

A lot of the response led to a merger mania at the local level. UNITE HERE engaged in a thoughtful process of merging locals with overlapping geographical jurisdiction, in the hope of committing garment worker resources to new organizing in the hotel industry. The Service Employees International Union (SEIU) utilized more blunt force to forge mega-locals that cover multistate regions. Such efforts were not limited to Change to Win unions. One of the projects I worked on at the American Federation of Teachers (AFT) was convincing nine New Jersey stand-alone locals of adjunct college faculty to merge into one statewide union in order to pool resources and hire a full-time coordinator of bargaining and contract campaigns.

More power and resources were concentrated at the international level. Constitutions were amended to give international leaders and staff more decision-making authority in organizing and even bargaining. Per capita dues were increased, giving the international unions (internationals) the power of the purse strings (and those internationals that left the AFL-CIO got even more money).

It is true that big campaigns against multinational companies can only be run with big resources and national coordination. But local unions with serious organizing programs (these do exist!) may have priorities that do not align with the international's plans. Too often, the hard work of hammering out a plan that works for both sets of interests is undermined by secrecy and manipulation. In her memoir, *Raising Expectations (and Raising Hell): My Decade of Fighting for the Labor Movement*, Jane McAlevey provides a good, if somewhat biased, view of this tension from the perspective of an SEIU local that was not entirely "on the program," as they say.

I saw some of these tensions firsthand while I was a young staffer at New York City's hotel workers' local, the New York Hotel Trades Council (NYHTC). The newly merged UNITE HERE's first major campaign was coordinating the expiration dates of as many citywide contracts as possible to end in the same year. This campaign was probably one of the biggest successes of the Change to Win era, as the threat of shutting down a significant percentage of hotel chains' business resulted in both substantial pay and work-rule improvements in the existing locals' contracts and neutrality deals that allowed the international union to grow in other parts of the country. (At their best, neutrality deals are legally binding agreements by employers not to campaign against employee unionization and to give unions reasonable access to bargaining unit employees for the purpose of organizing.)

But I do not think anyone at UNITE HERE told the leadership of NYHTC that the plan was to line up everyone's contracts with their 2006 expiration until after four or five cities' expirations were already aligned. And the chain that UNITE HERE most wanted to single out did not make strategic sense for the NYC local. Finally, those neutrality deals also involved signing away some locals' rights to organize other properties that the chains considered off-limits. Unfortunately, no one sought the locals' consent. I am not sure that any of these disagreements were properly aired until the day that NYHTC president Peter Ward and Las Vegas local president D. Taylor stood in the office of UNITE HERE General President Bruce Raynor and told him he would not be reelected (thus precipitating the disastrous "divorce").

The pressure to gain more members is one that international unions feel acutely, while many locals do not seem to feel that burden if they are able to continue to bring in decent contracts and get their officers reelected. This is particularly true for locals who represent only one employer or who have the lion's share of their membership in a handful of politically important shops. In fact, new members upset the apple cart. This is doubly true for new members who come in having learned the organizing model, and, therefore, have radically different expectations of their involvement in contract enforcement and future rounds of bargaining.

Another problem arises when comprehensive campaigns often feature confrontational tactics that may discomfort or embarrass local union leaders who are not used to them. What often results is a lack of local support, if not outright sabotage, and organizers are caught in the middle of a bureaucratic pissing contest.

Internal Organizing versus New Organizing

Positing internal organizing against external organizing is a false choice, borne out of prioritization forced by labor's declining resources. Both kinds of organizing are vital to labor renewal. But in the rush to find new money for new organizing, many unions targeted the vast sums that are spent on grievances, arbitration, business agent salaries, and shop steward training, expenses that do not tend to build union power absent a meaningful member mobilization plan.

At the risk of caricaturing, the "Organize or die!" logic essentially meant the following: We cannot grow if all we do is "service" our existing members and we cannot substantially improve pay and working conditions without meaningfully increasing union density in a given industry. Therefore, we should devote as much of our resources as possible to organizing for growth. Taken to its extreme, this resulted in quick and understaffed organizing campaigns under neutrality agreements, even quicker negotiations that prioritized union recognition and agency fees over detailed work rules, and new union members receiving business cards with an 800 number to handle grievances.

In such a framework, international unions jealously guarded resources meant for new organizing from being sneakily expended on contract campaigns. But here's the thing. Many organizers, including those on international staff, found it very difficult to organize new members into locals with poor reputations and weak contracts, and thus often prioritized reinvigorating legacy bargaining units with contract campaigns.

Because of vicious employer retaliation in union organizing campaigns, workers must have a sense that running the gauntlet of employer opposition will be worth it. Any organizer can vouch for how detrimental a worker with a "bad union experience" can be to a campaign. Conversely, if a worker had experience, or intimate familiarity with some other member's experience, in an organizing campaign with an informed and democratic organizing committee, a plan to win, and meaningful "asks" of worker activism, such a worker comes away a bit more radicalized and vastly more likely to take action in a new campaign.

The choice between internal organizing or new member organizing may be a false choice, but to the extent that unions have been making it so, there is a strong argument to be made that we have been choosing poorly. It is the visible resistance of organized workers that inspires people to join the labor movement. As a recruiter and trainer of new union organizers, I can recall very few new recruits in the last few years who did not cite as their "reason I want to do this work" either the Chicago teachers' strike or the Wisconsin protests. The Wisconsin protests were a failure, but the example of union members standing and fighting the right-wing agenda was still an inspiration. Of course, I am citing examples of workers who decided they wanted to work on the staff of unions, not stand and fight for a union where they currently work. Clearly, we have a long way to go toward inspiring an upsurge in spontaneous organizing.

In this regard, I agree with much of Richard Yeselson's "Fortress Unionism,"[36] which proposes that labor focus on preserving and strengthening existing unions "and then . . . wait" (his words). Except we must all take exception with his prescription for waiting for a spontaneous worker uprising. Our job is to inspire it! Unions should engage more in well-planned contract campaigns and job actions with the vast audience of non-union workers in mind.

Comprehensive new organizing campaigns are important for the same reason. Most workers in this country do not even know how a union gets formed. The assumption that workplaces either do or do not have a union by some kind of bureaucratic fiat is surprisingly pervasive. Non-union workers need to see big campaigns of workers standing up to their employer and demanding improvements and a voice at work to get inspired to do the same. We must talk more about this symbolic and inspirational value that comprehensive campaigns have because institutional support for them seems to be at a historic low. They are too often the victims of impatience, the changing priorities of new leadership, and the institutional conflicts outlined herein. But they are essential and must be revived.

Some Thoughts about Moving Forward

We need more training for union leaders and staff in the kind of facilitation and consensus-building that actually gets areas of disagreement and hesitation on the table and develops campaign plans with true "buy-in." This is some of our most difficult work, and yet we devote little attention to building these skills.

International unions, in partnership with their affiliates, should develop, or revisit, their own organizing models. Transparency, honesty, and a commitment to organizing must be the bedrock principles of any model.

There should be a greater openness to chartering new locals where an existing local, for whatever reason, is an impediment to new organizing. The kind of union-building that results in a leadership and a membership base that can stand on its own is time-consuming and resource-heavy, which is one reason why unions are loath to do it. But unions should only be engaging in organizing projects with long-term commitments to building power any way.

Unions must continue to raise their dues and implement special assessments for organizing and strike funds. Members will vote to raise their dues if it is presented as a real plan for increased power. Union dues should cost at least $1,000 a year. Many unions have already raised their dues to this level. Those unions who keep their dues "cheap" do the labor movement no favors.

And unions should continue to find ways to devote a larger percentage of their resources to organizing. We could certainly be more judicious about how and what we spend on politics. Doubling down on political spending in 2014 when, historically speaking, the president's party was inevitably going to lose the last midterm of the last presidential term, converted the Democrats' loss into labor's loss. That money could have been spent more wisely on organizing.

Finally, the AFL-CIO does have a role to play. The smaller international unions that have not yet engaged in comprehensive campaigns need the Federation's leadership. The AFL-CIO should take the lead in facilitating the development of organizing models and plans. A special focus should be placed on unions with similar jurisdictions that could be coaxed into combining resources in joint campaigns that result in new merged locals.

The great push to organize and grow that began twenty years ago with the start of the Sweeney administration, and which intensified ten years ago in the Change to Win split, has frankly and obviously stalled. Perhaps this discussion merely nibbles at the edge of the problem, but we need a thorough analysis of the institutional barriers that have kept unions from truly committing to organizing for growth and power.

FIVE

The Changes We Have the Power to Make

THERE ARE TWO BASIC PHILOSOPHICAL approaches that union activists—staff, leaders, and members alike—generally fall into. Both are variations of putting your nose to the grindstone, and both involve magical thinking that something will come along and save the labor movement.

The first approach is to view legislative labor law reform as a necessary precursor to labor's next upsurge. This entails running as many good campaigns as you can within a broken system, while shrugging "it is what it is" about the rules, and working to elect enough Democrats to Congress so that we somehow get a majority that will ditch the filibuster and finally repeal Taft-Hartley, pass a card check provision like the Employee Free Choice Act, and institute financial penalties for union-busting employers so that we can finally get on with the business of organizing the millions of workers who want and need unions right now.

The second approach is to take as an article of faith that there will be no legislative labor law reform absent a great upsurge of labor militancy, which it is our responsibility to spark. These comrades too shrug and say "it is what it is," accepting the rigged rules of our broken system as a given, and admonish us to "be better than the boss," run smarter and tougher campaigns, or find new leaders who will do so.

I don't mean to dismiss either camp. There are merits to both approaches. But let me suggest that we have more agency than that. As I said in the first chapter, our nation's current crisis of democracy and runaway inequality make this moment alive with possibility. We must be adroit and open to experimenting with even more approaches still.

We have to get past abstractions, and we have to stop conflating our legal rights with our human rights. We must pursue an internal debate that is crystal clear about what we can't control at the moment—Congress, capital mobility, and our psychotic president's attention span—and what we can—our strategy, structure, and demands. That is the focus of this chapter.

Labor's Bill of Rights

As soon as I left the American Federation of Teachers at the end of 2015, I began writing and publishing for the first time in years. I soon realized I had a lot of pent-up frustrations about unions' legal strategies and that I had to vent them.

Look, union organizers and labor lawyers have probably been butting heads since the dawn of the labor movement, and it's mostly a healthy tension. Disagreements, after all, can lead to strategic breakthroughs. But a kind of institutional inertia has set in, and at most unions, and in most campaigns, the lawyers get to have the final word on strategic decisions. All too often, it's without the benefit of a proper debate. And almost always the lawyers, particularly the general counsels and lawyers on retainer at the DC-based international unions, pursue a fundamentally conservative course of action.

They might not be wrong. The judiciary is traditionally hostile to workers' rights and collective action, particularly strikes and boycotts, and putting our campaign issues in the courts comes with the tremendous risks of new, awful court decisions that tighten the trap in which we find ourselves. Yet this seems to be happening anyway. The cautious strategy of losing more slowly in the face of this sustained corporate offensive should not be our default. Maybe—just *maybe*—we should try new offensive strategies based around positive assertions of our constitutional rights against the full weight of this trap we're in. Parts of our labor relations system have become plainly unconstitutional if we step back and look at it with fresh eyes and any semblance of fairness.

I began advocating a left-wing strategy of judicial activism for labor rights in *In These Times*. Look, I'm not great at branding. I didn't even come up with the name of this book! But that dreadfully unsexy framing of "judicial activism" landed with a thud (although I was steadily gaining an audience for such ideas).

Throughout 2016, I organized my thoughts on a series of constitutional challenges to the unequal and unfair application of labor law. The Century Foundation published "Labor's Bill of Rights" in the summer of 2017 as a white paper. That it's included as the appendix of this book instead of being reworked into a book of its own should be read as a sign of my own restless search for the right questions to help us figure a way out of this trap of a labor relations system. I never proposed "Labor's Bill of Rights" as a silver bullet. And, anyway, our enemy is not a werewolf. Rather than a magical solution or *deus ex machina*, I think that a conscious and deliberate strategy of challenging the rules that are enforced against unions but not corporations should be an arrow in our quiver.

The report was written in 2016 with the expectation of four more years of Democratic court and NLRB appointments. This doesn't mean that judicial activism is wrong or should even be put off until the next Democratic administration, or if there's ever a more favorable legal environment. When, where, and how we use the courts to agitate for workers' rights is something over which we do have a degree of control.

What follows is my attempt to point a fatter finger at the first campaigns we should run for a Labor's Bill of Rights and my thoughts on how to do so. Feel free to pause here and go to the back of the book to read the full white paper before returning to this slightly more practical coda. Or keep reading this chapter and get to that other bit at your convenience.

Part of the problem of the cautiousness of union attorneys is baked into the 1935 National Labor Relations Act (NLRA). Unions endured over a century of judicial meddling in union organizing campaigns and strikes. Judges invented and then prioritized employers' "property" right in their continued expectation that workers would continue to drag themselves to work every day. Judges prioritized this invented property right—and any "contracts" they forced non-union workers to sign in fidelity to it—over workers' constitutional rights to free speech and assembly in protest of their involuntary servitude.[37]

The NLRA created a system of private jurisprudence that emphasized collective bargaining and mediation and aimed to keep labor disputes out of the courts. At the time, this was a nearly unprecedented federal intervention in the workings of the free market. The framers of the NLRA justified this by Congress's constitutional authority to regulate commerce between the states.[38]

As soon as the Act was passed, employers immediately began challenging the legal framework for workers to organize and bargain collectively. They were in the courts arguing for their First Amendment rights of free speech. Unions were there defending the NLRB on the basis of collective bargaining's stabilizing effect on the economy and the principle of judicial deference to the new regulatory machinery. We have gotten our asses kicked on these terms of the debate ever since. It is time to flip the script.

Consider union certification elections. These are official legal elections conducted by an arm of the federal government. At stake is whether the government will enforce certain statutory rights of the workers who wish to form a union. The rules of the election are determined by the government through court decisions, congressional action, and NLRB rule-making—in other words, "through state action." In this simple "yes" or "no" vote about whether there shall be a union, only an employer—and only one advocating a "no" vote— can force voters to attend speeches where they will tell them how to vote. And if voters decline to attend, they can be fired. However, the party that advocates a "yes" vote has no equivalent right to respond. This is compelled political speech and a massive violation of workers' free speech rights!

How did this happen? Six short years after it was passed, the bosses succeeded in demolishing the Act's mandate of employer neutrality by strenuously appealing to the Supreme Court that the standard restricts the First Amendment right of employers to inform their workers about just how strongly they oppose unionization. Six years after that, a Republican Congress codified this unequal application of free speech in the Taft-Hartley Act: "The expressing of any views, argument, or opinion, or the dissemination thereof," the law now clearly states, "shall not constitute or be evidence of an unfair labor practice under any of the provisions of this Act, if such expression contains no threat of reprisal or force or promise of benefit."

For a brief time after Taft-Hartley, the NLRB enforced an equal time standard by granting union organizers access to talk to workers on the job when an employer conducted captive audience meetings. In an all-too-familiar pattern, the Board ping-ponged between different legal standards on employer speech and union access, depending on which political party was in the White House, until 1966.

That was the year of *Excelsior Underwear, Inc.*, the NLRB decision that established the right for unions to be furnished with a list of names and addresses of eligible voters. It was issued on the same day that the Board declined to reinstate the equal time rule. The case that we should have won that day was *General Electric Co. and McCulloch Corp.*, which would have restored the equal time provision of granting union organizers access to the employer's property when an employer conducted captive audience meetings.[39]

Loath to trample on management's rights and private property, the Democratic majority begged the unions in that case to try visiting workers at home and see if that effectively counterbalanced the boss's worktime campaigning. Anyone who has worked as a union organizer will tell you that an *Excelsior* list is no match for the mandatory round-the-clock campaigns of intimidation that union-busters consider "management's most important weapon"[40] in beating back an organizing drive.

To make Labor's Bill of Rights a campaign, every time an employer stages a captive audience meeting in advance of a union election, we should file an Unfair Labor Practice charge. And every time a union loses an election in which the employer conducted captive audience meetings (which is almost always), we should file an appeal to have the election results overturned. We should do this so many times that it becomes an obvious controversy that the next Democratic-majority NLRB must address. And the first time that the NLRB orders an employer to give a union equivalent access to bargaining unit voters in order to counterbalance their captive audience meetings, that employer will, of course, defy the order and get dragged to court. And then we're off to the races with a union free speech case in the wake of the *Janus* decision, which decided that every interaction a union has with the government is inherently political speech (of course, this was in order to invent a First Amendment right to avoid paying union fees).

One more example of what a campaign for Labor's Bill of Rights could do: restore the right to strike. Workers simply do not have a meaningful right to strike if they do not have a right to return to the job when the strike is over. This is currently the situation thanks to one of the most ill-considered and destructive Supreme Court cases ever. In *NLRB v. Mackay Radio & Telegraph Co.*, the Court gave employers the legal right to permanently replace striking workers. To do so, they deliberately ignored the plain language that "nothing in this Act shall be construed so as either to interfere with or impede or diminish in any way the right to strike."

In that 1939 case, the union's strike lasted all of one weekend. The employer continued operating by transferring workers from its other facilities, and when support for the union's goals failed to material-ize, the leaders called off the strike. When the strikers returned to work on Monday, four of the leaders were singled out and denied reinstatement.

Of course, the Mackay Radio & Telegraph Company didn't have enough time to hire permanent replacements in a weekend. It simply wasn't an issue in the facts of the case. The NLRB quickly ruled that the employer's actions were clear violations of the law and went to court to order the employer to reinstate the four fired strikers, with back pay. The Ninth Circuit Court refused to enforce the NLRB's order, as this was generally a period when many jurists considered the labor act, in part or in whole, to be unconstitutional. That's how the case got to the Supreme Court.

The case was an early constitutional test for the NLRA, and, ironically, the *Mackay* decision was hailed at the time as a victory for labor. It was yet another decision that cemented the constitutionality of labor law, and the Court also found *for* the union and the NLRB. The NLRA, after all, was meant to protect workers who engage in union activity from "discrimination in regard to hire or tenure of employment or any term or condition of employment." The Court agreed with the NLRB that these four workers were singled out for their strike activity and told that they no longer had jobs.

The issue of permanent replacements was gratuitously inserted by Justice Owen Roberts as an offhand comment, which I'll quote in full because it bears scrutiny:

> Although Section 13 of the Act provides, "Nothing in the Act should be interpreted to interfere with or impede or diminish in any way the right to strike," it does not follow that an employer, guilty of no act denounced by the statute, has lost the right to protect and continue his business by supplying places left vacant by strikers. And he is not bound to discharge those hired to fill the places of strikers, upon the election of the latter to resume their employment in order to create places for them.[41]

In other words, the employer in *Mackay* broke the law because it discriminated against the strike leaders by singling them out and firing them. But if the employer had found a non-discriminatory way to discriminate against the strikers (like, say, hiring scabs to replace them in the order of reverse seniority) then that would be hunky-dory.

In the four decades that followed *Mackay*, very few employers took the liberty to permanently replace striking workers, as it generally fell outside what was considered socially acceptable employer behavior in the postwar era. Which isn't to say that some employers didn't try to push the envelope in their union-busting attempts. Most judicial revisiting of *Mackay* comes from cases where the courts rejected employer attempts to go further. For instance, in a 1963 case, the Supreme Court rejected an employer's attempt to grant replacements a "super seniority" for their service as scabs by ruling that it was not "proper under *Mackay*."[42] It was this sort of right-wing judicial activism that pushed back on union rights and served to give a bad footnote the appearance of *stare decisis*, that is, settled legal doctrine. (I'm old enough to remember when Supreme Court Justices pretended to care about "settled law.") But the Court has never revisited the facts or logic of *Mackay*.

As Julius Getman points out in his book *The Supreme Court on Unions*, what is now considered the *"Mackay* Doctrine" is in direct conflict with the actual *Mackay* decision:

> The holding is that it is illegal to decide which employees are entitled to work after a strike on the basis of union activity. But the dictum insists that the employer may give employment preference to those who work during a strike over those who strike, which is precisely the same result, penalizing union activity that was outlawed by the holding.[43]

Mackay was weaponized by the Phelps-Dodge Corporation in 1983. The copper mining company bargained its Steelworkers local to impasse over drastic cuts in pay, benefits, and working conditions, essentially daring the union to strike. Exploiting the bad economic times, the company had no problem importing a permanent replacement workforce, for whom even the reduced pay was far better than most jobs available. After twelve very ugly months, the scabs voted to legally decertify the union.[44]

This Phelps-Dodge blueprint is how much of the deunionization of American industry occurred in the Reagan-Bush (and Clinton) era. Unions that survived frequently did so by capitulating to management's giveback demands.

So, what are our grounds to challenge *Mackay*? Let's do a close reading of Justice Owen Roberts's decision. First, the "right" to permanently replace strikers is only granted to employers who are "guilty of no act denounced by the statute." This is why unions try to frame their strikes as unfair labor practice strikes instead of strikes over economic demands, as the presence of ULPs can protect strikers from being permanently replaced.

But many anti-union acts are denounced by the statute! The very first unfair labor practice listed in the Act is "to interfere with, restrain, or coerce employees in the exercise of the rights guaranteed." In other words, basic anti-union animus is denounced in the statute! Hiring permanent replacements with the intention of busting the union violates *Mackay*!

We've forgotten this because throughout the wave of union-busting in the 1980s and '90s, the Reagan and Bush NLRB did their best impersonation of wrestling referee and looked away from the obvious union-busting that was taking place. We've also forgotten this because the AFL-CIO's first attempt to undo *Mackay* was a legislative push at the beginning of the Clinton administration. After that effort failed, to my knowledge, there was no effort to get the NLRB to simply revert back to a proper reading of the *Mackay* Doctrine.

Very late in Obama's second term, the NLRB did signal a shift in its approach to anti-union animus in the use of permanent replacements.[45] In a case called *American Baptist Homes*, the company's executive director and her counsel were stupid enough to put in writing that their use of permanent replacements was meant to "punish the strikers and the Union" and to discourage future strikes. The Board ordered the employer to rehire all of the workers it had permanently replaced. It was a pretty strong signal that the NLRB would return to an earlier Supreme Court–approved standard in which employers' rights to permanently replace striking workers may be "wholly impeached by the showing of an intent to encroach upon protected rights."[46] (Or at least do so when there are Democrats in the White House.)

Let's return again to a close reading of Justice Owen Roberts's decision. Second, hiring permanent replacements is also only protected if it is necessary for an employer "to protect and continue his business." That's a pretty high bar. Is it one that the NLRB has ever particularly investigated? Is it one that unions have ever asked them to? Could multibillion-dollar corporations like Spectrum Communications and Verizon prove that they would go out of business if they couldn't hire scabs and offer them permanent jobs? Should they be made to open their books?

What does a Labor's Bill of Rights campaign to restore the right to strike look like? It begins by filing a ton of unfair labor practice charges. Anytime an employer advertises for scabs, file a charge! Document every anti-union statement or action that the employer has taken by that point and charge them with planning to bust the union. Charge them with retaliating against members' union activity! Make them prove the economic necessity of their course of action. Do this even when a Republican majority NLRB will dismiss every case. Make it a controversy that the next Democratic majority NLRB will have to deal with. I guarantee you this: the issue will very quickly get in the courts. Employers who are ordered to rehire "permanently" replaced strikers will refuse to comply and the courts will await them.

Once we're in the courts, we should argue not just that *Mackay* was wrong the day it was decided by ignoring the plain language of the act. We should also be making historical arguments that employers' use of *Mackay* fundamentally changed in 1983, which had a direct and measurable impact on union density and bargaining power (*Mackay* has not been reconsidered by the Supreme Court since well before Phelps-Dodge, which weaponized the *Mackay* decision and unleashed the private sector union-busting era of the 1980s). Finally, we should be arguing that we have a constitutional right to strike based on the First and Thirteenth Amendments.

What happens if the right to strike goes before the Supreme Court and we lose? We already didn't have the right to strike, so what have we really lost? What we've gained is a powerful lesson for workers about how much conservatives and corporations fear the power of strikes. Maybe—just maybe—this gets more workers thinking about their power and how to use it.

Being More Thoughtful about How We Organize

Another key decision that is entirely within unions' power as union membership becomes voluntary is which workers to target for recruitment. The majority of states now ban the union shop in the private sector, and the *Janus* decision weaponized the First Amendment to turn the entire public sector right-to-work. Currently, most open-shop unions try to sign up all the workers they represent. Often, they fall far short of that goal.

Worse, however, is that the goal itself is shortsighted. When a workplace has few members, it makes the first union members de facto representatives, if not the actual shop stewards. But what if that early joiner is not respected by his co-workers? What if he's a sexist? What if he's bad at his job and his co-workers frequently have to pick up the slack? In its rush to pick up dues-paying members, a union could alienate ten times as many potential members.

I have a good friend who is a national representative at the American Federation of Teachers. His partner works for the federal government in a position represented by the American Federation of Government Employees (AFGE). She's a progressive and a union supporter. Federal employee bargaining units have been open shops for a long time. The shop steward for her union is an odious sexist, and she just can't stand to join and fork over dues to this guy.

In our rush to preserve our unions' revenue streams, the real pressure on organizers is to reach for the low-hanging fruit and sign up any warm body willing to pay dues. This is not how we structure new union organizing campaigns. In those, we target natural leaders. We look for workers who are brave, who ask smart questions, who are good at their jobs and respected by their co-workers. Often, the first worker to inquire about organizing a union, and from whom we learn as much as we can about the workplace and its leaders, is kept off the organizing committee because he doesn't fit the bill.

There are, however, other models.

I've had experience trying to organize grant-funded postdoctoral researchers in university settings. As much as I've read about global union comparisons, it's not been enough to claim expertise in that particular subfield of labor studies. But nothing has been more eye-opening than asking a foreign-born, relatively elite worker to sign a union card to get a gut-sense of how unions in other countries organize.

In a typical large union organizing card drive, the simple "ask" to sign a card is, far too often, at least in that conversation, the "big" ask, with the idea that we'll have a follow-up talk. In that scenario, the worker's response to the "ask" is amazingly revealing about how differently unions organize and are structured from country to country.

To a man (not so much a woman—more on that below), the Japanese scientists would have a slight look of panic in their eyes as they explained they simply didn't have the time that being in the union would involve. I never got the sense that this was a dodge. A postdoc probably spends 60 or 70 hours a week on his research. But, beyond that, the Japanese scientists all seemed to know from their experience, either directly or through friends or relations, that union membership also came with some commitment to be actively involved.

Indian scientists were usually hot or cold but rarely neutral. This is partially explained by the diversity of union ideology in that country. Every union, of which there are many, is closely affiliated with a political party, of which there are also many. This was most acute in the Uttar Pradesh state, which is periodically governed by communist governments with strong union backing. Scientists who came from middle-class (or higher-status) families blamed "unions" for every mild inconvenience their families had ever experienced. Everyone else from that state seemed to react delightfully and enthusiastically to a union card.

The French were the hardest nuts to crack. I've never gotten a French scientist to sign a card in a first conversation. They always weighed the matter soberly, and the conversations were always tortured, circular, and (to an American) bizarre. The objections were always I'm sorry, it's not for me, I don't have the time. They always supported there being a union for other people to join if they so chose. They hated the idea, as they understood it, that their not "joining" stood in the way of the workers who wanted to belong to the union. And they wouldn't believe us that in America joining a union didn't carry a commitment to be active.

This is a radically different way of viewing a unionized workplace. Union membership density in France is even smaller than in the United States, yet French unions are capable of organizing massive general strikes. There are many reasons for that, including the legal framework for bargaining, but the fact that French unions are *cadre* organizations is also a factor. Union membership is for workplace leaders and carries with it the duty to organize your co-workers to participate in union-sponsored campaigns and protests.

The open-shop drive that unions are facing is an opportunity to rethink our membership structure and strategies. We could strategically prioritize the recruitment of the best and most respected workers and the bravest and most class-conscious activists. We should measure our power less in "density" or in membership numbers, but by our leadership and through tests of how many workers in a shop will follow us into an action.

In the spring of 2018, teachers' unions led statewide strikes in West Virginia, Oklahoma, and Nevada. Those are all open-shop states, and yet the walkouts were virtually total. Thousands of workers who did not belong to the unions followed them out on strike because their demands were just and the action made sense.

Yes, unions need a financial base of dues in order to have the resources to be fighting organizations. But signing up every warm body just to get the money is putting your cart of a union treasury before your horse of workplace leadership.

Taking Advantage of the Breakdown of the System

The entire system of labor relations in America is under sustained attack from corporate forces, their dark money, and their allies in the courts and legislatures. The right wing doesn't want workers to have any power, individually or collectively. They want long lines of workers to queue up for a few hours of gig employment, for which they would sign an iTunes-length "Terms and Conditions" agreement. This waives their rights to occupational health and safety, talking to a lawyer, ever looking at a union card, applying to work for a competitor or for unemployment insurance, and signing a "voluntary waiver" of the Thirteenth Amendment right to be free from involuntary servitude. (This last will doubtless be encouraged by a 5–4 Supreme Court decision that Justice Alito will start drafting five months after this book is published.)

And that is a terrifying dystopia we should try our damnedest to avoid. But the default position of most unions to try to preserve and defend the system with some notion of rounding up all the king's horses and men to somehow put it back together again should be challenged as a strategy.

The thing about the vast right-wing conspiracy is that those in it have more money than brains. In attempting to make the union shop illegal, they are destabilizing and even directly threatening the system of exclusive representation. They've forgotten the history discussed in chapter 2. *They* wanted exclusive representation. *They* wanted to put an end to unions competing over who could make the bigger demands and lead the most disruptive job actions. *They* wanted to deal with one union that would mediate internal disagreements and present one set of bargaining priorities and then maintain labor peace through a no-strike clause for the length of the agreement.

If the exclusive representation model is broken, that would spell the end of contractual no-strike clauses. These would simply be unenforceable in an environment of competing, non-exclusive, members-only unions. Workers could simply drop their union memberships to participate in wildcat job actions, or else join new workplace organizations that have not signed agreements committing to labor peace.

I don't have any fantasy of some huge wave of potential strike actions that would occur tomorrow if only the enraged working class would stop being "repressed" by current union leadership and our current collective bargaining agreements. But these no-strike clauses go well beyond total shutdowns of production to include all manner of slow-downs, work-to-rule, and refusal to carry out selective duties.

Any experienced union rep reading this can recall at least one incident of having to talk his members off a ledge—out of refusing a new duty or everybody clocking out for lunch at the same time. These actions would be concerted protected activity in a non-union workplace, but under a contract with a no-strike clause they could result in all participants legally getting fired. How are we supposed to get workers who *don't* enjoy union protection fired up about taking action against their bosses when their unionized peers can't set any kind of example in terms of actually enjoying their supposed protections?

Janus only applies directly to the public sector, but the logic of the decision could extend to the private sector. Currently, the NLRB will only certify unions as exclusive representatives of *all* the workers in a bargaining unit, and only if the union can win a majority vote. Charles J. Morris argued in his book *The Blue Eagle at Work* that the early NLRB process of certifying minority unions as the bargaining agent for *their members only* is still technically open to unions. [47]

Morris wrote his brilliant book in 2005. Though it produced mild ripples of excitement in some unions about the potential to gain a foothold at more workplaces through card-check recognition of minority unions, only a handful of unions have politely asked the NLRB if they agreed with his analysis. To hell with that! We should *demand* it as our right. After *Janus*, how is forcing unions to represent workers they don't want to, that is, to represent workers who don't want to vote for or join a union, not compelled political speech? How is restraining workers who do want to join the union from doing so not a restriction of *their* political speech?

The end of exclusive representation could come to the private sector in an even simpler way. Unions in right-to-work states may simply stop representing the scabs. Many who do so will do it in the narrow-minded avoidance of the free-rider problem. [48] I don't endorse that motivation. However, once a union has ceded exclusive representation, it is inevitable that others will step into the vacuum. And that's where we have the opportunity to drive the bosses batty.

Let's look abroad for one example of how this could play out in the United States. Our peculiar union shop is, as we have discussed, not just unusual in American history but bizarre in a global context. It is only shared, in part, by two other countries and only then because American trade unionists literally exported their model to Canada and Japan. Following the Second World War, CIO union leaders helped Japanese workers craft their labor relations framework as a part of the U.S.-led rebuilding process. The Japanese unions took exclusive representation and evolved it into a system that's dominated by a peculiar model of company unions. For instance, there is no Japanese equivalent of the United Auto Workers union; that is, there's no union that seeks to represent all workers at every domestic factory in the auto industry. Instead, there's a union for Toyota workers and another one for Honda workers.

Although Japanese unions don't shy away from militant job actions—particularly when contracts are being renegotiated—they remain very loyal to the company. After all, increased profits and efficiency could mean higher wages. This loyalty is further enticed by Japanese firms offering jobs for life for their regular, full-time employees with a career track of promotions.

Women are excluded from much of this framework. This is partly explained by the proliferation of temporary and subcontracted jobs that are created to offset the costs of those well-paying lifetime jobs with an underclass of workers who just don't count in the companies' promises of mutual loyalty. But the reason that women more often fall into these substandard jobs is better explained by a patriarchal society that makes the United States look like a working-woman's paradise by contrast.

The traditional enterprise unions rarely filed grievances to defend women's jobs since they were politically dominated by men who believed that men need the jobs more in order to provide for their families.

Starting in the 1990s, a group of activists started new women-only unions to compete with the official unions and advocate for their members' rights, at work and in a profoundly patriarchal Japanese society. Anne Zacharias-Walsh participated in a transnational solidarity project and wrote about the Japanese unions' experience in her fascinating book *Our Unions, Our Selves: The Rise of Feminist Labor Unions in Japan*.[49]

These Japanese experiments with women-only unions are instructive about how new unions could even go about breaking the exclusivity model, and what might happen as a result. The members of the union join as individuals, not as collective groups. A worker would tend to join only when she has a grievance that the traditional union was not helping with or if she fell into any number of subcontracted or temp-work schemes that kept her out of union contract protections. The women's union would provide advice and counsel. By threatening legal action over employer practices that were plainly in violation of laws that were routinely flouted, the women-only unions could force a recalcitrant employer to the table over a grievance. Theirs would not be the strongest hand. Lacking the legal power of the collective bargaining agreement and the collective power of the woman's co-workers, most of these grievances would still result in a "voluntary" resignation, but also some financial compensation. In other words, workers who would otherwise have been totally screwed received at least that degree of justice and compassion.

Women who remained members of the women-only unions might do so openly and quit the official union. Many others might choose to quietly pay dues to the women's unions while retaining membership in the traditional union in order to go along to get along—a Japanese feminist slant on the American radical tradition of the "two-card man."[50]

An important point, and an instructive lesson for U.S. trade unionists, is that Japanese women's shift from exclusive representation to a competitive union model didn't come about through legislative reform, which is as difficult to achieve there as it currently is here. It was achieved by exploiting the very brokenness of the labor relations system.

To be clear, Japanese women-only unions face serious organizational challenges. Though individual women have won small measures of dignity and justice, these new unions have not yet won much power for women collectively nor established much of a permanent presence in many workplaces. One major challenge they face is that most members stop paying dues shortly after their grievance is settled. The union leaders' theory of change was that women who participated in prosecuting their own grievance would come away empowered and more active. Encouraged by their American sisters, the unions surveyed their current and former members and found that the opposite was true. The workers who joined because they had grievances were the *least* likely to remain members. The workers who joined to be a part of a social movement—as increasing numbers of younger women are doing—stayed for the long haul.

Part of this challenge is inherently Japanese. The women who founded the women-only unions intentionally embraced an individual membership model because they felt strongly that few women workers were ready to take charge and "act out" in union, which a more collective model must. But part of this dynamic is sure to pop up if new alternative unions experiment with workplace competition in the United States. There, if workers were to abandon exclusive representation, the traditional or dominant union would likely retain the loyalty of most workers in a shop, as they have the historical track record of wins in the past and as the official bargaining agent with a legal right to demand negotiations with the employer. Individual memberships in the alternative unions are more likely to be situational. Workers may switch unions or become dual-card holders when the alternative union is running a campaign that makes sense with a demand on the boss that resonates.

Imagine here a collective bargaining agreement that settles with no progress on paid family leave or childcare allowances. The minority of younger workers for whom this is a major issue break away to campaign for it. That campaign could now include slowdowns and work-to-rule actions that are forbidden by the union contract they now claim not to be bound by. While there are actions taking place, and as long as they provoke any management response, the alternative union may retain a loyal militant minority. But as soon as the union takes a break from the campaign or picks a new issue that isn't as important, it might see a decline in membership.

Now, this might read like the labor law version of a sci-fi spec script. We just won't know how a multiple competitive union model might play out in the United States until someone tries it. But the Japanese women-only unions provide a reasonable example. Most significantly, they provide the most important object lesson: They just did it. The system was broken, and they were daring enough to break it further because it just wasn't working for them.

In a model of multiple unions competing in a workplace, the best-case scenario is one contract for the unit, not a separate contract for each union or grouping of workers. If more unions experimented with *Blue Eagle*-style minority union certifications, the likeliest outcome is a contract-less labor zone where minority unions demand to bargain over changes in working conditions on a rolling basis.

What would this mean? Back to our labor law sci fi: If an employer has a duty to bargain "in good faith" with a members-only minority union that demands it, it stands to reason that the boss cannot refuse to bargain with another union with a different set of members. Assuming that the Unfair Labor Practice protections of the NLRA remain in place, an employer could not apply work rules on the basis of union membership. They could not punish one union by giving a different one a better set of terms. And they could not reward non-union members with better pay and benefits than members of a union. These responses would clearly run afoul of section 8(a)3 protections against "discrimination in regard to hire or tenure of employment or any term or condition of employment to encourage or discourage membership in any labor organization."

So, if one union raises an issue—a wage increase, a work quota reduction, paid parental leave—and wins it, that settlement would have to be applied to all workers in the bargaining unit. And if a different union regards that settlement as a sellout and continues to agitate and organize around it and somehow wins a better settlement, that would have to replace the old settlement as the new work rule for the entire unit.

In this scenario, I imagine that most unions will still see it as advantageous to seek a signed collective bargaining agreement, and that some employers might view signing one with a strong workplace leader as temporarily advantageous for getting a degree of peace. If they sign a deal, they'll find ways to avoid serious negotiations with other unions during the terms of the agreement, while the other unions spend the meantime shitting all over the deal so that they can jockey for workplace leadership in the next round of bargaining.

Here, I think, is where the potential for chaos comes into play. Those other unions? The ones that hate the contract and are organizing against it? Does the no-strike provision of the contract apply to them? Why would it? They're not members of the union that signed it. That union made a promise to keep its *own* members from striking, with the enforcement mechanism that the members who are a party to the agreement have signed off on the non-grievability of their firing should they violate the no-strike clause during the term of the agreement. I think this would be the effective end of no-strike agreements, which have been one of the greatest inhibitors to labor militancy in the last half-century.

We don't know where our breakthrough opportunities are going to arise. How we respond to and exploit anti-union legal pushes is within our control and holds the potential for good change. The bosses and think tanks that have doggedly pursued the right-to-work agenda and are now targeting exclusive representation itself are inviting chaos. Let's bring some noise.

SIX

Bringing Back the Strike

It's all about strikes now. So here's what's striking me.
— FUGAZI, *THE ARGUMENT* (2001)

CALL ME A BROKEN RECORD, but I'm going to keep repeating this: Our power comes from the work we do and our occasional refusal to do it. We need to bring back the strike. But that's a thing far more easily said than done.

We don't actually have a right to strike in America. A true right to strike would include the right to return to the job after the strike is over. As discussed in the previous chapter, the *Mackay* Doctrine has robbed us of this right, and corporations have exploited this ill-conceived, judge-made law for decades. Partly because of this, strikes have been on the decline, along with union power, since before the Reagan administration. There were 187 major strikes in 1980, involving 795,000 workers. By 2017, there were just seven, which only put 25,000 workers on picket lines.[51]

But maybe *strikes are back*. Since 2018, we've seen waves of major "Red for Ed" teachers' strikes, large strikes in the telecommunications industry, strikes at grocery store chains and McDonald's, and even a walkout by Google engineers. More workers in the United States went on strike in 2018—nearly half a million—than in any other year in the twenty-first century, than in any year since 1986 as a matter of fact![52]

But 1986 was a lousy year for strike activity, part of the long, slow decline of strike activity in the years since PATCO and Phelps-Dodge. And if you look only at the private sector, the historical decline is still dismal. Union researcher Eric Dirnbach crunched the numbers of the Federal Mediation and Conciliation Services' database of union contract expirations. He calculated an annual strike rate as the percentage of contract expirations that resulted in a strike. What he found was a strike rate close to half a percent for 2017 (the last year that data was available) down from about 1.5 percent in the 1990s.[53]

However, despite the recent uptick, by and large, unions have stopped using the strike weapon ever since Phelps-Dodge weaponized the *Mackay* Doctrine. How then do we revive the strike when few workers have even *seen* a successful strike, let alone participated in one?

Strikes Are Contagious

Union boosters were stunned and delighted by the statewide teachers' strike in West Virginia that took most of the country by surprise early in 2018 and that was possibly the beginning of the end of a long era of bipartisan mistreatment of teachers and the communities they serve. The walkout over rising health insurance costs and stagnant pay began on February 22 and appeared to be settled by February 27 with promises from the governor of a 5 percent pay raise for teachers.

Union leaders initially accepted that deal in good faith, along with vague assurances that the state would work with them on a solution for escalating out-of-pocket costs for workers' health care. But, dramatically, rank-and-file teachers refused to end the walkout.[54] Every public school in the state ultimately remained closed for nine days due to the strike, until the West Virginia legislature voted to approve a 5 percent pay increase for *all* state workers as well as a formal labor-management committee to deal with the health care problem.

That action was quickly followed by statewide strikes in Oklahoma, Kentucky, Arizona, Colorado, North Carolina, and Puerto Rico, although with varying degrees of diminishing returns. In May of that year, a wildcat job action by a group of AT&T technicians sparked a five-day strike against the company that put an estimated 14,000 workers on picket lines throughout the Midwest. By September, 6,000 hotel workers in Chicago staged the first industry-wide strike in that city in a century. By that summer, even *prisoners* across the country were waging a strike for better conditions and against slave wages.

In the course of all this, there were the ongoing one-day strikes staged by the "Fight for $15," which had begun in the year 2012, the same year that the Chicago Teachers Union won a strike that was a turning point in both the battle against corporate ed reform and austerity and in union members' dawning realization that strikes can still be planned and won. In short, strikes are contagious.

During brief revolutionary moments, thousands of workplace-centered grievances can cohere into a strike wave. In his classic text *Strike!* Jeremy Brecher explained that strike waves—of which there have been only a handful in our nation's history—also go beyond mere wage and hour demands to fundamentally challenge capitalist ownership and decision-making authority.[55]

The first strike wave in U.S. history is too often not acknowledged as even having happened. During the Civil War, when their slave-drivers and masters left the plantations for military service, thousands of slaves took the earliest opportunity to escape and make their way to Union battle lines—as volunteers. W. E. B. Du Bois dubbed this "the general strike of the slaves."[56] As much as the Battle of Gettysburg, this was the turning point of the war, as it inevitably compelled Lincoln to convert the war into a moral battle for freedom and provided the Union army with much needed reinforcements.

But those who were caught behind Confederate Army lines also went on strike. Rather than grow cotton and other cash crops for the absentee bosses' profit, the slaves who remained by and large converted the plantations to cultivation of fruit, vegetables, and livestock for their own consumption. Within this agricultural insubordination were the seeds of the proverbial battle cry for "40 acres and a mule." Breaking up those plantations and redistributing them among the freedmen would have been the most decisive conclusion to the Civil

War, and a ratification of the revolution that had already taken place. Alas, revolutionary time comes and goes with little forewarning.[57]

The first strike wave that was organized by bona fide trade unions came twelve years later, in 1877. It was sparked by the massive Baltimore & Ohio Railroad company continually cutting wages during an economic depression that had dragged on for nearly half a decade. The railroad brotherhoods called their members, from Maryland to Missouri and all points in between, out on strike.[58]

The railroads were the largest corporations of their day, playing the role that companies like GM and GE used to play in commanding the heights of industry, the roles that Amazon, Facebook, and the other tech giants probably play now. The railroad brotherhoods were, therefore, the largest unions of their time. They lasted until well into the twentieth century, although they remained aloof from formal union federations. The one big union of its time, the Knights of Labor, eventually joined the strike and sparked sympathy walkouts in industries as diverse as meatpacking and construction. There was even a general strike in St. Louis.

All of this was soon to be violently put down by state militias at the behest of conservative governors and court orders. The striking workers won little to nothing in material gains. This would be a common theme for the next half century.

If you've ever attended an art show or a rock concert at some ancient, landmarked concrete and iron building called an "armory" in the middle of a major city and wondered why there ever needed to be an arms depot in the middle of, say, Brooklyn, just know that it was probably constructed after 1877 in anticipation of the next time the workers rose up.

Nine years later, in 1886, the country was again racked by a strike wave, this time over the demand for an eight-hour day.[59] Unlike what was by then referred to as the Great Uprising of 1877, this was not a defensive battle against cutbacks. It was an aggressive demand by workers for a fairer share of the economic prosperity of the time. The lyrical demand for "Eight hours of work, eight hours of rest, and eight hours for what you will" captured workers' imaginations and loyalties in a way that no union demand ever had. It was the "Fight for $15" of its day, the numerical demands articulating a reasonable vision of a dignified standard of living that was worth fighting for.

Though the eight hours' demand had been around since the Civil War, the Knights of Labor popularized it and made it labor's signature cause. The organization that would become the American Federation of Labor contested for the loyalty and leadership of workers and soon eclipsed the Knights as the country's main trade union federation. It would not be the last time that union competition raised the stakes of worker militancy.

The strike wave was launched on May 1 by the AFL's predecessor, a craft union coalition called the Federation of Organized Trades and Labor Unions of the United States and Canada. To this day, unions and workers' movements around the world (and leftists and immigrants here) still celebrate May Day as the true Labor Day for the events that followed.

After police in Chicago murdered two striking workers at the McCormick reaper plant, a protest rally was organized on May 4. At the Haymarket Square rally, an agent provocateur threw a crude bomb into the crowd, and police responded in an orgy of gun violence. Union organizers, most of them anarchists, were tried and convicted of murder and finally martyred on the gallows.

Although some employers did briefly concede an eight-hour working day, few did so without reducing wages accordingly. This fight over how wages and hours were determined would continue for decades. In many respects, we're still fighting this fight, with some workers scrambling to get "more hours" at their many part-time jobs, and others forced to do mandatory overtime.

The three-year period that bookended the Panic of 1893 saw a huge rise of often violent labor fights that ended in state repression. In 1892, Andrew Carnegie decided to bust the union at his steel factory in Homestead, Pennsylvania, then the largest in the country. The union, the Amalgamated Association of Iron and Tin Workers, was one of the most powerful workers' organizations of its time. The workers basically determined and controlled the production process in the plant. They even controlled who got hired on a job! This had inevitably become an intolerable situation for Carnegie, who wanted to speed up production.

His lieutenant, coke baron Henry Clay Frick, pushed the union out on strike by basically ripping up the contract. He hired a private army of Pinkerton detectives who got into a shooting war with the thousands of strikers. The Pinkertons lost, but eventually the state militia was brought in to replace them. Five months later, the Amalgamated Association conceded defeat.[60] The factory was effectively being operated by a slimmed-down and sped-up workforce of scabs, as steel entered into mass production. But at least someone shot Henry Clay Frick in the neck for it.[61] (Oh, relax. He survived.)

Thousands of miners also went on strike against concessionary demands, in conflicts that also resulted in gunfights.[62] In New Orleans, streetcar workers struck for a ten-hour day. Solidarity was so great that it became a general strike.[63]

During 1894, three quarters of a million workers would go on strike, a number without precedent. Most of them were fighting back against wage cuts employers instituted as the economic depression deepened. The Pullman Palace Car Company did not cut workers' wage rates, nor did it lay off any workers. The factory lay at the heart of a model company town that was a civic-minded obsession of George Pullman. He reduced the hours of work in order to spread around what little work there was for his town's residents, but he continued to charge the same rent on the workers' homes.[64]

The response was an immediate strike of all the factory workers. The workers appealed to the new "one big union" of railroad workers, the American Railway Union, which had just won a strike against concessions on the Great Northern Railroad. Against his better judgment, union leader Eugene Debs followed his members' vote to boycott any train that carried a Pullman sleeping car, which was basically all of them. A quarter of a million workers participated in his strike and boycott, which put them in direct conflict with the federal government. President Grover Cleveland mobilized the U.S. Army to operate trains that carried mail cars, resulting in an orgy of violence around the country. The strike was put down and Debs was sentenced to six months in prison, where he spent his time reading up on Marxism. He emerged from prison the most famous socialist leader we've probably ever had in this country (so far).[65]

Although there continued to be unions and occasional strikes in the years that followed, strike waves would follow the boom-and-bust cycle of periodic economic depressions.

Workers again went on strike in huge numbers in the postwar year of 1919.[66] Union membership had increased dramatically—by some two million new members—as war production led to tight labor markets and workers began to feel their power. When the United States entered combat in 1918, the government created a War Labor Board to ensure that factories continued to crank out war materials. This was the first time that the federal government would enforce a legal right to join a union, as well as the first significant regulation of collective bargaining. Of course, it came with a no-strike pledge which most, but not all, union leaders complied with, and with restrictions on wages in a time of massive inflation.[67]

Pent-up frustrations were released after the November 11, 1918, Armistice and in the months that followed in a wave of strikes in the war industries. Thousands of coal miners, lumberjacks, textile workers, hotel waiters and cooks and shipyard workers struck for better pay. In 1919, general strikes broke out in cities as disparate as Kansas City, Missouri, Waco, Texas, and Springfield, Illinois.[68] A general strike in Seattle resulted for a brief time in a workers' council running the city as an alternative government, a development that put the fear of communism into the traditional rulers of America.[69] That same year a strike by Boston police that resulted in looting and rioting led to even more tut-tutting about the lawlessness of unions.[70]

The largest and most noteworthy strike was the Great Steel Strike of 1919. William Z. Foster, then at the peak of his organizing genius, secured funding from the AFL and a number of international unions to organize the steel industry on an amalgamated basis as he had successfully done in the Chicago stockyards in 1916.[71] In this approach, every union that staked a craft claim to a segment of the workforce would get the membership dues, but the union seeking to be the bargaining representative would be a council of all the unions.

Over 100,000 workers joined the twenty-four unions of the National Committee for Organizing the Iron and Steel Workers and waited patiently for their opportunity to strike.[72] Foster wanted to strike while wartime production was at its height, and the workers would have maximum leverage. Gompers would not permit this violation of the no-strike pledge he had made to President Woodrow Wilson, who continued to insist that the months following the Armistice were—for his purposes—"war" time.

When the strike was finally launched in September 1919, over 350,000 workers walked out. Far more workers than just the union members struck for better pay and union recognition. Unfortunately for the timing of the strike, the idled production was probably good for the steel companies' bottom lines as they contended with a postwar economic depression.[73]

Many of the companies that were subjected to strikes wound up laying off huge segments of their workforce due to the weakened economy. Its wartime needs satisfied, the federal government stopped supporting workers' rights, and industry launched an open-shop drive. Expired union contracts were not renegotiated. Union organizers were blacklisted. Other workers were made to sign "yellow dog" contracts promising not to join a union on pain of termination. The 1920s went on to be a historic low point for the unions of the American Federation of Labor.

And yet that low point was quickly followed by labor's great upsurge of 1934. By what miracle? Well, the work of the left in the 1920s was crucial, and it still often remains underappreciated. At Brookwood Labor College, legendary organizer A. J. Muste pushed a line of critical inquiry into union strategy and structure that had little patience for easy answers or sacred cows.[74] In the Trade Union Education League, William Z. Foster directed his acolytes to "bore from within"—not just the established trade unions, but to take jobs in the most important mass production industries and establish their leadership in the workplace.[75]

These cadre would be essential organizers when the Great Depression came along and created new opportunities for organizing.[76] It was not just that workers were desperate and angry enough to begin to take action, but that the Roosevelt New Deal administration gave them just enough encouragement to get things going. The National Industrial Recovery Act, signed into law in 1933, aimed to stabilize the economy through price collusion between competitive businesses. Contained within it was a (mostly) hollow promise of tripartite labor boards that could raise workers' wages and offer a degree of union representation.

The seventh section of the Act was a "right" to organize unions. That there was no enforcement mechanism meant that most employers refused to recognize the unions. Nevertheless, John L. Lewis, president of the United Mine Workers and soon to be leader of the CIO, twisted this weak statute into a federal endorsement of unions. He sent organizers into the coal fields who strongly implied that the president wanted workers to join the union.[77] Prodded by Lewis, the AFL began organizing thousands of new members in the mass production industries. When these new and energized union members grew frustrated with employer-dominated industry labor boards that refused to raise their wages, they began to go on job actions.

It started in Toledo. Workers at an auto-parts manufacturer called Auto Lite began a series of strikes for union recognition and a 10 percent wage increase beginning in February of 1934. They belonged to a temporary union chartered by the AFL but were under the influence of Muste and his American Workers Party. Six thousand workers went on strike. By May, they were engaged in street fights with the National Guard. By the first of June, workers across the city were threatening a general strike. The next day, Auto Lite recognized the union and conceded a 5 percent wage increase.[78]

On May 9, longshoremen up and down the West Coast went on strike for union recognition. Almost 35,000 dockworkers ultimately participated in the strike, which climaxed with a four-day general strike in the city of San Francisco in mid-July.[79] Longshoremen continued to stage "quickie" strikes around the various ports into the fall until they won 95 cents of the dollar-an-hour raise they were demanding *and*—crucially—a union-controlled hiring hall. One week after the West Coast dockworkers began their strike, Teamsters in Minneapolis shut down almost all commercial trucking in a strike that was soon joined by the Central Labor Council and converted into a general strike and finally resulted in union recognition in August.[80]

Later came the sit-down strikes. The most famous of these is the Flint sit-down of 1936–37. The new United Auto Workers union was attempting to organize General Motors on a company-wide basis. But the union had uneven support, with many if not most workers too scared to go on strike and the ongoing Depression providing the company with a reserve army of labor to recruit as scabs.

The union targeted a clear point of leverage: two factories in GM's massive production system that contained the die casts essential for making new parts. If they could shut just those two factories down, they could snarl production throughout the country. When the workers at the first of these, the Cleveland body plant, went on a wildcat strike over some unfair firings, GM recognized the threat and made plans to remove the die casts from its Flint #1 factory. This inspired a skeleton crew of union members to occupy the factory.[81]

Several factors contributed to making the Flint sit-down strike a success—the discipline of the occupiers, the support of flying squads of picketers and the women's auxiliary, a pro-union governor who refused to evict the strikers—but once it was a success and ended in union recognition at GM, the sit-down tactic proved to be inspirational and contagious. Workers across industries engaged in sit-down strikes in 1937. In one storied example, the mostly black and female retail clerks at the Detroit Woolworths—the Walmart of its day—staged a wildcat sit-down that won them union recognition, a wage increase, and overtime pay.[82]

The sit-down strikes were always illegal. The act is trespassing and theft, for starters. But when an action makes sense to the workers and they're feeling the wind at their backs, the law stops mattering.

The 1935 National Labor Relations Act finally put some teeth in Section 7's right to organize, by making pervasive union-busting tactics—including refusing to recognize and bargain with a union—illegal. Most bosses ignored the law, convinced that the Supreme Court would overturn it. The strike wave clearly compelled the Court to accept the law in order to channel this worker militancy and economic disruptions into a smoother regulatory process. Most employers, too, began to acquiesce to the National Labor Relations Board and to recognize majority-status unions before there was a need for a strike. Eventually, the 1934–37 wave of strikes subsided, and unions established a more permanent foothold in the economy.

Unions, as we've discussed, mostly observed a no-strike pledge for the duration of the Second World War. The wartime wage freezes and rampant inflation that workers endured made the countdown to V-J Day also the countdown to an inevitable strike wave.

Unlike every previous strike wave, however, there was little that was spontaneous or accidental about it. This was an example of union leaders responding from a position of strength to the militancy and demands of their rank and file and planning total strikes against their employers well in advance of their contract expirations. And these weren't just strikes for wages; the very nature of the postwar political economy was at stake. Recall the 1945–46 General Motors strike mentioned in chapter 3. The union demanded bargaining over the price of the cars in order to increase the spending power of the entire working class.

Nearly a quarter million UAW members walked out in that strike.[83] Nearly four and a half million workers—meatpackers, railroad workers, electricians, coal miners, and many more—struck at some point in the year and a half that followed the end of the war.[84] Workers made tremendous gains in these strikes—wages, benefits, hours reductions—and living standards continued to rise until many workers got delusions of middle-class grandeur as the postwar period went on.

The Empire struck back, of course. Republicans swept the midterm congressional elections and scapegoated the strike wave as dangerous and selfish with acts that threatened "the public" (which was who exactly if not the workers who were enjoying the rising standard of living that resulted from these strikes?). The result was the

Taft-Hartley Act of 1947, which began the transformation of our labor relations system, slowly and inexorably, into the trap it is today.

The last (or, I should say with a maximum of optimism, the *latest*) strike wave is perhaps the most interesting, because it took place within the context of our peculiar union shop and most of our current labor law regime. Two and a half million workers went on strike in both 1970 and 1971. According to the federal Bureau of Labor Statistics, which started tracking large work stoppages (defined as those involving more than 1,000 workers) after the post–Second World War strike wave, 52,761,000 work days (defined as one worker per day) were spent idled in 1970, twice as many as in 1947.[85]

Much of this is accounted for by the public sector employees' organizing boom, which started with the New York City teachers' strike for union recognition in 1960 and included the final fateful moments of Dr. Martin Luther King Jr.'s life, spent supporting the citywide strike of sanitation workers in Memphis. In one respect, this organizing boom represented exactly the kind of thoughtful deployment of union resources and strategic targeting that we hope and expect of unions organizing from a position of strength. Walter Reuther, still the president of the UAW, also directed the staff apparatus of the old CIO—now called the Industrial Union Department—that had been absorbed into the merged labor federation. He was approached by leaders of the Transport Workers Union, who had lost their collective bargaining rights when New York City took over the formerly private subway and bus companies, and of the American Federation of Teachers, who had yet to enjoy a legal right to collective bargaining but wanted to make common cause with the TWU, with a plan to win.[86]

Reuther was eager to revive the sense of a labor movement that had faded in the years since the AFL and CIO merged. He threw a ton of organizers and money at the campaign. The 1960s teachers' strike was merely a brief protest in which only about a thousand teachers took part (there's a joke that goes around in AFT circles that 60,000 old men still claim to have participated in it), but Reuther and legendary labor leaders like ILGWU president David Dubinsky and NYC

Central Labor Council president Harry Van Arsdale Jr. used their political leverage and the embarrassing spectacle of teachers on picket lines to convince Mayor Robert Wagner Jr. (son of the main sponsor of the 1935 National Labor Relations Act) to agree to a voluntary union recognition election, and eventually used their influence to pass a public sector collective bargaining law in New York.[87]

By the early 1970s, this movement had matured to the point that teachers and other public sector employees' unions that had won the right to collective bargaining were routinely striking to win better terms in new collective bargaining agreements, while teachers in cities that had not yet won collective bargaining were striking for it.[88] The year 1970 also saw a massive postal worker wildcat strike for better pay and collective bargaining rights that perhaps put over 200,000 workers on picket lines.[89] Many of these strikes were illegal, but states rushed to pass public sector labor relations laws that granted workers an orderly process for organizing and adjudicating unfair labor practices.

Some states legalized strikes, but only after unions had exhausted lengthy processes of mediation and fact-finding. Others passed statutes like New York's Taylor Law, which put in place draconian penalties for unions that engage in any kind of work stoppage. As public sector collective bargaining became legalized and routinized, the great wave of teachers' strikes slowed to a near-halt following the round of teachers' union contract negotiations in the late 1980s.

In private sector mass-production industries, something interesting happened during the 1970s. Large numbers of younger workers were rejecting the basic terms of factory work. Not all hippies became college professors. Many, to paraphrase Bob Dylan, took the day shift after their twenty years of schooling and hated the monotony, speed, and authoritarianism common in assembly work. The trade-off of excellent pay and benefits was not enough.

The UAW took its members across General Motors out on strike in 1970 as a pressure release valve for rank-and-file discontent, even though the company was throwing money at them.[90] This proved insufficient. When the contract was settled with more wage increases, but no language addressing the speed and structure of the assembly line, the young workers at GM's new Lordstown, Ohio, assembly plant rebelled through daily acts of sabotage. They managed to turn the company's pioneering "small car," the Chevy Vega, into a notorious lemon through their campaign of sabotage, which aimed to slow the pace of the line. Finally, in 1972, they staged a wildcat strike that has fascinated journalists and labor scholars ever since. Despite generous and rapidly rising wages, the workers rejected not just the inhumane pace of the assembly line but also their alienation from any pleasure at being the cause of an actual car driving off at the end of production. They wanted not just to slow down the speed of the line, but to spend more time with each car as it was assembled.[91]

They didn't succeed. As the economy soured and free trade and foreign competition threatened what are now, frustratingly, referred to as "good jobs," workers largely abandoned the existential demands that the Lordstown workers made in favor of continued job security.

The union-busting drive of offshoring, subcontracting, "freelancing" the work, and the weaponized *Mackay* Doctrine has really done a number on the American working class. We now beg for factory jobs that we used to reject when we had real bargaining power. This is why the modest return of strikes as a strategic choice for workers feels so radical.

What's been happening since 2018 is not yet a strike wave. Far from it. The West Virginia teachers' strike might not have happened, let alone been so successful, if it hadn't enjoyed the tacit approval of district superintendents and other managers who faced the same salary and health insurance squeeze. But it could be the long, slow start of something big.

Would workers have begun organizing and striking so quickly in the 1930s, if it had not been for the federal government's toothless Section 7a "right to organize" and John L. Lewis's deliberate inflation of that into the statement, "The president wants you to organize"? One thing we should be clear about is that American labor unions have historically *always* grown in short bursts of intense activity, oftentimes including a strike wave, and then declined slowly over time. It must be our goal then not just to organize predictable, legal strikes at contract expiration time, but to organize strikes and job actions that are potentially contagious; that could lead to great uprisings of workers.

"Legal" Strikes

A huge part of the trap that is our labor relations system is that by granting a "right" to strike—one that isn't meaningful because it lacks the right to return to the job—it puts a government that is typically dominated by business interests in charge of what strike behaviors are to be protected. It allows the boss to decide what a "legal" strike is.

What do the bosses want? A highly predictable, overly proscribed protest routine that gives them plenty of time to recruit scabs and keep his business going. Most of the spontaneous or surprise actions that workers undertook in previous strike waves are simply not "legal" today.

For starters, a collective bargaining agreement buys an employer years of guaranteed labor peace. Wildcat job actions will be punished by the employer, by the NLRB, the courts, and often by union leadership. Even when a contract expires, a legal strike can only occur after the union gives sufficient advance notice to the employer and to the federal Mediation and Conciliation Service. This isn't to say that mediation can't be helpful if both sides desire a good faith settlement. But if there is no settlement, mediation buys the employer time to prepare to operate on a non-union basis with scabs and middle management picking up the slack. It is difficult, if not "illegal," to surprise the employer with a "quickie" strike.

Due to the risks and restrictions inherent in "legal" strikes, one-day strikes have gained in popularity among unions. But even these involve advance notice. In order to avoid workers being permanently replaced on the day of the strike, a union must write to the employer and declare the end of the strike before it has even begun, simultaneously offering to return to work the next day with no conditions or demands.

Not only must one-day strikes be telegraphed in advance, they must be scheduled far apart from each other lest they be ruled "illegal" intermittent strikes. Going on strike on Monday, returning to work on Tuesday and Wednesday, going back out on Thursday and returning to the job on Friday and leaving the boss guessing what next week will bring would be tremendously disruptive. It would also keep the strikers from earning some pay, and it would leave more money in the union's defense fund. So of course it's illegal!

There are no clear rules about what will get a union slapped with an intermittent strike charge, so unions must err on the cautious side.[92] Not only must one-day strikes be spread apart over a long period of time, the union must find different pretexts for them. If the strikes are all staged in protest of the same issue, that could be deemed an "illegal" intermittent strike. For example, in September of 2018 the "Fight for $15" campaign staged a one-day strike at McDonald's in protest of its lack of protections against workplace sexual harassment. A worthy issue, for sure. But it's safe to assume that SEIU's lawyers were worried about McDonald's charging them with waging an "illegal" selective strike over wages or union recognition.

Partial strikes are also "illegal," thanks to NLRB rules. A partial strike is one in which some job titles or departments go on strike while other parts of the bargaining unit stay on the job. Partial strikes would be advantageous to unions. It's easier to pay out strike benefits to a smaller segment of the union's membership while everyone else continues to earn a paycheck. But also, if an essential group of workers go out on strike, it could leave everyone who is earning a paycheck with not much actual work to do.

As much as we venerate the 1936–37 Flint sit-down strike, all it did was bring GM to the table. It was a 1939 partial strike by the tool-and-die workers that won the UAW a contract.[93] After months of management intransigence on every issue important to the workers, the UAW's membership plummeted at GM, reflecting a demoralized workforce. The skilled workers who designed and made the tools and auto parts on the assembly line remained a stalwart base of support for the union, and so they led a partial strike that snarled production.

What was necessary to get a union at General Motors in the 1930s is illegal today. Is it any wonder that union density and union power have declined?

Back to the sit-down strike: How does a sit-down make the strike itself illegal? The actual occupation of the boss's physical plant by the workers was always illegal. It's trespassing and theft. The brave workers who sit down on the job are risking arrest and prosecution. But the fact that they are doing it together, to press for rights and wage gains for themselves and their co-workers, makes it concerted activity. It was meant to be a protected concerted activity under a labor act that explicitly states, "Nothing in this Act shall be construed so as either to interfere with or impede or diminish in any way the right to strike."

What should be the law—that is, the intent of the NLRA framers—is that when a sit-down strike is over, the employer is perfectly within its rights to call the police and press charges against the occupiers, but when the workers get out of jail they retain the right to return to the job. What the Supreme Court ruled in the 1939 *NLRB v. Fansteel Metallurgical Corp.* case is that workers who break the law in the course of otherwise protected concerted activity lose their right to return to the job if the employer chooses to fire them.[94]

This is why employers often encourage scabs to provoke fistfights on picket lines. The strikers who take the bait can be fired, so the scab can steal their jobs—a tremendously demoralizing action. But this also takes some necessary tactics off the table, or at least makes them risky for union members. A worker with access to business orders or other strategic documents would do well to steal them on the way out the door, for instance, and countless acts of sabotage may be necessary to win a strike.

Finally, "legal" strikes must comply with restrictions on when and where workers can picket. In practice, this means picketers must keep moving in circles within a protest pen that is far removed from the entrance. And it certainly means no picketing at secondary employers whose business your employer depends upon. We are so used to these restrictions that most people probably only think of picketing as symbolic protesting to raise awareness for the cause. But think of what a picket line is, what it was meant to be. The first picket lines—going all the way back to George Washington's first term as president[95]—were efforts to surround an unfair employer's place of business and prevent customers and scabs from entering. That's what makes a strike effective, so naturally it is now "illegal."

To hell with legality, you might say. Why follow an unjust law? Well, because the law has some real teeth. When the boss violates labor law, the NLRB must exhaust a lengthy internal unfair labor practice process before ultimately going to court to enforce its ruling on the employer. When a union is accused of committing an unfair labor practice, the Taft-Hartley amendments direct the NLRB to go straight to court to get an injunction. Violating that injunction comes with severe financial penalties. The union could be made to pay triple the amount of money that the employer alleges that "illegal" strike actions cost them. That's millions of dollars, and it would bankrupt any union.

Now if the employer commits an unfair labor practice (ULP) and the union strikes over that violation of the law, some of this is mitigated. Most crucially, the *Mackay* Doctrine does not apply to ULP strikes. Workers who go on ULP strikes retain the right to return to the job when the strike is over. Management can hire scabs, but those scabs cannot steal the strikers' jobs. Quickie, one-day, or intermittent strikes also enjoy a degree of protection when they are staged in protest of unfair labor practices.

Unions that are smart about organizing and striking try to draw and hold a ULP for up to the six-month statute of limitations in order to make their strike a ULP strike. But, by design, these are limited strikes. Once a ULP is mitigated or settled, the strike loses its protections.

Joe Burns, a veteran union negotiator and labor lawyer, has written extensively on labor's need to bring back the strike weapon. In his book *Reviving the Strike* he scorns one-day "publicity strikes" as no substitute for "an effective traditional strike." Burns urges unions to return to strikes that aim to totally halt production:

Today, the prevailing view of a strike is one of workers withholding their labor in order to pressure an employer to reach an agreement. In this conception of a strike, strikers force the market to determine the value of their labor as a group by withdrawing their services. The alternative view, held by trade unionists of the middle part of the twentieth century, viewed a strike as workers halting production in order to force the employer to agree to union demands. Understanding these different conceptions of striking is vital to labor's revival.[96]

To the extent that he's right about this, the "withholding their labor in order to pressure an employer" conception of strikes is yet another example of the labor movement allowing the boss's law to become our ideology. I think Burns puts too much emphasis on *totally* halting production at a time that global capitalism has restructured itself to make that goal nearly impossible. Offshoring, subcontracting, automation, and the proliferation of layers of supervision provide most corporations with ways to maintain some degree of production even in the face of a total walkout aimed to shut everything down.

Even the rather successful 2016 CWA strike at Verizon did not shut down production. Phones still rang, the internet still worked. Of course, when things broke, they took a long time to get fixed, which ultimately brought a lot of customer outrage, regulatory investigation, and political pressure down on the company's head.

Then, there's the fact—acknowledged by Burns in his follow-up book, *Strike Back!*[97]—that public sector strikes aren't, strictly speaking, economic strikes. Teachers' union strikes have been leading the way in our recent revival of the strike weapon, starting most prominently with the 2012 Chicago Teachers Union strike. But they don't cost the boss money in the way that strikes against private sector businesses do. What they do is create a political crisis, and if they are fought over issues that resonate with the community—such as smaller class sizes and more social workers in the schools—then they can be inspirational, and maybe a bit contagious.

Finally, while some on the left deride the one-day Fight for $15 strikes for being more like theater than an actual work stoppage, I think there is value in symbolic strikes. The average worker walking past a McDonald's on a day of a strike action has no idea which protesters actually had the day off or who is receiving strike benefits. All they see is a bunch of workers exercising some power and making their boss's day a little more miserable.

Would the slight return to union leaders weighing the strike option have happened if SEIU had not started a part-time strike movement with broad popular support? Maybe, but possibly not. Would rank-and-file teachers in West Virginia have started agitating for a strike without the little bit of electricity that the fast-food strikes put in the air? Workers have to take the notion, after all.

Cultures of Solidarity

We need to restore cultures of solidarity in working-class communities. Nothing accomplishes that quite like living through an intense period of putting your livelihood, dignity, and self-respect on the line and needing the support and protections of your friends and co-workers, knowing that they need the same of you.

Strikes do that. The Chicago teachers I know still feel a residual sense of accomplishment and pride in that 2012 strike. They have more-than-skin-deep loyalty to their co-workers. They are much more likely to join another union or community group's rally or picket line.

Union organizing campaigns—well-run ones, at least, with empowered rank-and-file organizing committees—similarly foster a culture of solidarity. The charter school teachers I keep in touch with also still keep in touch with their fellow OC members. Everybody might have switched schools two or three times, but they'll always remain brothers and sisters, quick to offer supportive words if not money, time, and muscle if an old comrade is in distress.

I'm not a sociologist, but I've got a theory about the culture of solidarity that the "Greatest Generation" built up, and how successive generations of union leaders and organizers coasted on an era of good feelings that they did not earn or successfully reproduce. The strike waves of the 1930s and the immediate postwar years meant that millions of workers experienced the kind of intense period of mutual aid and self-defense that fosters solidarity. It helps that most of those strikes were successful in materially raising workers' wages and standard of living. It's also worth noting that those strike waves bookended a war that put millions of workers into literal life-and-death situations where they depended on their comrades having their backs.

What developed was a culture of solidarity in which it was generally accepted that you just don't cross a picket line or buy a scab product. It's a culture that understands that poverty and want are threats to those of us who *have*. It's an environment where people cheer on workers fighting and striking for a new benefit or right, hoping that their example can help everyone win it everywhere. It's the kind of political culture in which massive new welfare programs like Medicare and Medicaid could be instituted.

The opposite of a culture of solidarity is one where workers can be goaded into slashing the social safety net to lower taxes. Or where minimally decent public employee pensions are vulnerable to scapegoating political attacks like, "*You* don't have that; why should *they*?"

Millions of baby boomers were raised by their parents to not cross a picket line or buy scab products. Of those baby boomers, many wound up in non-union jobs and non-union industries, as union growth was artificially closed by the trap of our system. Though many others did wind up in factory jobs or government employment, a far smaller proportion of them lived through the kind of life-altering organizing campaigns and strikes that their parents did.

Still, many of those baby boomers imparted the "don't scab" lesson to their kids, either drawing from their own experiences or those of their parents. And so on and so forth, and in this way, the Greatest Generation's culture of solidarity became faded like a Xerox of a Xerox of a Xerox. People gave it lip service, but if it wasn't a lived experience, it became a platitude too often dropped at the first sign of adversity.

I can't recall how many organizers I've seen strike out in an organizing conversation, digging for a change that a worker wanted to make at work through a union, only to lean on the intellectually lazy one-two combo of "Do it for your co-workers" (which is charity, not solidarity) and "The union was good for your family, so why not for you?" (which is nostalgia for a thing you didn't personally experience).

I think some union leaders have come to see this problem, albeit very late in the game. If we're going to revive a culture of solidarity, we're going to need more worker-led job actions. The unions, of course, have a role to play. I have more to say on that below. But, first, let's grapple with what the proper role of the political left is.

First of all, it's completely amazing and a potential game-changer that we even have a left to speak of. Tens of thousands—and I have no reason to doubt it will soon be hundreds of thousands—of people have embraced some version of the socialist project in the wake of the dispiriting Clinton campaign and the horrific Trump administration.

One of the most urgent needs is some basic trade union education so that new socialists don't, as Bill Fletcher Jr. says, "treat the labor movement as a panacea or as some sort of hideous creature."[98] This requires studying the history of both labor and the left, as well as the law. Leftists must have a structural critique of the labor relations system in addition to their complaints about union strategy and politics as they weigh their own role as organizers.

I've seen some talk online of a rank-and-file strategy, which is certainly well intentioned. I do think it's a mistake for leftists to seek out *careers* as union staffers. Although I would also argue that a year or two as a union organizer, if you are young and footloose, can provide a valuable education.

In general, our place is where the workers are. However, as much as I've seen proponents advocate for a variety of rank-and-file approaches to organizing, what seems to translate most clearly and embraced most eagerly is the idea of taking a union-represented job and getting involved in the union with an eye toward contesting for power. I think this might be a waste of our opportunity. It's another example of how many in the labor left have become the new traditionalists, just instinctively following the same formulas that have been tried and failed for the last forty or fifty years. Finally, thinking of Stanley Aronowitz's personal account of his experience in *Death and*

Life of American Labor, any leftists who did manage to take the reins of leadership would find themselves just as trapped by the system as everyone who has come before.[99]

I find a bit more promise in the work that some smart activists in the extant Industrial Workers of the World are doing. Within that would-be historical society, there are also some thoughtful comrades who spin off new organizing projects—like Brandworkers, the Burgerville Union, and the Jimmy Johns union—and support the workers in organizing something new while experimenting with protest tactics like quickie strikes and innovative boycotts.

If class-conscious left-wing activists intentionally took jobs in industries and at companies that are politically essential to be organized, but that no union is currently focused on—much as the Trade Union Education League (TUEL) activists of the 1920s "salted" the auto and steel industries—well, we might have the start of something.

With no union treasury to be sued and no clearly identified "leaders" to pin the blame on, cells of activists would have a much freer hand to get creative in their organizing and protest planning. Perhaps the least intimidating way to go about organizing at Amazon or within Google is to think small. Taking on the entire company all at once is too daunting a task, though we obviously have to get there. But what about your immediate co-workers in your department, your unit or team, or your building? What are small protests you can take to win the issue of the day, whatever the issue of the day is, be it bathroom breaks or building a database of faces for law enforcement?[100]

In Silicon Valley, for example, is it everyone on the team routinely leaving campus to take an extra long lunch break at the same time? In an Amazon warehouse, is it a coordinated slowdown, or even a five-minute strike of unauthorized silence and rest? From such small actions, bigger things can grow. Plus, these companies are so unused to worker pushback that any sign of concerted activity is likely to get some kind of a response from management, some tiny concession that could give hope to others that bigger demands can be made and won.

In fact, Google engineers engaged in a brief global walkout in November 2018 to protest employer sexual misconduct.[101] From this distance, it looks like Google management tacitly approved the walkout as a pressure release for simmering tensions, and the company quickly responded by ending its policy of forced arbitration over employment disputes, including sexual harassment.[102] But the walkout has emboldened the Google workers; they continue to organize and expose the company's dirty employment practices.[103]

One strike tactic that needs to be revived, but can only be revived outside of an official trade union structure, is sabotage. Now, this can be a scary word and it has historically been scapegoated and demonized in the press and among respectable types, who often conflate it with acts of violence or a willful disregard for health and safety. In his classic history of the Industrial Workers of the World, *We Shall Be All*, Melvyn Dubofsky described the contested, occasionally confused, and often surprisingly clear-eyed advocacy for sabotage on the job by early twentieth-century labor radicals:

> One forceful method explicitly advocated by the Wobblies—indeed, the tactic with which they are most indelibly associated—was sabotage. To most Americans, sabotage implied the needless destruction of property, the senseless adulteration of products, and, possibly, the inexcusable injuring of persons. Wobblies did not always dispel such images. The [IWW newspaper] *Industrial Worker* suggested to harvest hands in 1910, "Grain sacks come loose and rip, nuts come off wagon wheels and loads are dumped on the way to the barn, machinery breaks down, nobody to blame, everybody innocent."[104]

"For the next three years," Dubofsky explains, "the paper continued to urge this method upon its readers, telling them, 'Sabotage is an awakening of labor. It is the spirit of revolt.' This campaign culminated in 1913 with a series of twelve editorials fully explaining the methods of sabotage and when they should be used.

"Most stressed sabotage's nonviolent characteristics," according to Dubofsky, and

> repeatedly, IWW speakers asserted that sabotage simply implied

soldiering on the job, playing dumb, tampering with machines without destroying them—in short, simply harassing the employer to the point of granting his workers' demands. Sometimes, it was claimed, the workers could even effect sabotage through exceptional obedience: Williams and Haywood were fond of noting that Italian and French workers had on occasion tied up the national railroads simply by observing every operating rule in their work regulations.

The "exceptional obedience" that Ben Williams and "Big Bill" Haywood described is today called a "work-to-rule" job action, one of the few forms of sabotage that remain "legal" under our union shop, and one that is still widely practiced by unions today. Indeed, when successfully implemented, "work-to-rule" actions can be huge morale boosters.

Even minor acts of sabotage reveal to workers how much power they have through their mastery of the job, and how much the boss depends upon their willingness to participate in teamwork and continued tolerance of adverse situations. It also helps if the actions are fun and funny.

In 1992 Martin Sprouse collected "Anecdotes of Dissatisfaction, Mischief and Revenge" in his book *Sabotage in the American Workplace*. Compiled in the 1990s, many of the actions that Sprouse collected were individualistic, but still contained the potential to become contagious.

For example, Joey was a waiter at a small cafe who would find ways to sneak free meals for friends. And he was not alone. "It was a thrill to recognize that other people were doing it."[105] When Judi and her co-workers at a postal bulk mail center faced a speed-up in the late 1970s, they recorded most of the day's mail as lacking a zip code, which caused a system-wide backup and no short amount of downtime. Another time, they sent most of the mail to a facility in New York where the workers were on a wildcat strike.[106] Tad, a farmhand, would intentionally jam up his International Harvester combine giving him and dozens of his comrades in the wheat fields a few hours of idle time while the machine was repaired. Management never even suspected sabotage. "I think this is true for most non-unionized off-the-street labor," Sprouse noted. "They generally assume that you will never pull any stunts."[107]

"As long as people feel cheated, bored, harassed, endangered, or betrayed at work," Sprouse stated, "sabotage will be used as a direct method of achieving job satisfaction—the kind that never has to get the bosses' approval."[108]

Going back to Lordstown in the 1970s, the sabotage by assembly line workers was aimed at shutting the line down for five blissful minutes of silence. A few loose screws tossed into a gas tank could accomplish that. Once it was discovered toward the end of the line at quality control, the entire line would be paused to investigate what went wrong. Workers could only do this a couple times a day, and only in situations where there was little way for a foreman to figure out that it was intentional or who did it. It was just a little way of taking back a tiny amount of control over the pace of work, a protest against the inhumane expectations of the job.

Today, Amazon probably tracks their warehouse workers to such a degree that there's no credible way for one worker to deny an act of sabotage. But what if an entire shift of workers at one location overwhelmed the company with acts of sabotage that are imperceptible until after the action is taken? How hard is it for one worker to accidentally put the wrong shipping label on a box, and how easy would it be for *every* worker on a shift to put the wrong labels on all the boxes for an hour or two? When would that be discovered? When a couple thousand customers complain about receiving the wrong item two days later?

This might be a flight of puckish fancy, but I imagine that corporate would be more likely to punish the shift supervisors than the actual mutineers. First of all, an entire shift of warehouse workers is hard to replace if Amazon wants to maintain its commitment to overnight and two-day delivery times. But perhaps more important, Amazon probably doesn't want to call attention to both the grueling working conditions in its warehouses and the unpredictable nature of worker protest against those conditions, which might undermine consumer confidence that their packages will arrive on time. It is not hard to imagine that Amazon would scapegoat and punish the site supervisors for "letting things get out of hand" and maybe even offer small concessions like longer or more frequent restroom breaks.

There is no shortage of anonymous internet forums for workers to share stories and trade ideas so that any tactic leading to a concession or to a raising of workers' morale for a day or two might be tried in more locations. And from these experiments, a movement could grow. It's certainly worth trying.

What Can Unions Do?

As noted in chapter 4, picking between new organizing and internal organizing is a false choice. But if we're going to revive the strike, unions are going to have to give more strategic attention and allocate more resources to internal organizing campaigns that could lead to inspiring and winnable strikes. More international unions should be running comprehensive internal and community organizing campaigns in advance of major contract expirations with the goal of staging, if necessary, major strikes that would serve as an example for all workers of how to fight and win.

At this point, it's been years since I worked for the American Federation of Teachers so I'm hardly privy to any of the internal deliberations, but the teachers' unions—the AFT, in particular—have clearly pivoted after rank-and-filers started the "Red for Ed" movement. The West Virginia strike of 2018 initially caught them by surprise and they struggled to maintain leadership of it. Since then, AFT leadership seems to actively seek out potentially game-changing local contract campaigns and support them with on-the-ground organizers and build toward a credible strike threat.

The Hotel and Restaurant employees continue to try to line up the expiration dates of their big citywide contracts in order to target powerful national chains like Marriott and Hilton in nationwide strikes that threaten a huge percentage of the hotels' revenue. The union staged the largest nationwide hotel strike ever late in 2018 when 7,700 Marriott employees in Hawaii, San Francisco, Oakland, San Diego, San Jose, Detroit, and Boston ultimately walked out and won substantial pay increases.[109] The union organizes around demands that go far beyond wages to include automation, the misuse of customer data, and the protection of room attendants from potential sexual predators. These are fights that are more likely to resonate with the public and show that strikes can be fought for higher causes.

The Communications Workers of America have also strategically approached their major landline contract expirations with serious plans to be ready for a strike. And they likewise have demands that resonate with workers *and* consumers to keep customer support human (not automated) and based in the United States. They won two major telecom strikes in 2018, although Verizon settled quickly and fairly in order to avoid another costly strike after taking a drubbing in 2016. In union shop talk, we call that the "strike dividend," when long memories of a hard-fought strike win quick settlements in future rounds of bargaining. Nevertheless, Verizon and its predecessor companies' track record is such that they tend to forget after a decade, making future strike prep essential. The Verizon contract is clearly a perennial flashpoint and always contains the potential for inspiring internal organizing fights.

As does the Teamsters' UPS contract, which is why *Labor Notes* and Teamsters for a Democratic Union reformers fixate on it. Over a quarter of a million UPS workers went on strike in 1997 over demands that the company promote thousands of exploited part-time workers to full-time jobs with benefits. It was the signature campaign of the Ron Carey reform administration, and the contract campaign and strike preparation represented years of hard work beforehand. It was a watershed moment after the nearly two decades of the weaponized *Mackay* Doctrine had convinced most outside observers (and, indeed, many union members and leaders) that strikes couldn't be won. That the strike inconvenienced so many consumers and still retained broad public support—thanks largely to its central challenge to the ongoing degradation of "good jobs"—was an inspiration to many.

Every round of bargaining with an employer like UPS should be approached as an opportunity to fight a big fight and inspire more workers to take the notion that our labor and occasional withdrawal of our labor is the source of our power. Every international union has their version of a UPS. So much of what the union is able to enforce as industrial standards, so much of what the union is able to convince members to pay in dues and so much of the union's reputation at non-union competitors is wrapped up in what could be won or lost in the next round of bargaining with big, powerful, influential employers. Why would a union not prepare for a strike every time?

Another thing that the international unions should do is to finally act upon an idea that's been floating around the AFL-CIO for over a decade: invest in new "start-up" unions to take on the challenge of organizing new industries. The idea was boldly proposed by the American Federation of Teachers during the AFL-CIO debate over structural change that preceded the Change to Win split of 2005. Harkening back to the Mineworkers' sponsorship of the Steelworkers Organizing Committee and the United Auto Workers' and Industrial Union Department's funding of their own drive for collective bargaining in the 1960s, the AFT proposed "creating new unions from scratch and even adopting unconventional tactics unencumbered by the restraints of current labor law."

The implication here is that a new union that lacks a treasury would be freer to engage in "illegal" strikes banned by the Taft-Hartley Act:

> The AFL-CIO could explore the legal and financial avenues for building institutional firewalls for donor unions (or for the AFL-CIO as a donor organization) that would be responsible for providing money, logistical assistance, long-term loaned staff and other help without the expectation of an organizational quid pro quo.[110]

It's an exciting idea that was quickly forgotten in the aftermath of the messy split in the labor movement. It is time to revive the idea. The official unions badly need a *cause célèbre*, and a signature new organizing campaign aimed to inspire workers to take the kinds of "illegal" job actions that led to the great upsurge of the sit-down era.

Finally, and although it might seem a minor issue but in fact is not, we have to consider the role of organizers. I'm not just talking about campaign decision-makers. The thousands of paid organizers—full-time, release-time, short-term project—who collectively talk to hundreds of thousands of workers every year play a large role in shaping how workers think about strikes.

I had an eye-opening experience late in the game of running the AFT's charter school organizing division. For most of my tenure, we thought we were covered by public sector labor laws, where strikes are either completely illegal—punishable by termination or crippling financial penalties—or so heavily regulated that a "legal" strike could not be conducted until after exhausting many months of mediation and fact-finding. During that time, our general approach was to organize escalating pressure tactics inside the building and at school board meetings and throughout the community.

As for strikes, my belief and general experience was that key organizing committee members would raise the idea with their lead organizer if several months of the routine of first-contract bargaining had convinced them that management wouldn't strike a fair deal until the workers upset the whole dynamic. I'd usually have that lead prepared to respond—in as confident and as easygoing a manner as possible—with questions like, "Do you think it's come to that?" and "Do you think your co-workers would agree?" You never wanted the idea of a strike to be something that a staff organizer just dropped on the committee all of a sudden at a meeting. And we'd map out the next one-on-one conversations with fellow organizing committee members to build support for moving toward a strike. It was almost like forming a new OC, a committee of the committee, if you will.

But once the NLRB took jurisdiction over charter schools and we found ourselves in the private sector, we needed to talk about strikes much earlier in the organizing process. To my great surprise, I found many of our organizers were uncomfortable—scared, even!—with the idea of pushing workers to think about going on strike.

Although it makes sense when you think about it. It's one thing for a worker to knowingly risk her own job. It's another thing entirely to feel like you're risking someone else's job. And organizers (good ones, anyway) constantly feel sick to their stomachs about how many workers' jobs are at risk during the course of an organizing drive. The best an organizer can do is achieve a kind of Zen realization that, in the end, it's up to the workers. There's something about workers making a campaign decision—any decision—for themselves after weighing all of the information and the possible risks and rewards that is empowering. Trust the process and trust the workers.

So, what we tried to shift to was to respond to the very first time that a worker said the s-word with a simple and forthright, "There may come a time that you and your co-workers decide that a strike is necessary. You'll put it to a democratic vote, and you'll need just about everybody to agree if you're going to be at all successful. But I don't think we're there now." If the organizers did that, they turned striking from a fear that we had to inoculate against into a campaign strategy that was on the table and within the workers' control.

And bosses really do hammer away at the threat of strikes in their union-busting campaigns. The union will *make* you go on strike. They can fine you if you don't go on strike. You'll never make back the money you would lose by going on strike. These are all routine boss messages during an organizing campaign. They're plainly ridiculous, but they can scare off a lot of workers if they're not prepared for them.

One of the most powerful fears that workers have in an organizing campaign is the fear of losing agency, of losing control. It's one of the reasons we make plans with our organizing committees. "If the boss does X, then we respond by doing Y." Having a planned response to a termination or a captive audience meeting takes away some of the fear of these things. But on strikes, all too often we don't make a plan.

And the subject comes up, early on. It's usually brought up by a worker in the first or second conversation about forming a union. Let's lean into it. If you are an organizer on staff, I implore you not to peddle a self-defeating defensive line like, "Actually, strikes are really rare" or "Most contracts are settled without a strike." We need to instill the notion that going on strike is an option that workers have the power to choose, that it's their choice and they have the power.

SEVEN

An All-In System of Labor Relations

IF YOUR RIGHTS AS A WORKER are dependent on the company you work for and the worksite you report to, then you have no rights that are durable or bound to be respected by the boss. Any system of labor relations that allows a boss to veto his workers' choice of union representative or to secede from the system entirely is hopelessly broken.

Many of the most exploitative employment practices—from misclassification of "independent contractors" and overuse of temp agencies and subcontractors to forced arbitration and more—are driven by an employer strategy of avoiding coverage in our current employer-based labor law and collective bargaining system.

The solution is not merely to plug holes in the National Labor Relations Act and other federal workplace protections, but to build a new system. I don't propose to replace enterprise-level collective bargaining, but rather to build a new system around it to raise the floor on basic standards and rights and help make collective bargaining work again.

This new system should emphasize universal standards of rights and industrial standards of pay and benefits. It should foster new forms of democratic, pluralist, and voluntary worker representation.

The "How Can You Pay Your Dues Blues"

Throughout this chapter and those that follow, I'm going to throw out ideas for how unions could gain new members outside of the process of NLRB certifications and union contracts with dues check-off provisions. These will require new forms of organization for unions.

For starters, we should be thinking of new ways for workers to join unions that aren't dependent on a collective bargaining agreement with a union shop provision at their particular workplace. I can already hear some of you scoffing at the notion of unions running around and chasing voluntary dues-paying "at-large" members. Would we even bring in enough dues revenue to justify the organizing expenses? How do we possibly go to scale?

Let me just say that a federal dues check-off by law is an essential part of any reform or reimagining of our labor relations framework. Voluntary contributions are difficult to maintain without access to payroll deductions. While I appreciate the romantic turn-of-the-twentieth-century history of Wobbly dues stamps and "walking delegates" hand-collecting union dues, modern experiences with alternative forms of dues collection have proven to be wheel-spinning exercises that can't properly fund unions.

I spent years organizing with the United Teachers of New Orleans after all the teachers were fired in the wake of Hurricane Katrina. With no collective bargaining and little access to payroll deductions, we were asking union supporters to rejoin and pay their dues through credit cards or bank account debits. In our new age of inequality, even supposedly "middle-class" teachers bounce checks and miss monthly credit card payments with distressing regularity. In a typical year, we would sign up 500 new members for a net gain of 100 new dues payers.

Harvard professor Richard B. Freeman has spent decades parsing public opinion survey data on unions and workplace representation. This is a necessary project because our system is so mystifying. For instance, as of his last report in 2007, 32 percent of non-union workers would vote for a union tomorrow. Combined with the percentage of the unionized workforce that would vote to *maintain* their union representation, Freeman estimates that 58 percent of all workers want union representation. One poll he had to interpret—a 2004 Zogby survey—found that 45 percent of workers would "join" a union if they could.

Finally, a crucial finding:

> Three-fourths of workers desire independently elected workplace
> committees that meet and discuss issues with management, which
> some see as a supplement to collective bargaining (having both)
> and some see as useful as a stand-alone mechanism for voice. Very
> few workers (14 percent) are satisfied with their current voice at
> work and seek no changes, although another 10 percent are unsure
> about what they want.[111]

This is obviously a bit of a jumble. It is, however, a reflection of how
opaque the union organizing process is to most workers, and how
much workers struggle to understand how our peculiar union shop
works. The key takeaways are, first, that our current levels of union
membership are artificially lower than they ought to be, due to procedural noise and employer opposition. Second, most workers want
some form of institutional representation, or voice, at work. Third, a
massive number of non-union workers would join a union as dues-
paying members today if there was a reasonably easy mechanism
to do so. And, finally, if unions had a representational role in every
workplace by default, even more workers would join unions and pay
dues to support the campaigns that they run on behalf of all workers
in an industry, a workplace, or the economy at large.

Back to the Future of the Past

Let's do some more sci-fi thinking and imagine a world in which the
National Industrial Recovery Act (NIRA) was never declared unconstitutional by the Supreme Court. The Act was the signature initiative
of Franklin Delano Roosevelt's first New Deal, and it was the administration's first stab at labor law. The law's major goal was to get companies to stop their race to the bottom on prices and wages, which was
worsening the economic crisis. Those that complied displayed a Blue
Eagle on their products and advertising.

Again, this law is where that Section 7a "right to organize" originated. But it's the tripartite industrial boards that are of interest in this section.

The National Labor Relations Act is often misunderstood as the "replacement" of the NIRA. Roosevelt signed the labor act a few weeks after the Supreme Court—which simply abhorred any federal intervention in the magic of the broken and depressed marketplace—overturned NIRA. But the bill was drafted by Senator Wagner with the expectation that the new law would exist side by side with the federal industrial labor boards, as well as the state-level wage boards that had proliferated in the first New Deal. It was meant to be an enforcement mechanism for Section 7's "right to organize," by outlawing pervasive union-busting techniques and threatening the power of the state to restrain "unfair labor practices." Significantly, all it demanded was that employers bargain in good faith when workers declared themselves to be a union.

In our alternate universe, John L. Lewis still signs a members-only collective bargaining agreement on behalf of the Steelworkers with the massive US Steel corporation the day after the Supreme Court rules the NLRA constitutional.[112] The union could then have used that base of power to pressure the steel industrial board to extend their wage and hour gains to the "little steel" companies. In any universe, "little steel" would violently resist unionization for years until they were forced into collective bargaining by the federal government's need for smooth wartime production.[113] At least with the wage board, the workers would have made tangible gains earlier, joined the union in greater numbers, and taken on the steel industry as a class.

Some of these vestigial state wage boards still exist. For the same reason that the National Labor Relations Act was rooted in Congress's authority to regulate interstate commerce—that reason being to try to find an argument for constitutionality that the conservative Supreme Court would accept—so too was the minimum wage. But until the civil rights era, interstate commerce had a much narrower definition. A hotel, for instance, sitting entirely within the boundaries of one community, was not considered to be under federal jurisdiction.

So progressive states passed baby Wagner Acts and created tripartite wage boards to deal with minimum wage and overtime protections.

University of Michigan law professor Kate Andrias has tried to shine a light on the extant wage boards still on the books in states like California and New Jersey. She proposes that they could be used to pioneer a new form of social bargaining in the here and now. This is not pie in the sky. Governor Andrew Cuomo dusted off New York's wage board system in response to the Fight for $15. He was looking to take some heat off himself, and it was by no means assured that the public and industry representatives on the fast-food wage board would approve a full wage increase to $15 an hour. But the union ran a smart campaign and won.

Toward Federal Industrial Labor Standards

So how about bringing back the Blue Eagle for labor relations? We need a new federal system of tripartite industrial labor boards that cannot just raise the minimum wage for particular job categories and economic sectors but also settle big ticket work rules and benefits across entire industries and take those issues out of competition entirely.

It's easy to be cynical about Democratic politicians and their willingness to break a sweat on behalf of the legal rights of the American worker. The phrase that's perhaps most commonly mumbled under the breath of union lobbyists on Capitol Hill is "The Democrats don't love us as much as Republicans hate us." And, yes, that kind of lazy lesser-evilism has freed two decades of political hacks from having to engage in the kind of nitty-gritty details I'm trying to draw out in this book, or from working particularly hard to free us from this trap that they had no small role in baiting.

But something has changed. There have been too many election nights that went drastically against Democrats' expectations. Centrist politicians and shapers of public opinion who have hardly been friends to the working class are slowly waking up to the role that unions play in political education and voter turnout. The Trump moment was particularly disastrous. By around March of 2017, when the dust settled and it was clear that while Trump might be too stupid and lazy to overthrow our democracy a lot, Democrats on Capitol Hill finally had their "Oh shit" moment (to quote one staff member of a U.S. Senator and 2020 Democratic candidate I spoke to). Trump might be temporary, but if Democrats begin to grasp that if they can't assemble a robust and durable coalition of voters, centered on working families of all races and deliver real wins for working families, they are doomed to get turned out of office all over again in 2022 by a racist and demagogic death cult.

How do I know? Because I started getting calls from staffers of marquee progressive names in the House and Senate. And I'm nobody! That's how desperately they're casting about for good ideas. And that's how cautious and conservative unions had gotten about proposing reforms. At least that was a few years ago. Watching even the centrist candidates in the Democratic primary endorse reforms like just cause and wage boards have opened some unions to the possibility of demanding more.

So what to do with this realization? Well, let's stop nibbling at the edges of workers' legal rights with narrow technocratic "fixes." Consider the Employee Free Choice Act, for example. The basic theory of the Act, as best as I can understand it, was that card check and compulsory arbitration of first contracts would somehow lead to rapid increases in union density and put unions in a position of power to demand greater improvements in the labor law regime.

Apart from how little sense that makes from anyone who's been in the trenches on new union organizing campaigns, the theory also suffers from a basic political miscalculation.

In our current system, unions organize from a position of strength. That means that in our winner-take-all system of exclusive representation on the enterprise level, unions will tend to focus on non-union firms in already heavily unionized industries and markets. And that means that card check would lead to union organizing gains in a handful of deep blue states like New York, New Jersey, Illinois, and California.

There are states where right-wing media stoke popular resentment toward unions as islands of privilege. This gave the space for accidental Republican governors like Wisconsin's Scott Walker or Michigan's Rick Snyder to gut public sector collective bargaining and to sign private sector right-to-work laws. These are states where milquetoast Democratic governors like New Jersey's Jon Corzine and Illinois's Pat Quinn slashed hard-earned public sector pension and health care benefits and then lost office to otherwise unelectable schmucks like Chris Christie and Bruce Rauner because they had thoroughly demoralized their base by slashing their benefits and campaigning on the threat that the next jackass would do worse.

So let's embrace partisan cynicism. What sense does it make to add thousands more new union members merely to the handful of states where unions are still powerful and exercise an inordinate amount of influence that seems to engender resentment from our purported political friends?

So if this "oh shit moment," as we might call it, has any political force, it's twofold. First, any political ask that we have of the Democratic political establishment needs to put thousands of new union members in *every* state of the union as quickly as possible. If there were a new industrial labor board that could raise wages in the hospitality industry overnight, then it would make sense for UNITE HERE to deploy full-time organizers to, say, New Orleans, to build a base of support to win those wage gains. And if there was an education labor board that could shore up pension obligations and force school boards to enact reasonable paid family leave policies, then it would make sense for the two major teachers unions to double down on their organizing investment in Louisiana. And if there were a telecommunications labor board, then maybe the Communications Workers of America (CWA) would see fit to send another half-dozen organizers into the small towns of Louisiana where various subcontracted call centers have set up shop, secure in the belief that they are beyond the reach of unions under our current labor relations model. Having a couple dozen full-time organizers from just those four unions would create an unforeseen multiplier effect as neighbors who had good organizing conversations with staff organizers or co-workers would have more good organizing conversations with neighbors, co-workers, and family members.

Louisiana was a swing state until neoliberal Democrats teamed up with G. W. Bush Republicans to fire all the teachers in New Orleans public schools. That busted one of the biggest unions in the state—and, not coincidentally, one of the biggest institutional legacies of the civil rights era—the United Teachers of New Orleans. They had around 10,000 members before Hurricane Katrina. Are 10,000 new union members enough to turn Louisiana back into a swing state? How many new union members could four international unions deploying a few dozen organizers gain in a system where they're agitating for immediate wage and benefit gains on an industry-wide basis with immediate access to payroll dues deduction? And what if we repeated that experiment in every state of the union?

Secondly, a system of industrial labor boards creates the possibility to make real wage and hour gains for workers quickly. Like, before-your-reelection fast. Do you want to win office and stay in office and have a bigger voting bloc in the next legislative session? Well, put money in workers' pockets. Right now. *Yesterday*. Give them free stuff, sure, but also give them the power to take what they deserve—what they *earned*—from the boss.

Two Against One?

American trade unionists might hear "tripartite" and think, "Oh great. Two votes to one against the workers." But think of it this way: what do you call a group of decision-makers who *could* vote to give you and your peers a wage increase or fairer scheduling practices or the right to several weeks of paid family leave but resists doing so? I call that a boss—a big one that we can run campaigns against. Except unlike in our current system, where workers are siloed in their bargaining relationships with individual employers, unions could take on entire industries as a class.

As this idea gets bandied about among union leaders and think tankers in Washington and up and down the Acela corridor, there are many people who struggle mightily to keep it within a two-party bargaining framework (or "bipartite," if you're curious). Let me just say something slightly heretical: What if surrendering bargaining power is a step toward freedom? I don't mean to give up on collective bargaining entirely. Again, I think a reformed structure of NLRB-certified collective bargaining still has a role in the economy, and there are a great many workers who want to be able to bargain over shift assignments, uniform dry-cleaning allowances, and health and safety initiatives.

As discussed in the first two chapters, there are political dynamics of collective bargaining within a framework of exclusive representation that are in the bosses' interests, far more than they are in those of the unions. The dynamics of our routine of collective bargaining are such that bosses get way more credit for workers' contract wins than they deserve, and unions take way more blame for concessions than they deserve.

The unions are the ones that *take the deal.* They're the ones that *settle.* And as soon as the ink dries on that bottom-line signature they have a political need to go out and *sell* that deal to their members as the best they could get. This dynamic is the same regardless of whether it was some sweetheart deal cut in a back room or a hard-fought win after a long drawn-out strike with no shortage of rank-and-file input.

The boss? He just gets to endlessly badmouth the deal. He can immediately turn around and complain that what he voluntarily agreed to is going to bankrupt him and might lead to layoffs. He can grouse that he wanted to do more for certain categories of workers—merit pay or targeted raises—but the stupid union leaders wouldn't let him.

In the non-bargaining scenario of industrial labor board rule-making, this script is flipped. The unions demand, say, $15 an hour. Hell, let's demand $25 an hour. If the labor board votes to increase an industrial minimum wage by anything at all—a dollar, fifty cents—the unions can claim a win. It's money that workers wouldn't have made if the unions hadn't pressed the demand and if they hadn't waged a campaign.

But the unions are also free to charge that *those cheap greedy bastards still aren't giving us what the workers deserve*. It's more grist for the mill for a membership drive. We need your support so that next time we can win the minimum wage that we deserve. *Join us, wear this button, pay your dues.*

It's important that these industrial labor boards do much more than establish minimum wages. First of all, Congress can do that. (I mean, technically they can. Obviously their track record of doing so has been less than stellar.) Let's tap into the expertise of a worker representative who has done the work and an employer representative who has 20,000 incredibly specific fears about unintended consequences of any new policy or regulation. More important, let's give workers issues to rally around that could not be solved by bosses alone and that are put into competition by companies who try to gain an edge over each other by exploiting their employees.

How about paid family leave for teachers? There is considerable inequality in such leave between suburban and big city school districts. Some provide paid leave, but not all. In many places, a new mother has to take an unpaid leave of absence. Charter schools are driving down what standards exist, treating new parents like thirty-year-olds in *Logan's Run*. If there was an education labor board that could make a minimum enforceable standard of paid leave for new parents, there would be many teachers who rush to build the campaign to win it.

And that raises some questions: How do you carve up the economy into distinct industries? How many industries? How many boards? Would an education labor board also cover higher ed? Would it go from pre-K to postdoc? Would bus drivers be under its jurisdiction or a transportation labor board? I don't know. It seems to me that there would need to be some flexibility built into this system. Perhaps the boards have the authority to create subcommittees or to designate authority for a subset of workers to another board for questions where that other board might have more technical expertise.

Regardless, the principle has to be that we're all in. Whatever your craft or profession, regardless of part-time or temporary status, regardless of whether you work for a Fortune 500 firm or a subcontractor of a subcontractor, there is an industrial labor board that can vote to raise your wage and a union that wants you as a member.

Let's Spitball a Few More Scenarios

Let's imagine a hospitality industry labor board. What kinds of companies are covered by the hospitality board? Well, hotels and restaurants for sure. Maybe fast food is under the jurisdiction of a retail industry board, or maybe it's spun off to a subdivision of hospitality. Is airline catering here, or under transportation? Again, I would expect a certain degree of forum-shopping by the employers as some industrial boards prove to be particularly deft and aggressive in improving standards for workers, while others might be less aggressive on sectors that are outside of their bread and butter or have weaker unions.

For now, let's think about hotels and restaurants where there is a long history of worker organizing efforts and some pockets of union strength. This labor board could do anything from raising the minimum wage of hotel housekeepers to abolishing the practice of tipping in restaurants. It could, and should, take on more than mere paycheck issues. It could ban "clopens," which is the practice—more prevalent in fast food and retail—of assigning an employee to work the first shift of the day after she just finished the last shift of the night before, leaving little time for rest between closing and opening. It could take on issues of harassment in the workplace like granting cocktail waitresses the right to refuse to wear "uniforms" that are too sexually exploitative. Or it could extend a standard that unions have managed to win here and there through collective bargaining, but is a necessary right and a fight that would resonate across an industry. A good example would be mandating that all hotels—not just the union shops that have won it so far—install "panic buttons" for housekeepers to call for help when a customer is being creepy or aggressive.

The workers' representative on the board—nominated by the secretary of labor or the White House or anybody with the appropriate authority and picked from among the handful of organizations that represent hospitality workers—could force a vote on any of these issues. Maybe it's on a schedule, maybe it's on demand, maybe there's a limit of how many new issues can be raised in a year. Regardless, once a vote is scheduled on an issue of importance to the workers in the industry, every union and workers' center with an organizing stake in the industry would agitate for a yes vote.

What would this look like? Surely there would be a lot of petition-signing (on paper in the shops, as well as online) and asks to call or email the industry and public representatives on the board. Hopefully, there would be some visibility actions—buttons and T-shirts and that kind of stuff. Rallies and hand-billing in key locations. Every union and worker center campaigning on the issue should definitely be organizing workers into dues-paying membership.

One would expect the unions would have an analysis of which major employers would have the most outsized influence on the other two board members and target them for disruption—including slow-downs, consumer boycotts, and rolling strikes.

When the industrial board finally votes, maybe the unions win their demand. Maybe the board goes for a compromise measure—a $1-an-hour wage increase where the demand was for $3, for instance. Or maybe the worker representative gets outvoted and the workers get nothing. The unions have still gained members in new shops, and there might be enough activist energy at some of those shops to run an organizing campaign to win collective bargaining through the NLRB or some other method.

Let's consider a more concentrated industry. What if there was a telecommunications industrial labor board? Again, this could have jurisdiction over everything from whoever owns Ma Bell's ancient network of copper landlines to cable and satellite TV providers to whatever the hell gets Netflix in front of people's eyeballs that isn't Ava DuVernay.

But let's narrow our focus to cellular phone companies, of which there are basically four that dominate the industry: AT&T, Verizon, T-Mobile, and Sprint. I type these corporate names fully convinced that I'll have to revise this section before this book is published, or else this will be the first handful of paragraphs to be hopelessly out-dated a few years later, given how rapidly this industry is consolidat-ing and transforming.

But, as of this writing, only one of those major cell phone provid-ers is—within the limits of our peculiar union shop—more or less fully unionized. That's AT&T. The union that represents AT&T—the Communications Workers of America (CWA)—also represents much of Verizon's hard-line phone and cable business, and has had a doggedly persistent organizing campaign among the corporation's wireless workers for well over a decade. They've also tried a number of approaches to organize T-Mobile's workers, including a voluntary associate membership program that is still ongoing.

So let's imagine a world where CWA can leapfrog their AT&T Wireless collective bargaining demands (and wins) into campaign demands against the telecommunications industrial labor board. Should CWA demand that the telecom board set a wage scale for the entire industry that's at least as high as the AT&T contract? Sure, but why not demand higher? Why should the AT&T workers care about what particular mechanism—bargaining over a soon-to-be-expired contract or a wage standard set by some public board—got them more money in their pockets?

How about pressing the industrial board for a rule that all customer service workers should be based in the United States and also subject to an industrial minimum wage scale? Or abolishing sales quotas in the stores?

So again with the petitions and buttons and dues authorization cards and consumer boycotts and rolling one-day strikes. But here's where the fun starts. When does CWA hold back a demand on the industrial labor board in order to line it up with the AT&T contract expiration? When does it take a demand to the AT&T bargaining table first, and concentrate its protest activity on one of the other three companies while making a recent AT&T settlement the new demand before the industrial board?

Win, lose, or draw, the workers in cellular are fighting for their demands as a class against the entire industry. Regardless of outcome, we've turned what is currently an inexact and opaque process—the "spillover effect" of union contract gains being matched by non-union firms—into something more direct, and far more obvious and worthy of solidarity activism. Beyond that, how many cycles of leapfrogging the contract bargaining at AT&T with the targeted protest actions at the other big three before, say, Verizon starts feeling out CWA about a neutrality agreement so that they can get in on some of the sweet, sweet no-strike action that AT&T has enjoyed for two or three years at a time?

Betriebsverfassungsgesetz

Industrial labor boards would be an all-in system of labor relations, but it's very much a macro-economic representation. Workers need, want, and deserve micro-economic representation. They want representation that is focused on the nitty-gritty, day-to-day decision-making at their individual workplaces. Moving toward an all-in system of workplace representation—one where employees in every workplace simply enjoy representation on day one with no debate or vote on the fundamental democratic principle that all workers in all workplaces deserve representation—might require slaughtering the sacred cow of exclusive representation.

Unions must be political organizations. We shouldn't run away from that fundamental necessity. Unions need to have and express viewpoints about the work that members do (or refuse to do), the priorities, products, and business practices of corporations, as well as the politicians that those corporations buy and sell.

So if we try to make all-in representation automatic at the workplace level and then default to the organizational model of our peculiar union shop with exclusive representation and agency fee, we're going to have a constitutional problem. Even with a liberal majority on the Supreme Court, we're either compelling people to join a political organization as a term of employment or we're depoliticizing an organization that workers desperately need to be political in order to compel membership in it.

So one thought is to return to the basic intention and plain language of the NLRA. Which is that anywhere that two or more workers declare themselves to be a union, the employer is bound to negotiate with them in good faith over changes in the terms and conditions of employment. That wouldn't put workplace representation in every workplace on day one, but we could probably get there by Thursday afternoon. Getting two or more workers in every workplace to turn to each other, do a little fist-bump and say, "I got your back if you got mine. Now we're a union" is an organizational challenge that I think we're up to. I'll return to this idea in chapter 10.

Another idea is this: *Betriebsverfassungsgesetz.* The word describes the German works council model, which has elements that might be right at home in America. One of the most peculiar things that our peculiar union shop does is create a kind of government in the workplace. But that government is a one-party system. It's just philosophically un-American, and we—union organizers, advocates, and allies—just don't appreciate how much noise it adds to our organizing challenge.

A German works council is an elected group of workers at a firm who meet with management over a broad set of workplace issues that get much closer to the "core of entrepreneurial control" than what is currently beyond the legal scope of bargaining for U.S. unions. The operations of the work council are funded entirely by the employer. The council members might be proud and openly identified members of their unions, but they could just as easily be independent.

The works council operates alongside voluntary unions and multiple levels of collective bargaining—including industry-wide and firm-level. Any agreement that a works council makes with management has the force of a contract, provided it does not undercut the terms of the industry-wide agreement.

I've simplified this a bit, but the main idea should be clear. And, like almost every labor relations system in the world, the German system is under stress and subject to change. I don't propose that we slavishly re-create German works councils in the United States. I do suggest that we seriously consider a model of workplace government within which unions operate as political parties and that coexists with traditional contract bargaining *and* industrial labor board standard-setting.

It should be a law that every employer should have a works council to allow for corporate-wide worker representation. The employer must release elected representatives from their work duties when the workers decide to conduct their works council duties, and the company must pay for reasonable expenses of operating the works council.

It's a government. In order to fund this government employers' profits are what's being taxed. But the voters remain, exclusively, the workers. Let's say the term of office is one year or maybe two years at a time. All non-managerial workers can vote in the representation elections, and any non-managerial worker can run for office regardless of what—if any—union she belongs to or what unions might or might not have collective bargaining rights within the enterprise.

What kinds of decisions or work rules must an employer discuss with a works council? It must be a matter that is currently considered off-limits as a matter of management's rights or "the core of entrepreneurial control." So, for instance, where a union can only bargain over the impact of an employer's decision to subcontract bargaining unit work, a works council should be able to weigh in on the decision itself.

Could the two processes happen simultaneously? Could the works council oppose a decision to subcontract and slow it down through painstaking negotiations and information requests while the union demands to bargain over the impact while ramping up protest actions? Damn right it could. Twice the power for workers is still unequal to the far greater economic power of employers. But at least this dual power would be fairer than the limited tools that workers currently have at their disposal.

The corporate-wide works council should also have the ability to create smaller works councils for discrete worksites of the enterprise. These may be based on departments, geography, or work shifts. Whatever makes sense.

Here's another heretical proposal: it probably makes sense for the worksite-level works council to take jurisdiction over some items that have been the prerogative of traditional collective bargaining. I'm thinking specifically of health and safety and employee discipline.

This is important stuff but it's also resource- and time-intensive. In chapter 4, I described the institutional tensions as unions tried to focus more on external organizing but shifted resources from grievance work like this. One of the tensions I didn't describe is personality-based. There are union activists who are temperamentally more suited and really do prefer to represent workers who need help, and then there are rabble-rousers who want to agitate around issues and organize job actions. Both roles are vital to the workplace. One should be handled by an elected works council and funded by the boss, leaving the union with more of its own time and resources to focus on internal organizing.

That's where there *is* a union. Where there *isn't*, workers still deserve a process to defend their jobs and their health and safety. We need works councils as a part of an all-in system of labor relations. And, as I'll discuss in the next chapter, unions can gain footholds in non-union workplaces by defending key workers' jobs using formal processes like this.

EIGHT

A Right to Your Job

WITHOUT A UNION, A WORKER can be fired for a good reason, a bad reason, or no reason at all. A non-union worker is entitled to no advance warning or opportunity to improve or any recourse, appeal, or severance.

Perversely, many union activists seem perfectly okay with this. The basic thinking goes something like this: Unions provide job protections through a collective bargaining agreement. Workers who want job protections at work should form a union with their co-workers. If workers have a right to their jobs as a part of an "all-in" system of workplace rights, then what incentive would there be for workers to form and join unions?

This way of thinking is yet another example of how we tend to not question the rigged rules of the system and of how we allow the boss's law to become our ideology. Worse, it's an example of how we sometimes unwittingly prop them up. That American workers lack this basic workplace right, so common in the rest of the world, is a shame. That unions have abandoned and even discouraged fighting for this right is bizarre.

The fact that most workers could be fired at any time for just about any reason is not driving workers to form unions in hordes. It's doing the opposite. It is what gives anti-union campaigns of terror—with their pervasive threats of widespread job loss, sprinkled with actual retaliatory terminations—so much of their power. It is, in part, what holds so many workers back from everyday acts of protest on the job.

As a movement, we have to fight for a legal standard of "just cause" employment. We have to fight for a right to your job.

The "At-Will" Doctrine

Explained simply, "just cause" is the principle that an employee can be fired only for a legitimate, serious, work-performance reason. Most union contracts contain a "just cause" clause. The alternative to just cause is the current mess of affairs euphemistically referred to as the "at-will" employment doctrine. Basically, that means that you are free to quit your job. But it also means that your employer has the right to fire you.

Because as a society we don't actually believe that an employer should be able to fire a worker for a *bad* reason, we do have a number of laws that protect employees from being fired discriminatorily for, say, their race or religion or in retaliation for being a whistleblower. Unfortunately, these cases are hard to win. They involve lengthy regulatory processes and expensive legal bills. They put the onus on the fired worker to make the case that she was fired for a bad reason. Just cause does the opposite. It puts the onus on the employer to establish that a termination was for a good reason, for a "just cause."

"At will" is judge-made law. The concept was imported by conservative—or, rather, "classical liberal"—jurists to wave away all of that pesky talk of free assembly and due process that the framers of the Constitution meant to apply far more broadly to society than the narrow way it defines "government" these days. It was a betrayal of the workers who fought the Revolution for America's independence.

It happened because the American Revolution was rapidly followed by the Industrial Revolution, which totally altered the relationship between employers and their workers. Pre-industrial production was marked by small shops and a pathway to self-employment for every free worker. A master craftsman would work alongside his journeyman and apprentice, as he taught them the craft in preparation for eventually moving on to be masters themselves. But as masters formed corporations and amassed capital, they hired larger work-forces of apprentices and soon dispensed with teaching them too many tricks of the trade. The master craftsmen became bosses and everyone else became wage workers with less and less of a chance of breaking out into self-employment.

It's in that context that workers formed the first unions in America in the early 1800s. And it's in that context that workers who were now dependent on wage work for their survival started the first strikes and boycotts and also began to argue that they had a right to their jobs.

The judiciary was incredibly hostile to this. In her book, *Private Government: How Employers Rule Our Lives (and Why We Don't Talk About It)*, Elizabeth Anderson writes:

> Preindustrial labor radicals, viewing the vast degradation of auton-omy, esteem, and standing entailed by the new productive order in comparison with artisan status, called it *wage slavery*. Liberals called it *free labor*. The difference in perspective lay at the very point Marx highlighted. If one looks only at the conditions of entry into the labor contract and exit out of it, workers appear to meet their employers on terms of freedom and equality. That was what the liberal view stressed. But if one looks at the actual conditions experienced in the workers fulfilling the contract, the workers stand in a relation of profound subordination to their employer. That was what the labor radicals stressed.[114]

Conservative judges today, of course, still think in terms of one lone worker (or consumer) entering into a fair negotiation of equals with massive corporations.

Unions, however, spent generations resisting the "at-will" doc-trine and fought for employment rights for all workers. In fact, in the years just before the passage of the National Labor Relations Act in 1935 there were many in the labor movement espousing a legal theory of a worker's property right to his job. This was in some ways a tit-for-tat reaction to the bosses' most effective legal tactics at the time. Before the 1930s, employers could routinely convince judges to issue injunctions against strikes, boycotts, and picket lines by arguing that those protests interfered with their property right to expect their workers to report for duty everyday.[115]

The union theory of a property right to the job was just enough of a legal fig leaf to justify the sit-down strikes.[116] The sit-downs, of course, were eventually ruled to be illegal, but not before they put enough fear of revolution into the Supreme Court to allow the NLRA to stand. Our current labor rights regime was ushered in; the property right to your job angle was dropped; and the labor movement's DNA was fundamentally changed.

With just cause routinely negotiated into collective bargaining agreements, unions evolved to accept that job security is something a worker only gets for being in a union. Even today, many union leaders and organizers might even have a slight preference for retaining "at-will" in order to drive more unrepresented workers to organize for a union contract at their place of work.

Attempting to legislate job protections for all workers regardless of whether they are dues-paying union members would be a departure for the postwar U.S. labor movement. The labor movements of other countries strike more of a balance between negotiating rights and benefits for their members and legislating them for all workers. And when rights are enjoyed by all, they are defended by most. Conversely, recall how easily the corporate "ed reform" movement was able to demonize teacher tenure, which is simply "just cause" by another name.

"Just Cause" in Practice

One of the key questions in designing a just cause law is whether or not to include a formal progressive discipline policy and appeals process. There are benefits to both approaches. In a union contract, progressive discipline typically consists of a verbal warning of an infraction or unsatisfactory performance, followed by a formal written warning, then a suspension without pay, and finally termination. The progressive steps of discipline reflect an increasing seriousness of infraction or inability to improve following warnings and remedial supports. Lower levels of discipline might be accompanied by new training or counseling to help the employee improve. Some matters might go through the entire progression of discipline. Other, more serious infractions might go straight to a higher level of discipline. (Theft, for example, almost always leads directly to termination.)

So that would be the natural model for a legal standard of progressive discipline. As for an appeals process, that would probably also look a bit like a union's grievance procedure, with appeals to higher levels of management authority, leading finally to a "hearing" by the employer that results in management's "final answer." It would make sense to give workers and their employers access to mediators like the Federal Mediation and Conciliation Service to encourage negotiated settlements over expensive (for the worker) lawsuits. But only by mutual agreement of both parties, and the employee must have the right to reject any terms and proceed with a lawsuit.

The benefit of this approach—of spelling out the legal standard of progressive discipline and the appeals process—is that everyone would understand the process and their rights and responsibilities under it. It would normalize a system of employee rights across all workplaces. Employers will likely cry foul over such an unprecedented federal intervention into the workplace, so it could be too difficult politically to win just cause *and* progressive discipline.

There is also benefit to not spelling out progressive discipline under the law, and leaving it to employers to figure out how they will comply with the law. With a legal just cause standard, companies *will* professionalize their human resources departments. They *will* institute forms of progressive discipline and document it. They *will* create internal appeals processes, because they'll want to fire people and they'll want those terminations to stick. They don't want to be successfully sued every three days.

And that's good news for us, because left to their own devices they will inevitably botch it. Absent a negotiated collective bargaining agreement, companies are not going to consistently apply the same standards or give every worker the same transparency and communication. When unions file grievances over a termination or other form of discipline, we're grieving not just the fairness of the discipline but also the fairness of the process. So a messy, inconsistent employer-controlled process would give unions and workers' centers more opportunity to save workers' jobs. And that would create all kinds of organizing possibilities.

A worker who receives warning that her job is in peril might reasonably want to contest a write-up and seek help and representation. One possibility here is that unions create a category of membership for individuals to join on an at-large basis. A union would be providing a tangible benefit and service at that point. There are many workers who would consider it reasonable to pay $15 or $20 a month for telephone counseling and advice.

If the "grievant" works at a company that the union is interested in organizing, providing on-site representation could be a good way to make inroads with other workers. We did exactly that in a charter school organizing campaign in New Orleans, and it helped us win the first collective bargaining agreement for any group of teachers in that city since the city tore up the United Teachers of New Orleans (UTNO) collective bargaining agreement when they fired all the teachers in the wake of Hurricane Katrina in 2005. (Technically, the teachers weren't "fired" as much as suffered from the biggest reduction in force in history and nearly every public school was "closed" and then reopened as new legal entities—a state takeover of the district and a proliferation of charter schools.)

The AFT kept a crew of staff organizers in the city—for over a decade. We didn't have collective bargaining, but in the state-run "Recovery School District" and in the five and a half schools that remained in the old Orleans Parish Schools system, we had that non-union union system that is so common in the South called "meet-and-confer." Management would meet with us as a worker representative. We could raise issues that were important to our members. It wasn't bargaining; there would be no contract. But it was a degree of collective voice and representation, and there was payroll deduction for voluntary union dues. In the charter schools, it was worse. No meet-and-confer, no payroll deduction, and no rights that bosses were bound to respect.

We organized the workers into voluntary dues-paying membership using credit cards and bank drafts. As I described in the previous chapter, this was a Sisyphean effort. These workers had—and then lost—the protections of a collective bargaining agreement. They knew exactly what they had lost and how vulnerable they were.

Our membership levels were terrible and prone to a very high turnover rate. We labored under the impression that we were under the jurisdiction of Louisiana's public sector labor laws, which weren't so much a "system" as a kind of "speakeasy" rule. Management could voluntarily recognize a union and bargain a contract, but there was no labor board to compel them or police the rampant unfair labor practices in the system.

The bosses brought back (verbal) yellow dog contracts, telling workers in their job interview that maintaining a job was contingent on not joining UTNO. Captive audience meetings were conducted on a routine basis over the school intercoms during the breaks between classes. It was a mess. There was no model that the workers could accept to organize. Strike for recognition?!?—"They'll just fire us!"

The historically elite Benjamin Franklin High School—the state's top performer and a magnet school before the storm—became a charter school but largely retained its pre-Katrina faculty. It had low membership numbers when it was a district school in the collective bargaining (but still right-to-work) era of Orleans Parish Schools. But they had had some pretty bad experiences with dictatorial, sometimes cultish and incompetent management by 2014.

Then the principal tried to fire the popular Latin teacher, Stephen Pearce (his co-workers nicknamed him "Prof"), and suddenly—finally—we gained a few members at the school. We had recently gotten a National Labor Relations Board decision out of Chicago indicating that the NLRB was inclined to take jurisdiction over charter schools as private sector employers with little meaningful accountability to voters or governments. We could file ULPs! We could even file for a certification election if an employer refused to voluntarily recognize us. I was hungry to test our new legal powers.

Our on-the-ground campaign director, Audra George, stubbornly argued with me against rushing to an NLRB election drive. UTNO needs to demonstrate efficacy, she insisted. Franklin High had adopted a sort of bootleg due process and grievance procedure when it became a charter school in 2005 and were still afraid of the specter of unionism. It remained in their by-laws. Audra wanted to defend Prof in a hearing before the charter's governance board.

Okay, I relented, let's try it, but I want to be moving toward majority support for collective bargaining in the building. Audra got the workers circulating a petition to the governing board in support of Prof's continued employment and brought some of them into the hearing to testify about his excellent teaching and faculty leadership. Amazingly, the board agreed to her participation as Prof's representative. And management backed down! Prof's job was saved.

The petition circulators turned into an active rank-and-file organizing committee. Before the school year was over, they had signed up 90 percent of their colleagues for the union and marched on the principal. After another crazy governance board meeting in which hundreds of students and alumni turned out to hear teacher testimony about why they had formed a union, management voluntarily recognized the Franklin chapter of UTNO as the teachers' bargaining representative.

Contrast that story with what almost always happens today when a non-union worker whose job is in peril calls local unions for help. The worker is most often told, "They're allowed to do that" and "We can't help you." The union usually writes off the shop as an organizing prospect because how can you start a campaign with a worker who's about to get fired?

Remind me again how the "at-will" doctrine encourages workers to organize unions.

NINE

Get the Boss Out of the Doctor's Office

THE DAYS OF UNIONS TAKING labor costs out of competition are largely over. Unions increase the amount of money that companies spend on payroll costs. In so doing, they make unionized firms less competitive. It's an uncomfortable truth that union supporters don't like to acknowledge, but it's also a huge part of the trap we find ourselves in. We have to grapple with it.

Fringe benefits at a unionized firm can add more than 40 percent to payroll costs. Some of that is things like Social Security, workers compensation, unemployment insurance, and taxes that all employers pay. But for a unionized firm, it can include things like pension, health and dental insurance, life insurance, and contributions to an employee benefit fund that provide all kinds of welfare.

As an illustration: If I write up a grant proposal to bring on an extra researcher at my labor center, the university wants me to incorporate a 42 percent fringe benefit rate. That is to say that instead of needing, say, $60,000 in grant funding to pay the salary of a new researcher, we need to find $85,200. As a worker, you're a number on a spreadsheet to your boss. But that number is way higher than what you see on your pay stub. And it's even higher if you're a union member.

As we've discussed, unions never actually stopped organizing for new members in bargaining units. In fact, unions in the 1970s sought to organize roughly half a million private sector workers a year in NLRB elections. But, for the first time since the NLRB was established in 1935, unions began to lose a majority of all representation elections, a decline that has continued to the present day. Lane Windham recently wrote a valuable history of this period, *Knocking on Labor's Door*.[117] The late 1960s and into the 1970s saw an attempted organizing wave led by women and workers of color in the South and across varied industries get smacked down by a new corporate open-shop drive.

Egged on by a then-new cottage industry of "union avoidance" consultants and anti-union law firms, employers aggressively pressed against the limits of labor law when campaigning against union organizing drives. They skirted the prohibition against threatening the jobs of union supporters by phrasing those threats as predictions of the negative impact that a union would have on the company's bottom line. They threw out fantastical scenarios about how unions might trade away benefits. They swore that the unions would make no gains unless the workers went on strike, and if they did strike, the company would permanently replace them. They froze planned pay increases and told the workers that the unions and the law forced them to do so.

When they got caught actually breaking the law—by being too obvious in their espionage of organizing activity or materially punishing a union leader—the paltry punishments that were meted out sparked a new union-busting revolution. Why obey the law at all? Paying an illegally fired union activist just the wages she was owed—minus whatever unemployment insurance or moonlighting money she earned in the years it took for the case to get adjudicated—was far less money that a successfully negotiated union contract would cost.

At the heart of American corporations' renewed resistance to union organizing was the increase in foreign competition. This was not strictly the dumping of products made cheaper in overseas sweatshops, which we tend to think of as the driver of inequality in the global economy. The first pangs of competitive anxiety were triggered by German and Japanese manufacturers who had finally recovered from the Second World War and could export quality products at affordable prices. Their competitive edge was that the cost of their workers' health and retirement benefits were not loaded onto their payroll and then passed on to consumers at a higher retail price—those social welfare benefits were the responsibility of the state.

Since most U.S. corporations were, and are, unlikely to embrace social democracy, those in the 1970s resolved to fight the global pressure by fighting their own workers. But union supporters must grapple with an uncomfortable fact about our peculiar union shop and routine of collective bargaining. In any industry that is not mostly unionized, the decision by workers to form a union really can make a company less competitive. And high union-density industries are just juicier targets for capitalist vampires like AirBnb and Uber to compete by undercutting those standards.

By hook or by crook, we must take these vital benefits, such as health care and retirement security, which are really human rights, out of competition. However, there is an embarrassing and frustrating political reality. While making Medicare a universal right from cradle to grave and expanding Social Security enough to provide everyone a dignified retirement is a common-sense necessity, the unions that have managed to survive into the twenty-first century will likely be obstacles toward those goals.

As institutions, unions are risk averse. More than that, as discussed regarding job security, union leaders and members alike have inherited some hard-to-shake notions that good benefits are something you get by having a union. They ask, if everybody had health care and retirement security as a right, why would people continue to form unions?

Union Benefit Funds

The first union I worked for took special pride in the health care it provided its members. Considerable space was devoted in the union's weekly newspaper to touting its benefits, explaining its benefits, and promoting its benefits. Was this service model unionism? Hardly.

The New York Hotel Trades Council is a direct lineal descendant of the Wobblies. The union was born from a series of infamous industry-wide strikes in the fancy dining rooms and kitchens of the hotel industry in 1912 and 1913. That last strike lost public support when Wobbly organizer Joseph Ettore infamously warned, "It is the unsafest thing in the world for the capitalist to eat food prepared by members of your union."[118]

The workers dusted themselves off and formed a new independent union inspired by IWW organizing techniques but chastened by the fallout from the P.R. carelessness of the organizers who has trained them. Their Amalgamated Food Workers was, in turn, supplanted by a Communist Party–affiliated union, the Food Workers Industrial Union. By the late 1930s, they had organized a few more citywide strikes. At that time, the industry was basically suing for peace. The Communists and anarchists merged into the AFL-affiliated Hotel Trades Council and continued to organize into one big union nearly all of the housekeepers, food service workers, craftsmen, and professional staff in almost all of the firms in the city's hotel industry.

This union was, and is, unique. I was lucky to have worked for the Hotel Trades Council at an early stage of my career and political development. It defied clichéd and rote organizing in a way that made the lazy "it is what it is" attitude among most unionists particularly unappealing to me when I encountered it later on.

As discussed previously, during the Second World War unions that were fenced in by no-strike pledges, wartime inflation, and wage freezes were freed by the "Little Steel" formula to bargain for fringe benefits. It was mostly the craft unions of the AFL that took advantage of this temporary loophole. The CIO unions, which had more of a social democratic orientation, held out, presuming they could push the New Deal Democrats to expand Social Security to cover health care after the war was over.

Well, what are a bunch of AFL Communists to do under the circumstances? They bargained for employer-funded health insurance during the war and quickly chafed against the costs involved and lack of control that Blue Cross and Blue Shield afforded them. So they focused on forcing employers to fork over the money for a jointly run Employee Benefit Fund that would build and staff a network of health care clinics.

Today, it is the crown jewel of their union-negotiated benefits. The doctors, nurses, and technicians are all salaried employees. They're well compensated. Many but by no means most are in earlier stages of their careers, a little past their residencies and internships. Many also prefer the arrangement of being a salaried medical professional for a mid-size group practice that is more focused on the care and treatment of patients than cost-cutting and profiteering. They didn't want to be relatively new at a very demanding and complicated profession and also have to deal with starting a new small business.

It's easily the best health *care* (as distinguished from health insurance or that wretched centrist term of art, "access to health care") that I've enjoyed in my life. It's not just that co-pays were low or zero and prescriptions were dirt cheap. The group practice aspect of the network of NYC hotel industry health clinics—doctors, nurses, and technicians actually consulting with each other about a patient's symptoms and medical history and developing a holistic approach to diagnosis and treatment. It is what we all hope to get when we visit a doctor. We don't get it under our current mess of a health care system. But the NY Hotel Trades Council has somehow managed to win and maintain just such a miniature form of socialized medicine for its community. And it's amazing.

One of my best friends probably owes his life to the health care we both received as staff of the NYHTC a decade and a half ago. A routine blood workup at his annual physical showed a slightly elevated amount of iron in his blood. It's the sort of thing that goes altogether ignored by doctors when the cost of lab tests is a consideration. But the benefit fund's doctor could easily do a follow-up lab test in-house, which led to a diagnosis of hemochromatosis, an uncommon metabolic disorder. It's probably more commonly discovered in autopsies, after a seemingly healthy person drops dead at around the age of fifty after an excess of iron in the blood has poisoned a vital organ like the heart or liver. If it's caught early enough, as it was for my friend, treatment is as simple as donating a pint of blood every six weeks or so.

So, I appreciate the pride that union leaders like the NY Hotel Trades Council's take in providing excellent health benefits for their members, and their reticence about making big changes. Yet all that moving to a Medicare-for-all system would do is alter who pays for the health clinics, not who hires the medical staff or who the patients are. In fact, moving to a single-payer system might enable more unions to create group practice health clinics for their members.

The Hotel Trades Council was able to organize its miniature system of socialized medicine because they were smart enough to take advantage of a political moment in time when employers wanted labor peace and were willing to pay for it. They've managed to hold on to it because they have maintained a very high level of union density and because the economics of the system work for the employers.

There are other unions with benefit funds, of course, and they play an outsized role in the thinking about labor law reform. There are some who propose technocratic solutions for union growth, by having unions take on the administrative burdens of benefit administration and offering economies of scale to entice employers into a bargaining relationship.

There are two problems with this approach, and they should be obvious. First of all, this requires organizing from a position of strength, and there are not many places where we are institutionally strong. In recent years, the Hotel Trades Council has begun to organize workers outside of the five boroughs of New York City. The fact that unionized hotels that pay into the benefit fund wind up spending less money on better health care has been helpful. That's great for hotel workers in New Jersey and upstate New York. But what the hell do we do about grocery store workers in Arizona or adjunct professors in Texas?

The second problem is that operating a benefit fund requires willing employers, and employers are mostly *not* willing. They're not eager to have unions in the workplace and they're not willing to engage in collective problem solving with their competitors. Employers spent the last forty years breaking out of multi-employer bargaining everywhere that they could.

Most unions go to the bargaining table with one employer at a time, and that employer puts the high cost of health insurance on the table on the first day of bargaining. Before they can even try to make any gains, most unions are already fighting concessions on their health insurance.

Dr. Boss

If we had industrial labor boards, we could mitigate some of this defensive bargaining by taking the cost of health insurance out of competition in each industry. Or, I should say, out of domestic competition, because we would still have the same problem of American-made products and services being made unnecessarily more expensive compared to those of countries with government-sponsored health care.

We would also still have the Hobby Lobby problem of bosses getting all up in their employees' vaginas. You might recall that our nation's second-most trusted purveyor of scrapbooking supplies[119] refused to comply with the Obamacare mandate that insurance plans cover contraception. Their case went all the way up to the Supreme Court, and they won under the newly weaponized First Amendment.[120]

Now, Hobby Lobby hid behind Jesus, but the plainer truth is that bosses are gonna boss. It is simply in boss nature to assume that their paycheck entitles them to way more than your time on the clock. If you let the boss into the doctor's office, he's going to have opinions about your medical treatment.

Sometimes it's not even nefarious, but it is nevertheless your employer having literal life-and-death power over you. When I worked for the American Federation of Teachers, I had what I thought was excellent health insurance until my wife and I had difficulty conceiving. Our doctors eventually determined that we would need to do in vitro fertilization if we had any hope of having children. And that's when I found out that my employer-sponsored health insurance wouldn't cover one red cent of the procedure. My employer had what's called a self-insured plan, which essentially means that they write up a list of procedures, tests, and prescriptions that will be covered, and Blue Cross hands them a bill for their employees' usage of the benefit.

In the time that IVF went from being considered a weird and rare experimental treatment to a fairly routine medical procedure, my employer never updated its self-insured plan to add IVF to the list. The union that represented the AFT's staff didn't want to reopen the plan out of fear that management might use that opening to make less desirable changes. Management took the position that it was incumbent upon the staff union to propose any increase in benefits. And so it sat there in a stupid stalemate.

That's just my story. How many people out there are similarly denied health care they need or want because their boss has a veto? This is why I detest the argument, made typically by political centrists, that we should not upend the entire health care system and a huge chunk of our economy because most people who have insurance are satisfied with it. Sure, they're satisfied with it—until they really need it. Then they find out they don't have as much coverage as they thought. How are we a free people if we allow our employers such intimate control over our care, over matters of life and death? Let's get the boss out of our doctors' office.

Pensions

We also have a burgeoning pension crisis. I write here not of politically motivated attacks on defined benefit pensions, particularly in the public sector, but of the shortsighted way too many unions deal with those attacks. Our vesting periods are too damn long, and that is undermining younger workers' confidence and participation in pensions, which further undermines the solvency of the pension funds themselves.

There is a tendency of older workers, particularly those in union leadership, to view the fact that people will work a variety of jobs over the course of their worklife—the median tenure of employment is a little over four years[121]—as a part of the sickness of our economy; something that unions aim to "fix." And there is some truth to that. Absent any organizing for collective action, one of the main forms of protest against poor treatment available to a worker is to just quit the job. However, something deeper is at play in society as well. A great many younger workers—let's say those under the age of forty—simply don't see staying at one employer for thirty or even twenty years as desirable. They want a variety of experiences. They want the freedom to switch fields altogether.

When I went to work for the State University of New York, I was faced with a dilemma. I could enroll in the state pension plan, which takes ten long years to vest, or I could opt for a defined contribution plan with a much shorter vesting period of a year and a day. Under the pension plan, after ten years of employment I would be guaranteed a *partial* pension. I'd have to work for twenty years to receive a full pension. If I left before ten years, I could withdraw the 5 percent of my salary that I had to contribute to the pension fund but none of the employer's contribution. If I opted for the defined contribution plan, I could leave with all the money that both I and the employer contributed plus interest.

I'm a union guy and a strong believer in the need for retirement security through a pension, so I signed up for the pension. But I sure swallowed hard at ten years. I've made it to my forties without working anywhere for that long. How many younger employees at the university opt for the defined contribution because they don't know where they want to be in ten years? And how does their opting out undermine the pension plan for everyone else?

In fairness, we have some pretty lousy public sector labor laws in New York, and unions don't have the right to bargain over pensions. The state has imposed reduced-benefit tiers and extra-long vesting periods on generations of new hires. But I also haven't seen the public employee unions raise much of a ruckus about the diminishment of benefits for new hires.

At least a job at another state agency could be combined with my tenure at the University to make up the vesting period and the twenty years to a full pension. And many state workers do just that, particularly the idealistic good government types who spend careers bouncing around various social and constituent service agencies. In that way, it is a bit like a multi-employer pension plan.

In the private sector, multi-employer pensions are largely all that is left and all that we are capable of defending. Although jointly managed by equal numbers of employer and worker representatives, these plans are essentially creatures of the unions. They were devised for industries marked by itinerant work (what we now call "gig" employment) like construction and entertainment where a particular job might not last for thirty months, let alone thirty years. In my opinion, this makes them a model for how to deal with retirement security in our new world of work.

The employers pay into the fund at some formula that is bargained in the union contract, based upon what the pension fund board says it needs to be properly funded. The pension board is the steward of the money, investing for growth and stability. For the workers, retiring is a matter of earning enough pension credits, that is, spending enough time working for employers that paid in to the fund.

Multi-employer pension funds have also been created by unions that organize in industries with small and mid-size firms, where pooling funds and reducing risk to an individual employer is advantageous. It also helps with organizing. When the New York Hotel Trades Council organizes workers at a new or previously non-union hotel, the workers win a pension because the union is able to bargain the employer into the industry-wide benefits fund. SEIU locals like 1199 and 32BJ also have robust multi-employer pensions that they can bargain newly unionized employers into. Their existence is probably the best argument for the "bigger is better" mega-local merger spree the union went on a few years back.

Without a healthy multi-employer pension fund, a union that does manage to organize a new employer will not win a pension for the workers. No employer is going to agree to the obligation of guaranteeing a defined retirement benefit all by itself. Indeed, many employers that have legacy pension plans are trying to dump the obligation on the federal Pension Benefit Guaranty Corp. and switch new employees over to 401(k) plans.[122]

And yet we talk about the era when strong unions meant good pensions with the implication that bringing the unions back will also bring back pensions. But that's magical thinking without a plan. Or, literally, without *pension* plans.

As tempting as it is to treat our retirement security crisis like our health care crisis and just write off employer-based solutions like pensions and switch to a vastly expanded Social Security retirement system, it's not quite right. We certainly should tax the Richie Riches on all of their income—not just up to the current salary cap. And we should expand Social Security to cover all workers who are currently excluded from the system, mainly misclassified "independent contractors" and state employees of stingy, money-grubbing places like Illinois (!) who still exempt their retirees from the New Deal.

But the value of pensions is not just the guaranteed income they provide to retirees. They are also our financial arsenal on Wall Street. Boston University law professor David Webber shines a spotlight on the role of pension fund activists in altering the rigged rules of corporate governance and executive compensation in his book *The Rise of the Working Class Shareholder*.[123] Thanks to our pensions, worker representatives control hundreds of billions of dollars in Wall St. investments. Webber points to a few examples of how workers' billions have been leveraged to supplement labor power:

> A UFCW leader used his position on the governing board of the California Public Employees Retirement System to successfully campaign for the removal of members of the Safeway supermarket chain's board of directors who were loyal to its CEO in the aftermath of a difficult strike in 2003-04.[124]

Public employee pension funds in New York City passed a policy that bars investments in companies that promote job-destroying privatization of government services and prioritizes investment in "responsible contractors." The national building trades unions used the carrot-and-stick of their NYC pension funds' $160 billion to get Blackstone's $100 billion infrastructure investment fund to sign on to union "benefits, wages, working conditions, and training opportunities" for all of its projects.[125]

Used wisely, we could have much say over issues of corporate governance, executive compensation, and pro-worker investment in infrastructure. And if we manage to win a labor relations system where we're swimming with the sharks to set labor standards across entire industries by squaring up against the combined power of the entire *Fortune* 500, we'll need a bigger boat.

So pensions matter. And getting every worker in the country covered by a pension has to be a part of any "all-in" system of labor law.

One solution that some public employee unions have been toying with is opening up the various state pension funds to participation by private sector employers. This would obviously be a win-win, with workers who heretofore lacked retirement security winning a defined benefit for retirement and the state pension funds winning a larger constituency of workers and voters who depend on those pensions and will (not literally!) slit the throat of any politician who comes after them.

A cousin of this strategy is passing laws—on the state, federal, or even local level—that mandate employers to provide (and pay for!) defined benefit retirement plans for their workers. Under such a framework, both the state employee plans and the multi-employer private sector plans could be waiting in the wings as the ready-made solution to such a mandate.

History's Punching Bag

I would argue that we are in a philosophical crisis as deep as the inability of the craft unions of the 1920s and '30s to grapple with mass production industries. The craft union strategy historically had been one of job control. The union trains its apprentices as certified workers who have proven they have learned their trade. The goal is to have a monopoly on skilled workers so that employers must contract with the unions for their staffing, but the union controls the quality and pace and the price of the work.

Mass production completely de-skilled the jobs and broke them down into a tightly controlled series of a handful of sped-up tasks. In so doing, the mass production industries broke free of union control (the massive amount of violence that the hired Pinkerton guns rained down on protesting workers did their part, too). The big factories and major industries of auto, steel, and more operated on a non-union basis in the first decades of the twentieth century.

In the 1920s, the craft unions couldn't get past go on the question of organizing in mass production. They quibbled over which workers "belonged" to which trade union, and how they would divvy up the homogenized jobs after they somehow organized the plants. In the 1930s, after autoworkers began to join a new temporary "federal" union that the AFL created, the crafts immediately pushed to tear up the one not-so-big auto union so that they could reclaim the members they claimed belonged to each of them. This was one of the main disputes that led to the decisive split between the new Congress of Industrial Organizations and the older AFL.

The final break came, somewhat hilariously, when Carpenters union president "Big" Bill Hutcheson tried to block an industrial charter for rubber workers, another of the mass production industries clamoring for a one big union approach at the 1935 AFL convention. John L. Lewis accused Hutcheson of "small potatoes" proceduralism, then punched him in the face and led the CIO delegates out of the convention hall.[126]

To the extent that history remembers Hutcheson and the craft union leaders, it's as a literal punching bag. But what gets lost in history is that the craft unionists had a coherent philosophy and something approximating a strategy. Those factory jobs, with each worker's task broken down into a handful of tightly controlled and monitored movements on an assembly line, were to them degraded crafts. The craft unions didn't merely intend to arbitrarily divide up the bargaining unit into different union jurisdictions. They thought they would organize and fight and bargain with the employers to restore the craft skills of the workers.

They were not wrong, per se. If the workers knew better than the boss how to build a car or forge steel, they would have had tremendously more power than unions that represented a mass of workers who could more easily be laid off or replaced. And the workers would surely enjoy more pride in their work if their craft expertise and collaborative work with their comrades left more of a mark on the product. It's a wonderful vision of a more satisfying work environment. But this was capitalism, and, given this, the industrial trajectory could not be reversed. Time and capitalism had simply moved on.

In trying to reconstruct thirty-year careers at one employer and the private welfare system of employer-sponsored benefits that were a highlight of the vaunted postwar economic triumph, are we not similarly stuck in the past?

TEN

And We Have to Fix the Labor Board . . .

LET'S NEVER DO EFCA AGAIN. Not just the bill, but the theory and process that created it. The Employee Free Choice Act was pushed hard by the AFL-CIO from the tail end of the George W. Bush administration until it died of a Senate filibuster in Obama's first term. It was an ill-conceived effort to "tweak" the National Labor Relations Act in the vain hope that card-check certifications would somehow help unions grow by the millions of new members, who would then have the power to push through bigger, more necessary reforms.

First, given the system that unions are trapped in, card check alone will simply not result in a meaningful bump in organizing wins. Look, I've organized under card check. It's nice. It happens to be more democratic, as it requires the active approval of an overall majority of workers in a bargaining unit in a process where every voter functionally starts as a "no." All card check does is help workers who already know they want a union limp across the finish line of an exclusive representation certification process. If we had managed to win EFCA, I'm convinced we would have been humiliated by how little unions would have grown as a result.

We're not going to get any labor law reform by watering our demands to win over moderates and Republicans, which seemed to be the basic theory of EFCA. For the purposes of this chapter, I encourage you to think about the maximal demands that we should make for fixing the National Labor Relations Act and the National

Labor Relations Board should a crisis open an opportunity for real reform.

At a bare minimum, we need to repeal Taft-Hartley. That's the 1947 amendment to the National Labor Relations Act that turned it from a law that affirmatively defends the right of workers to organize and encourages the process of collective bargaining into a legal road map for union-busting.

Many writers point to Taft-Hartley's so-called "right-to-work" provision, which allowed states to pass laws forbidding unions from negotiating union shop clauses, as its most pernicious attack on union rights. That was bad, but it's not the thing that's been killing us.

The outlawing of solidarity protests—what the law neutrally refers to as "secondary activity"—is possibly the best explanation for the long decline of the labor movement.

But also we've got problems with policies and procedures of the National Labor Relations Board itself; with how it "balances" the interests of two very unequal powers in the best of times and gets turned into a union-busting operation when Republicans are in the White House.

But let's start at the beginning.

Findings and Policies

The preamble to the Taft-Hartley Act is actually a big deal and needs to be fixed. The original preamble, which was written with an eye toward justifying what was in 1935 a relatively unprecedented federal intervention in the private sector marketplace to a conservative Supreme Court that was usually hostile to such things, was a bold statement:

> The denial by employers of the right of employees to organize and the refusal by employers to accept the procedure of collective bargaining lead to strikes and other forms of industrial strife or unrest, which have the intent or the necessary effect of burdening or obstructing commerce by (a) impairing the efficiency, safety, or operation of the

instrumentalities of commerce; (b) occurring in the current of commerce; (c) materially affecting, restraining, or controlling the flow of raw materials or manufactured or processed goods from or into the channels of commerce, or the prices of such materials or goods in commerce; or (d) causing diminution of employment and wages in such volume as substantially to impair or disrupt the market for goods flowing from or into the channels of commerce.

The inequality of bargaining power between employees who do not possess full freedom of association or actual liberty of contract and employers who are organized in the corporate or other forms of ownership association substantially burdens and affects the flow of commerce, and tends to aggravate recurrent business depressions, by depressing wage rates and the purchasing power of wage earners in industry and by preventing the stabilization of competitive wage rates and working conditions within and between industries.

Experience has proved that protection by law of the right of employees to organize and bargain collectively safeguards commerce from injury, impairment, or interruption, and promotes the flow of commerce by removing certain recognized sources of industrial strife and unrest, by encouraging practices fundamental to the friendly adjustment of industrial disputes arising out of differences as to wages, hours, or other working conditions, and by restoring equality of bargaining power between employers and employees.

It is declared to be the policy of the United States to eliminate the causes of certain substantial obstructions to the free flow of commerce and to mitigate and eliminate these obstructions when they have occurred by encouraging the practice and procedure of collective bargaining and by protecting the exercise by workers of full freedom of association, self-organization, and designation of representatives of their own choosing, for the purpose of negotiating the terms and conditions of their employment or other mutual aid or protection.

Taft-Hartley added the word "some" to the line about "denial by employers of the right of employees to organize." It goes on to add,

"Experience has further demonstrated that certain practices by some labor organizations, their officers, and members have the intent or the necessary effect of burdening or obstructing commerce by preventing the free flow of goods in such commerce through strikes and other forms of industrial unrest or through concerted activities which impair the interest of the public in the free flow of such commerce."

It's sort of the congressional legislative equivalent of a Twitter troll smugly coming at you with a dumb "Well, actually . . ." Except that this *matters*. It turned the law into a balancing test between the very unequal powers of labor and management. It has hamstrung the NLRB itself, as Republican members have leaned heavily on the Taft-Hartley language to justify their attempts to roll back workers rights, and Republicans in every special and regular committee to oversee the Board have harangued Democratic appointees who had the temerity to try to extend the protections of the Act and encourage collective bargaining.[127]

All of that Taft-Hartley crap has to come out of the preamble, which should be restored to the full-throated defense of workers' rights that it was and should be. However, we need to go further to rhetorically and constitutionally protect our rights in the preamble.

The decision to base the constitutional authority of the NLRA exclusively in the Commerce clause was a strategic mistake. And it wasn't an oversight or a lightly considered choice. It was, in some ways, a preview of our current problem of labor lawyers—particularly the general counsels and DC- and NYC-based firms on retainer—muscling organizers and other risky thinkers out of the strategic conversation in order to pursue their conservative, pragmatic approach.

Andrew Furuseth, the American Federation of Labor's main representative in the NLRA drafting process, loudly insisted that labor law should be rooted in the section of the Thirteenth Amendment that tasked Congress with passing legislation to ensure that "neither slavery nor involuntary servitude . . . shall exist within the United States."

Furuseth was simply outmaneuvered by Louis B. Brandeis, whose pragmatic concern was getting the law past judicial review by a conservative Supreme Court that was overturning all of the New Deal economic legislation that intervened in the economy. The Court did find the NLRA constitutional in *NLRB v. Jones & Laughlin Steel Corp.*, but the wave of sit-down strikes that had roiled the country probably had more influence on the Court's 1937 decision than Brandeis's rhetorical strategy.[128]

Brandeis's strategic choice is at the root of labor's legal problems. When union activity and workers' rights issues wind up in the courts, the judges are weighing the impact on business—not the civil rights and free speech of the workers.

Andrew Furuseth was not being a crank when he insisted that labor's right should be rooted in the Thirteenth Amendment. Union activists had long seen the amendment's prohibition against "involuntary servitude" as labor law enshrined in the constitution. Unions campaigned for their rights and cited the Thirteenth Amendment when resisting injunctions and other anti-union judicial action. The preamble to the NLRA ended that history, but we should embrace the Thirteenth Amendment.

We live in a time when corporations routinely force employees who are privy to such trade secrets as how to assemble a mediocre fast-food sandwich to sign non-compete clauses that forbid them for working for any other minimum wage–paying purveyor of borderline-inedible sandwiches.[129] These same employers might email or stuff in an interoffice mailbox terms of an "arbitration agreement" that forbids employees from suing over stolen wages or workplace discrimination—especially from joining a class-action lawsuit. No response will be legally accepted as "agreement" to this "contract."[130]

Whatever the conservative majority of the Supreme Court might claim, these are hardly terms and conditions of employment that are voluntarily agreed upon by equal bargaining partners. I don't know how any clear thinking person could see these working conditions as anything but "involuntary."

An amended preamble should also include a positive statement about the right of workers to band together in protest and in bargaining being a First Amendment right of free speech and assembly.

We probably also need some language harkening back to the bad old days of anti-union injunctions when the labor movement's top aim was to get a law that plainly stated that your boss does not have a property or contract right to expect you to drag your sorry ass into work tomorrow morning.

Definitions

While we're being wonky about the Preamble, let's also split hairs over "Definitions," the next section in the Act. By legally defining "Employees," "Employers," and "Unions" the framers of the NLRA opened the door to three-quarters of a century of hair-splitting over those definitions. Most of it is the work of employers trying to carve as many workers and workplaces out of the protections of the Act as possible. Some of it is the vast right-wing conspiracy of think tanks and union-busters trying to subject workers' centers, community organizers, and other effective alternative forms of worker organizing to the same trap unions find ourselves in by defining them, too, as "unions."

And yet the solution, it seems to me, is to broaden the definitions as widely as possible. Everybody should be covered by the National Labor Relations Act, either as an employee or an employer, and in some cases as both simultaneously. The definition of "employer," in particular, should be expanded as widely as possible. Someone did a service for you for money? You're an employer. Someone did work for you for free? You're an employer (and probably violating the Thirteenth Amendment; see Appendix). You hired another company to boss your workers around? You and your subcontractor are joint employers.

Did you hire the teenager across the street to babysit your kid for three hours? Well, in that specific interaction you were a boss. I hope you weren't a jerk to her and, yes, she *does* get to bargain over how many bottles of pop she can raid from your refrigerator. We have to plug the holes in the Act and take away the incentives and wiggle room that permit employers to secede from the responsibility of being the boss.

Another hole to plug? How about organizing rights for "supervisors"? The original NLRA did not define "supervisors." They were "employees" like anyone else who wasn't Henry Ford or Walter P. Chrysler. There were far fewer supervisors in corporate America in 1935 than there are today, and it's not like they rushed to organize with the workers who were daily challenging managerial authority with their hard-fought and newly won union contracts.

In the 1940s, however, assembly-line foremen, squeezed by their subordinates' union demands and their bosses' penny-pinching, began to organize unions of their own.[131] Aghast at this development, the National Association of Manufacturers pressed to make sure that the Taft-Hartley amendments ripped supervisors out of the Act's protections and enshrined their dubious status as "management."[132]

These days, the questionable "supervisory status" of certain workers is used to force hearings that delay union elections and tie unions in knots over concerns that "supervisory taint" of union activists who are subsequaently (and erroneously) ruled out of the unit could cause a successful union election to be overturned. The bloat of middle management is one of the major inefficiencies in the U.S. economy, and union avoidance is a primary culprit.

Supervisors should be defined as a specific subset of "employees" under the Act. They should be allowed to form unions of their own with no procedural objection, and even to join the unions of their lower-ranked co-workers by mutual consent.

This suggestion might raise the hackles of some good old-fashioned unionists who might see it as an opening for company unions or other forms of unfair domination. But, in fact, *not* having supervisors in unions is more of a historical oddity than would be reestablishing their rights. Think back to the history I laid out in chapter 3. The early craft unions didn't make a distinction between workers and supervisors. The building trades today still manage to have foremen and lead employees in their bargaining units.

I spent a substantial portion of my organizing career helping supervisors with little real power win their union voice at work. This was largely in the public sector, where the law often recognizes rights for them that the NLRA denies private sector workers. In some cases, the state laws were pretty specific about making supervisors form bargaining units of their own. In others, the "one big union" approach was allowed.

My current union, the United University Professions, local 2190 of the American Federation of Teachers, represents full-time tenure-track faculty, adjuncts, and professional staff of the State University of New York in the same bargaining unit and collective bargaining agreement. Are there occasionally conflicts of interest? Sure, but we can work them out internally and democratically. And with one union, we stand a far better chance of doing so than if (potentially) powerful supervisors were exluded. In a university setting, we're talking about department chairs and principal investigators on research grants that fund various postdocs and graduate employees' positions leaving them to be squeezed by the college bureaucracy.

So, in the case of *private* sector supervisors, we've just let somebody else's law become our ideology. This happens in other situations as well. Remember that babysitter from a few paragraphs back? At the moment, she can't bargain over the pop bottles not just because NLRA doesn't recognize her as an "employee" just because she's an "independent contractor" or a "domestic" worker, but also because she has no co-workers. That's an arbitrary and ridiculous distinction. Yet the idea that a bargaining unit must be "two or more" workers and that a worker who is making any kind of complaint or demand has to "do it with a co-worker" has been absorbed as union ideology.

As much as we on the left want workers acting collectively if we want to get something started in this country, we need to work with some of the selfishness and shortsightedness of many workers. Too many unfair labor practice charges are dismissed because a belly-aching employee didn't bring a co-worker along to raise his gripe or wasn't quick-thinking enough to phrase it as a demand that affects more than him.

As for the definition of "employee," there is a subclassification of "professional" employees. This was an arbitrary distinction made by a Supreme Court that had little concept of solidarity and probably bristled at the thought of men in suits and ties being "forced" into the bargaining units of the sweaty unwashed automatons on the assembly line.[133] It's a bunch of elitist nonsense that's out of step with the twenty-first century—or any century, for that matter. I'll explain more below, in the section about undoing the damage the Supreme Court has done to the NLRA.

Finally, in the current definition of "employee" there's a clause that begins, "But shall not include" and then goes on to list a whole slew of exclusions from the Act. Delete this. Some of these, like domestic and agricultural employees, were carved out in order to gain the votes of racist white Democrats to get the NLRA passed in the first place. This is a shameful injustice that needs to be corrected. Others, such as supervisors and independent contractors, are just massive holes in the system that need to be plugged.

But the final categories require a strategic leap of faith by unions if we want the National Labor Relations Act to be a kind of "all-in" system of labor protections. One exclusion is workers who were already covered by an older federal labor law, the Railway Labor Act (RLA). I've never done any organizing or bargaining under the RLA, so I can't speak with much authority about the ways in which it is superior or inferior to the NLRA. Mostly, it's just different.

One way it's different is that a new bargaining unit certification election must clear a majority of the entire workforce, not just a majority of voters. Also, the RLA has a preference for the largest bargaining unit possible, while the NLRB will certify "an appropriate unit" of a smaller subdivision of worksites or job titles. This is the reason why FedEx is an entirely non-union company. They've deliberately gotten themselves covered by the RLA's jurisdiction to thwart organizing efforts by the Teamsters.[134] That sort of forum shopping leads to traps, which is why I think an "all-in" approach to the NLRA makes sense.

Public sector workers are currently covered by a patchwork of state laws or local ordinances because governmental subdivisions were excluded from the 1935 Act, again, in order to get the votes to pass the thing. (Unions for thee, but not for me? Color me shocked that any Congress could be so hypocritical.) We've now watched

Republican governors and state legislatures routinely and system-
atically roll back union rights laws on the state level as if someone
had paid them to do it. They have done it with a ferocious velocity in
Indiana and Wisconsin and very nearly did it in Ohio and Michigan.
And union membership has plummeted in these states, as did votes
for Democrats. It's plain to me that the solution is to extend the NLRA
to cover public sector employees.

Here, however, strong public sector unions (particularly, I'm sad
to admit, in New York) are, unless there is sufficient debate, likely
to oppose such an effort. It is, in some ways, still 1979 in New York.
Unions here have the illusion of control. We may gripe about our
Public Employment Relations Board, but it's the devil we know. (In
my experience it is an inept bureaucratic mess—and that's before we
even consider the draconian anti-strike provisions of the Taylor Law.)

Meanwhile, the NLRB ping-pongs between different standards of
employee and union rights, and when Republicans control the executive branch it gets converted into a union-busting agency. This is all
true, but the point is to change that. And part of changing it is making
it everybody's law so that there's a greater coalition of people fighting
to preserve it and make it better.

To union leaders in New York who view gaining federal labor protections as a risky proposition, my rebuttal is this: Scott Walker. The
ease with which he was able to wipe away the nation's oldest and most
established public sector labor law should shock us out of compla-
cency on this question. It is precisely because the public sector labor
law was a "special right" that he was able to "divide and conquer" and
get them first before eventually going for a right-to-work bill. It is
clear that the Kochtopus of dark money will knock out public sector
labor laws wherever it can muster the votes. And if you think that
can't happen in New York, I've got a bridge to sell you.

The Right to Strike and Engage in Solidarity Actions

The right to strike must include the right to return to the job once the
strike is over. And that means we must overturn the *Mackay* Doctrine.

Legislatively overturning *Mackay* was the top political goal of the AFL-CIO in Bill Clinton's first term in office.[135] The César Chávez Workplace Fairness Act would have made it an explicitly enumerated unfair labor practice for an employer to "promise, threaten, or take other action to hire a permanent replacement for an employee" who participated in a strike and "has unconditionally offered to return to work for the employer."[136] The House of Representatives twice passed the bill, but it was twice filibustered in the Senate. I'm not sure who got spooked more by that failure, the unions or the Democrats, but it's notable that there was no similar effort as a part of the Employee Free Choice Act. Repealing *Mackay* has *got* to be our number-one demand in any negotiations over amending the NLRA.

But, again, it was the outlawing of solidarity that was the most insidious anti-union provision that got inserted into the NLRA by the Taft-Hartley amendments. The Act somewhat coolly refers to what it outlaws as "secondary boycotts." Secondary means not primary, and primary means your actual employer—the company you and your co-workers are seeking to bargain with. The secondary employer is a company that your employer had an important business relationship with, so much so that messing with that relationship could put real pressure on both firms.

And boycott means a lot more than handing out flyers in a parking lot asking consumers not to buy a certain product. The ban makes it an unfair labor practice for any union or worker "to engage in, or induce or encourage any individual employed by any person engaged in commerce or in an industry affecting commerce to engage in, a strike or a refusal in the course of his employment to use, manufacture, process, transport, or otherwise handle or work on any goods, articles, materials, or commodities or to perform any services."

The reason this ban is so effective is that it comes with crippling financial penalties. The NLRB is directed to go straight to federal court to enjoin the union's boycott and implement triple damages. Those penalties could easily be millions or even billions of dollars. They would break any union that got fined. In 1959, the Landrum-Griffin Act inserted more restrictions on solidarity activism in the form of a ban on what were then called "hot cargo agreements." These agreements were clauses in collective bargaining agreements.

The power of such solidarity activism should be obvious, as is why a right-wing Congress would make them illegal in 1947 and add further restrictions a decade later.

A few years ago, the Nabisco corporation shut down a unionized plant in Chicago that made Oreo cookies and moved production overseas. An obvious counterattack to that action would be for the union that represents grocery store workers to encourage its members to leave the unopened boxes of scab cookies in the stockroom and to bargain with the supermarket chains to have them communicate to Nabisco their intention of no longer buying Oreo cookies as long as they remained the subject of a labor controversy.

That is precisely what is illegal. And yet corporations can and regularly do engage in secondary boycotts. How many times have you turned on the television to watch a baseball game or an episode of *Mad Men* to find the station blacked out and replaced with the name and number of a corporate CEO to call and complain. The owners of that channel were blackmailing the cable provider into paying them more money and relying on pressure and complaints from consumers like you to win their demand.

Unions must be allowed to do the same if they are to have any economic power. It's not just defensive fights like the Oreo cookie situation. The prohibition on solidarity activism prevents unions from organizing from positions of strength, and from using the power where they have it to help non-union workers get organized.

Why did unions do such a poor job of expanding beyond their postwar economic bases of manufacturing and construction, and their regional bases of the Northeast and Midwest into new parts of the economy and the country? This is the biggest factor. If we want to have more unions and more collective bargaining, we have to remove the bans on secondary boycotts and hot cargo agreements from the NLRA.

What the Supreme Court Did to Us

Mackay v. NLRB is just one of many examples of the Supreme Court butting into labor relations and inserting their patrician values and assumptions into the law. So there are lots of terrible court decisions that need to be explicitly rejected, reversed, and invalidated with a clear statement of congressional intent. Furthermore, the intent of the NLRA was to create an autonomous regulatory system that kept these issues out of the courts entirely. Employers figured out that by refusing to cooperate with an NLRB order they could force the NLRB to take them to court for enforcement, and through that process the employer could relitigate its case. The courts were all too happy to take the cases and insert their pro-business biases while ignoring the plain language of the Act.[137] We need language to discourage that.

And, finally, we need some policy language in the Act that would serve as clear congressional intent, giving the courts guidance about how to prioritize conflicting values should a labor case come before them.

One creative solution was floated by Richard N. Block in the early 1990s. It included a statement in labor law reform that the NLRB "is not bound by a previous decision of the board or any court." His argument was as frankly practical as it was deeply radical:

> It will provide employers and unions with the opportunity to argue that old doctrines should be changed or retained. . . . Releasing the reconstituted NLRB from precedent would, over a period of several years, probably develop a system that is fair to all parties and takes into account the needs and interests of employers and unions.[138]

Since so much of the damage that conservative judges have inflicted upon the post–New Deal regulatory regime was made possible by an ostensible absence of clear legislative intent, such an approach would be a brilliant way of compelling the courts not to step on the legislatures' constitutional turf. (It is *they* who are charged with making law, not the unelected judges.) It would instantly strip a whole body of judge-made labor case law of precedential preemption, allowing unions and the NLRB to proceed to expand workers' rights with a clean slate. Moreover, it would be a clear statement that when courts disobey Congress's directive to stay out of the business of judging economic disputes the Congress believes the courts tend to get the facts and interpretation wrong.

Let's turn our attention back toward union certification elections. The rigged process that I described earlier in the book, which lets the employer force employees to attend mandatory "vote no" presentations or be fired, while leaving the union no right to respond, is the result of numerous bad Supreme Court decisions. In all of them, the Court privileges the boss's free speech over that of workers and privileges his property rights above all.

The Court ruled that bosses have a First Amendment right to express their views against unionization shortly after the NLRA was passed, and that principle was enshrined in the Taft-Hartley amendments. In our current system it's hard to imagine a court majority that could ever endorse the outright state repression of a boss's speech, but we will need to explicitly reject some other Supreme Court cases in order to enshrine a principle of equal time in the Act.

In the 1956 case *NLRB v. Babcock & Wilcox Co.*, the Court made an arbitrary distinction between "inside" organizers and "outside" organizers—that is, union organizers on staff—and ruled that management has a property right to ban union organizers on staff from the premises.[139] In 1992's *Lechmere Inc. v. NLRB*, the Court ruled that organizers can be banned from the parking lot across the street.[140] Both decisions need to be explicitly rejected. But going further, there should be a new unfair labor practice for an employer to conduct a mandatory meeting on union organizing or collective bargaining without affording union representatives equivalent access to employees.

Again, to counter the outrageous class biases of most judges, there should be a policy statement somewhere in the Act that should get the point across that if employers' property rights and employees' rights under this act are ever alleged to be in conflict, it is the intent of Congress that employees' rights under the Act shall be considered paramount. And, again, if we're amending the preamble of this act strategically, employees' rights are explicitly free speech and assembly rights. (We'll return to this in the Appendix.)

Speaking of free speech, the Court ruled in the 1953 *NLRB v. Electrical Workers (Jefferson Standard)* that workers can be fired for protest activity if their speech is too critical of the employer's product. "There is no more elemental cause for discharge of an employee than disloyalty to his employer," thundered the majority decision signed by a bunch of rich white men in silly black robes.[141] This decision should be explicitly repudiated in the amended Act.

But we also need a broad policy statement of congressional intent here. Something like "any judicial assumption that an employer is entitled to a property right or expectation of loyalty or continued service, or that any agreement made on the unequal basis of terms dictated by an employer outside of collective bargaining are hereby superseded by this Act."

Finally, although the following matters should be cleared up in "Definitions," as I propose above, these two Court decisions merit a specific Bronx cheer. In 1980, the Supreme Court ruled in *NLRB v. Yeshiva University* that private sector college and university faculty are inherently managerial because of all of the meaningless committees they sit on and the academic senates in which they vote on resolutions that wind up in the recycle bins of the corporate executives of the school.[142] It's possible that faculty governance in some ivory towers was not yet a dead letter in 1980. Today, anyone with a real understanding of power who works at a university would laugh at the notion of being a part of some giant management collective. And many would form unions if they could. *Yeshiva* should be called out by name as wrong on the day it was decided.

Similarly, in a 1958 case, *Leedom v. Kyne*, the Court ruled that the NLRB cannot certify a bargaining unit that contains both "professional employees" and "employees who are not professional employees" unless the "professional employees" vote in the majority for such class status miscegenation. Let me give you a specific example of how this dunderheaded, elitist protectionism will hobble twenty-first-century organizing unless it is specifically rejected in a policy statement in the amended Act. We were organizing several sites in a network of charter schools in Cleveland a few years ago. We had a super-majority of support on a public petition and a mail ballot election scheduled for a two-week period in the summer. The NLRB ballots were in the mail. The teachers, who were on year-to-year employment contracts, had all received and signed renewal contracts for the upcoming school year. Then the charter school corporation began firing people during their summer vacation—during the union certification mail ballot election—ostensibly for issues with their "provisional" teacher certifications.

The retaliatory nature of these terminations was as obvious as the chilling effect they were meant to have on the voters. We filed an unfair labor practice charge and the NLRB promptly brought the election to a halt. To my great surprise, the NLRB agents we were dealing with were immediately talking about a Gissel bargaining order—with us *and* with the boss—and pressing hard for a settlement that could result in a fair election. A Gissel bargaining order is the unicorn of NLRB case law. It's when the Board says it is clear that the union had majority support in the bargaining unit until the employer broke the law in such an egregious way that there is no way that a fair election can be held. The NLRB therefore certifies the union without an election and orders the employer to bargain with them.

It would have been the first and only Gissel order of my career, and it was warranted. We had 90 percent of the workers providing pictures and quotes on a brochure and a Tumblr campaign website plus a public petition offering personal essays about why a union was needed at their charter network. And the terminations were so beyond the pale for an employer in an industry where they could have simply "non-renewed" teachers in June and sufficiently muddied the waters. Instead, the employer waited until union election ballots were in the mail in July to fire the workers. There really was no way to have a fair election any time soon.

Then the draft Gissel order landed at the NLRB General Counsel's office in Washington, and someone noticed that this would be a "combined" unit of "professional employees" and, I dunno, *regular* workers. Silence. Delay. Finally, we were asked if workers had signed anything indicating that they understood they were organizing a "combined" unit. Now, why would we do that? They understood they were organizing a union with their co-workers—all nineteen or twenty of them, depending on the campus and unit. Well, the Supreme Court told the NLRB in 1958 that they cannot certify a combined bargaining unit without an assurance that the "professionals" agreed to getting lumped in with the lumpen.[143]

Again, this is where Richard N. Block's brilliant idea to wipe the slate clean by directing the NLRB to be "not bound by a previous decision of the board or any court" would really cut through the crap. Because here's the crazy thing about the Supreme Court's twentieth-century factory logic in twenty-first-century union organizing: in a school, the professionals are the majority. What the midcentury Court was worried about was the couple of hundred engineers and tool-and-die guys getting lumped in with the tens of thousands of assembly-line workers against their will. So, they gave the professionals the privilege of a two-pronged ballot. First question: do you want to have a union? Second question: do you want to have a union with your stupid, stinky co-workers?

If a majority of the professionals vote yes on question one, then their votes on question two will be lumped in with the rest of the votes on the overall question of should there be a union at this workplace. If the professionals vote no on question one, then that's game over for the professionals, while the rest of the workers get to have their ballots counted alone on the question of whether there should be a union for everyone else.

But in a charter school—or, really, many modern workplaces—this whole thing is turned upside down. Our charter school units were, basically, fourteen teachers—"professionals"—plus a lunch lady, secretary, janitor, and part-time bus driver. Or some variation thereof.

If the "professionals" vote yes on question one, they're also voting yes on question two (honestly, no matter how many trainings you do on these two-pronged ballots, workers basically double down on their basic instinct of whether there should be a union or not; it's "yes, yes" or "no, no" but almost never "yes, no"). So if the professionals vote "yes" there's going to be a union because they make up the vast majority of the bargaining unit.

But if the principle of the Court's *Leedom v. Kyne* decision is that a minority that may not have the same interests as the majority shouldn't be forced to bargain together, here's what happens to the "employees who are not professionals." If the lunch lady, secretary, and part-time bus driver outvote the janitor about whether to form a bargaining unit, but the majority of the "professional" employees voted in favor of a combined unit then the four votes of the "employees who are not professionals" get lumped into the overall bargaining unit vote for a net loss of one measly vote. In effect, the professionals "forced" the non-professionals into their union under the Supreme Court's cockamamie formula.

Except, in the real world, it was three out of four non-professionals who supported the union in solidarity with three out of four professionals. Yet they had to wait two more years to win their union because the Supreme Court forbade the NLRB from certifying a combined unit under the circumstances. So the workers had to endure two more school years of renewal/non-renewal letters and an organizing pressure campaign that finally resulted in a "code of conduct" election agreement with the charter management company that let the workers—finally!—freely and fairly vote for union representation.

Procedures

I can't say that I'm intimately familiar with the internal life of the National Labor Relations Board. I've never worked for the NLRB, although I've got friends who have, and they've got stories to tell. I've never argued a case before the Board or even an Administrative Law Judge (ALJ), although I've been on many frustrating conference calls with them or about the unpredictable or unreliable way that the agency was handling a case.

It's clear that policies, rules, procedures, and staffing are crucially important "minor" details that deserve major attention when we finally get to amending the National Labor Relations Act. Veterans of the NLRB and other experts should certainly weigh in on any reforms of the Act, but here are a few thoughts I have about what should be under discussion.

For starters, there is an asymmetry between management's ability to force their objections into the courts and that of workers. Unions are generally dependent on getting the support of the progression of NLRB staffers, administrative law judges, regional directors, the NLRB general counsel, and finally the National Labor Relations Board itself, before finally getting into federal court to compel a boss who has refused to voluntarily settle or comply with the NLRB's orders. Compounding this is that all levels of the NLRB bureaucracy are massively understaffed, which means the process moves at an excruciatingly slow pace and involves increasing pressure on unions and workers to take a weaker settlement for expediency's sake. A boss, on the other hand, has to simply keep saying, "No. We disagree," and the entire NLRB process glides its way into the courts where employers will argue against the very constitutionality of the Act.

So, one strategy is to find some language, like the instructions to the NLRB to ignore Supreme Court precedent, that sets a higher bar for the federal courts. Another is to give unions a clear shot at taking their challenges to employer lawbreaking directly to the federal courts. One model to look at is California's Private Attorney General Act. By the time you're reading this, there may be other states that have passed similar statutes. It allows private individuals—often, groups of individuals organized by workers' centers—to sue companies for wage theft or discrimination using the power of the state. It does require some sign-off by the state that the case has merit so that the Attorney General is justified in "deputizing" the plaintiffs.

A private enforcement mechanism in the NLRA would still require some investigation by the NLRB's staff, as well as hearings and briefs that provide an employer an opportunity to defend its position within an NLRB process. But once, say, a regional director has issued a decision, the union would have the option of taking the employer to court at its own expense but with the legal powers of the NLRB to win speedier justice.

This would also likely lead to quick settlements of more cases. Employers that know an unfair labor practice charge has merit and that the union is willing to pay to go to court over it are going to be more willing to cut their losses and make reasonable settlements. It could significantly free up resources at the NLRB as fewer appeals would be lodged within the system. Nevertheless, it is essential to increase funding and expand the staff of the NLRB if we're going to reform the organization itself. There should be enough investigators working at the agency to not just get to the cases that come before them in a timely manner, but also to go out and find unfair labor practices that are taking place at non-union workplaces all the time.

An agency that in some corners of the country can be a bit moribund requires an infusion of fresh blood. There are thousands of union organizers who have burned out and no longer work for unions. They are subject-matter experts on the ways that employers break and evade the law, and they are passionate advocates for justice. Swelling the ranks of the NLRB with crusading investigators would change the culture of the agency for the better.

The Board is tied up in knots over three-quarters of a century of precedent. They're supposed to retain legal consistency, but that is simply impossible with the way the economy has totally reordered itself and how Republican appointees have consistently tried to hamstring the Board's mission to encourage collective bargaining.

Does fixing the National Labor Relations Act's preamble to return it to an active and unqualified statement of workers' rights, with a mission to encourage collective bargaining, free the Board from bad or useless anti-worker precedents? Does the "not bound by a previous decision of the board or any court" language do it?

Because the NLRB needs a freer hand to restrain employers from conducting unfair labor practices, from issuing bargaining orders, from certifying unions through card-check elections, and from rec-ognizing micro and minority bargaining units, we need an NLRB that will embrace whatever it takes for workers to have a voice. This includes the power to issue financial penalties to union-busting employers that should serve not just as remedial justice but as a pow-erful disincentive for employers to break the law. The law should be amended to give the NLRB the explicit authority to issue penalties as it sees fit, No guidelines, no hard dollar limits, just their expertise and their charge to protect workers' rights and encourage collective bargaining.

"Right to Work"

We should outlaw "right to work" as well. I do think we tend to over-focus on it as a cause of unions' decline and as a silver-bullet solution to rebuilding the labor movement. And I have my doubts about the wisdom of unions sticking with the organizational model of exclu-sive representation, that I've shared in this book. But the fact is that exclusive representation doesn't work without the union shop. The political obligations of representing all workers in a bargaining unit, of mediating and prioritizing workers' demands, of selling and main-taining labor peace must be compensated with mandatory represen-tation fees.

Moreover, leaving this issue to the states has been a policy disas-ter. It is a road map for resource-draining attacks on unions in order to maintain "red state" hegemony by a cutthroat Republican Party. "Right to work" is simply wrong for the United States.

ELEVEN

Conclusion

THE LABOR MOVEMENT ENTERS the third decade of the twenty-first century ripe with potential. Despite all the barriers to the exercise of worker power, in spite of the trap that has ensnared unions as legal institutions, this is an exciting—and frightening—period of change. As in electoral politics, so too in workplace governance: the status quo will not hold, and the old order cannot be restored.

One of the reasons I rushed to write this book is that it was clear to me that Senate and congressional Democrats—led by those on the left, but trailed by centrists who are simply out of ideas—will soon launch the strongest effort to overturn the Taft-Hartley Act in over forty years. My fear is that union leaders who have spent their entire careers in the political wilderness, and activists who are looking for straightforward solutions, will jump on the "Better Deal" or the "Protecting the Right to Organize (PRO) Act" (or whatever they're calling it by the time you read this book) as the solution to labor's woes.

Even if that bill somehow passes (and I'm not totally pessimistic that it *won't!*), it will not be enough to radically alter the course of labor relations and worker power. The trap that unions find themselves in— from winner-take-all workplace-by-workplace certifications to overly broad management rights and no-strike clauses in contracts to the hostile treatment of workers' rights in the courts—cannot be reversed by one good bill. If we fail to grow by leaps and bounds, radically expanding union membership in every state and every industry after doubling down on our temporarily restored political influence, we may squander the moment.

Conversely, "not enough" might be just enough to change the attitudes of more workers to spark the kind of self-organizing and job action experimentation needed to create a true crisis for capitalism. There is something to be said for the powers that be raising—and then dashing—the hopes and expectations of the working class. And anything that changes the discourse on unions and workers' rights makes the air a little more electric.

The symbolism of Ronald Reagan firing the air traffic controllers in 1981 was enough to embolden an epic union-busting drive by corporate America and gave cover to the thousands of scabs whose willing participation was necessary to chip away at union power and density. Likewise, Franklin Roosevelt's endorsement of the "right to organize" through (the ultimately toothless) Section 7a was enough to inspire a small organizing wave that led directly to the sit-down strikes of 1934–37 that, in turn, brought real change to many workplaces.

Now imagine what might change in workers' imagination if a president really does put on "a comfortable pair of shoes" and joins a workers' picket line or two, as candidate Obama had promised and President Obama failed to do.[144] Or imagine an enormously popular senator crusading against union-busting employers, grandstanding in special hearings that excoriate corporate executives, and attaching riders to tax bills that mess with their money?

Even if prominent politicians engage in class warfare insincerely, it could create an environment in which more workers are emboldened to make demands that go far beyond what any party or labor union can control. But that requires leftist activists and campaign strategists to be quick to adapt to barely perceptible changes in the political environment and the workplace. This is my warning to messianic leftists waiting for the nigh-mythical general strike before even contemplating changes that might finally be possible in the law: Don't let a good crisis go to waste.

Our ongoing crisis of democracy and rampant inequality have

made it clear to at least the more liberal faction of the ruling class, the one that casts its lot with the Democratic Party as the country's best hope for order, fiscal responsibility, and inclusion, that unions and workers' rights are an essential solution. Leftists and veterans of union organizing should play an active role in developing the bookshelf of reform proposals *now*, not *after* our hard work of fomenting revolt creates a deeper crisis. By that point, the powers that be will be rushing to implement *someone else's* solution.

In the 1930s, while communist and socialist cadre were doing the hard and dangerous fieldwork of the CIO's great organizing drives, John L. Lewis famously said of them, "Who gets the bird? The hunter or the dog?"[145] I will be no one's dog. Why should you?

I believe that the labor movement needs a much wider discussion about what unions, workplace rights, and collective bargaining should look like in the twenty-first century. I think we should make deeper and more profound demands. The principle we should pursue is that *there will be unions*. Period. Full stop. Not subject to debate, election, repeal or secession.

Every worker, in every workplace, at every company, in every industry, and in all parts of the country should have systems of representation and the ability to join a union on day one to do so. And those unions must have the legal power to bargain for more than wages, hours, and (some) working conditions. Workers deserve, at long last, co-determination with owners and managers.

But we're not waiting for legal reform to change the way we organize and fight. We do have changes within our control. The first and most obvious is that we control our organizing strategies. We can choose to run more comprehensive campaigns. We can choose to seek out new union partnerships to go after new and related industries. We can pick campaign targets and protest activities that aim to inspire workers outside of our immediate campaigns to think about their potential power at work. We can choose to focus on natural workplace leaders, in both new organizing and internal campaigns, and to create representative and empowered organizing committees to drive our campaigns.

Also within our control are our bargaining strategies. We can and should go back to viewing our collective bargaining agreements as temporary truces instead of as permanent workplace constitutions. Let's put those no-strike and management rights clauses back on the table. Scratch out the lines you don't like; delete, delete, delete. Make the boss earn his language in each new successor agreement.

We should be crystal clear about which parts of our peculiar union shop and routine of collective bargaining work for us, and which parts are in management's interests. Where the system works for them and not for us we must be willing to try, to resist, to experiment, and to generally blow the system up.

Exclusive representation is one of those areas where we have the power to make change. Exclusive representation is *always* in management's interests. Now, it might be in many—if not most—current unions' interests as well. But think of what it gives management: peace. Now ask yourself: Do most bosses deserve peace?

Exclusive representation forces unions to mediate innumerable workplace disputes in order to curate a smaller, prioritized list of changes that workers would like to see.

Exclusive representation allows an employer to settle the items on the whittled-down list of demands and let them stay settled for years. They remain settled because every worker is bound to the terms of a no-strike clause that is only enforceable through the principle of exclusive representation. And, ultimately, most employers don't have to deal with any union at all because of the rigged rules of NLRB certification elections—elections that are only necessary if a union is seeking to be the exclusive representative of all the workers in a bargaining unit.

Our movement needs some leftist experimentation with minority unionism, be it in new organizing campaigns or in breakaway rebellions within legacy bargaining units. And, thankfully, we finally have a left that is worth speaking of! That, in and of itself, was the other major impetus I had for writing this book.

I became a teenage socialist in the 1990s, when a couple hundred younger workers joining left organizations was considered a B.F.D.

Today, that many join the movement every couple of days. For the first time in forever, we have a socialist left in the United States that is growing, dynamic, and contains the potential to change the world for the better.

The last thing that these new comrades should do is surrender to the "it is what it is" way of thinking about unions and the labor movement. I don't only mean following the rigged rules of the "official" NLRB-sanctioned labor relations system or succumbing to "business unionism" as usual. I'm also worried about too many of us following old formulas of salting traditionally organized industries, waging opposition caucus fights within the too-few surviving unions, or simply following the best practices (as they are currently known) of comprehensive strategic campaigns driven by union staff. All of that has its role, but none of it adds up to the complete solution to the labor movement's woes.

The opportunity of the moment calls for activists to take (or remain in) jobs in the unorganized industries and to experiment with new (or abandoned) forms of worker protest, like sabotage and quickie strikes. The opportunity of the moment calls for bolder demands for workers' rights and workplace governance. The opportunity of the moment demands a program of popular education to get the working-class majority to see that our power is rooted in the work we do and our occasional refusal to do it.

Finally, I'm tempted to thank you for sticking with me until the end of this book. But then I am reminded of another persnickety bit of union organizer training: never say "thank you" at the end of an organizing conversation. This is difficult for many people since it's only basic politeness to thank someone for their time. But do you thank someone for allowing you to help them make improvements at work and in society? Organizing is about solidarity, not charity.

So I will close this book as I would end any halfway decent organization conversation: I look forward to working with you.

Labor's Bill of Rights

These are dark times for labor. The Republican majority that now controls all levels of the federal government has made it clear that they plan on rolling back labor and employment protections, while also not funding and enforcing the currently existing laws. Judicial conservatives have regained their fifth vote on the Supreme Court, and have weaponized the First Amendment to overturn the constitutionality of public sector fair share agreements.[146] House conservatives have introduced a national right-to-work amendment to the National Labor Relations Act of 1935 (NLRA), and other restrictions on union activity are likely to be moved in the House.[147] All of this will come at a time when the power and reach of organized labor is at historic lows.

Today, *fewer than 11 percent* of workers in America are members of a union, including 6.4 percent of private sector workers and 34.4 percent of public sector workers.[148] The dramatic drop in union representation since the 1950s, when over a third of the workforce was unionized, has resulted in stunning income inequality, wage stagnation, continued wage discrimination against women, tens of millions of Americans working for sub-poverty wages, and widespread gaps in basic health, retirement, and family leave benefits.[149]

Traditionally, the courts have not been kind to labor. From the very beginning of our nation's history, the earliest union efforts were treated by conservative jurists as criminal conspiracies and interferences with

employers' property and contract rights and with Congress's responsibility to regulate interstate commerce. Unions spent the nineteenth
and early twentieth centuries decrying "judge-made law" and seeking,
essentially, to get the government and courts out of labor disputes.

For a brief time this worked. The Norris-LaGuardia Act of 1932
sought to prevent the federal courts and military from enjoining or
interfering in union protest activity, and many states passed similar
laws to keep their courts and police out of the fray. The NLRA made it
the official policy of the United States to encourage the practice of collective bargaining. The Act established a federal agency, the National
Labor Relations Board (NLRB), that would certify the existence of
a union at a workplace and sanction employers who refused to deal
with a bona fide union.

Much of the thrust of midcentury labor law was to encourage a
private system of jurisprudence: contract negotiations, arbitration,
and the occasional industrial warfare of strikes, boycotts (and, later,
lockouts). Though unions point proudly at the legislative and regulatory successes they have achieved since the nineteenth century, they
retain a vestigial bias against legislating and litigating our rights and
benefits.

Unfortunately, labor rights have been gutted by bad court decisions
and worse legislative action. The courts quickly waved away legal job
protections for striking workers (particularly for those who engage
in what had been the unions' greatest strategic weapon in the 1930s:
the sit-down strike), granted employers wide "free speech" latitude
to conduct campaigns of terror to break their employees' resolve to
form unions, and removed large categories of workers from protection under the Act.

Pro-union labor law reform has been largely unachievable since
the passage of the NLRA in 1935, and Congress has instead twice
amended the Act to severely restrict unions' ability to engage in
solidarity activism in the form of secondary boycotts and sympathy
strikes, to protect and enforce union shop agreements, and to enhance
employers' rights to fight back against their workers' demands for a
better quality of work life. In more recent years, Congress has severely

underfunded the NLRB, cutting agency staff and essentially giving employers wider latitude to break the law with impunity.

Simply put, unions are hampered by rules that would never be applied to corporations or to any other form of political activism. One of the root causes of this injustice was a conscious decision by the framers of the NLRA to root its constitutional authority in the Commerce Clause, not in the First Amendment right of free speech and assembly nor in the Thirteenth Amendment right to be free from "involuntary servitude."

As Rutgers law professor James Gray Pope has detailed, tying the NLRA to the Commerce Clause was a conscious, "pragmatic" decision of progressive lawyers to reject a half-century of a rights-based campaign for labor law waged by the American Federation of Labor.[150] Unfortunately, this decision is not just a historical footnote. It has the perverse effect of judging workers' rights, which should be a matter of human rights, within the frame of the impact on business of workers' actions, to the exclusion of free speech and other considerations. The last half-century has demonstrated that, in such a framework, the courts will tend to have more sympathy for business interests.

Labor rights should be rooted in fundamental constitutional rights, from First Amendment freedoms of speech and association to Fifth Amendment protections from unlawful takings, to Thirteenth Amendment freedoms from involuntary servitude. However, labor's foes have perversely used these constitutional rights against labor. This is seen most often in the push for "right-to-work" laws, which prevent unions from collecting fair-share fees to cover the expenses germane to collective bargaining.

It is the time for unions and their allies to return to the rights-based rhetoric and constitutional legal strategies that preceded the passage of the National Labor Relations Act and the development of our current labor law regime. The rights of working people to unite, to protest, to withhold their labor, to boycott unfair businesses, and to demand change in all areas of business and society precede and transcend individual labor statutes. Our rights are fundamentally rooted in the Bill of Rights and the Reconstruction amendments. Where the labor law regime, through statute or judicial fiat, restricts our constitutional rights, it should be resisted and challenged as such.

Let's look at this in some detail, by outlining the ten rights that, together, must constitute Labor's Bill of Rights.

Labor's First Right: The Right to Free Speech

Over the course of a few weeks in 1949, ten unionized technicians at the Jefferson Standard Broadcasting Company distributed handbills criticizing their employer. The workers were in the middle of protracted negotiations and had been without a contract for some time. The Charlotte, North Carolina, company was one of the first television broadcasters in the country. The handbills criticized the company's substandard technical equipment and lack of local programming, and charged that Jefferson Standard considered Charlotte a "second-class city."[151]

The corporation swiftly fired the ten technicians. The workers filed an unfair labor practice charge at the NLRB, arguing that they were participating in what they considered to be legally protected concerted activity to advance their contract campaign. The NLRB disagreed and ruled that the technicians' actions were not protected, because they were not obviously and explicitly connected to the union contract campaign. Upon appeal, the U.S. Supreme Court issued *Labor Board v. Electrical Workers (Jefferson Standard)*, one of the most anti–free speech decisions in the realm of labor law, that thundered, "There is no more elemental cause for discharge of an employee than disloyalty to his employer,"[152] henceforth known as the *Jefferson Standard* dictum.

Interpretation of *Jefferson Standard* has for decades led to a hash of confusing and contradictory NLRB and appellate court decisions, which continue to chill the rights of workers to speak out about their workplace.[153] The idea that union activists can be fired for making what employers consider "disloyal" statements about their employer seriously undermines organizing campaigns, and is used as a tactic by union-busting firms to delay and derail legitimate organizing activities.

In *Jefferson Standard*, an arm of the federal government (the NLRB) declined to enforce workers' statutory protections based on the content of those workers' speech. Such a decision in any other realm would not pass constitutional muster; it should not in the workplace either. This truth should be self-evident, despite how contradictory it is to so much current labor law: working people do not shed their free speech rights simply because they desire to join together as a labor union.

How to Restore This Right

To restore this right, unions and their allies must raise more First Amendment challenges to the labor law regime. Unions, workers' centers, individual workers, and law firms could, and should, challenge any governmental restriction on workers' pure and simple words. If a flyer, tweet, or online post, in and of itself, is challenged by a government agency to violate the Taft-Hartley Act, a state labor law, or some obscure and ill-considered court decision, mounting a First Amendment challenge must become a primary strategic consideration.

Ironically, one area of labor law where the courts often consider free speech in the realm of labor is with regard to the employer's speech rights.[154] For instance, the Supreme Court has taken free speech into consideration in carving out an employer's right to conduct captive audience meetings. Employers use these mandatory meetings—held in all-staff, small-group, or one-on-one formats—to "educate" employees about the disadvantages of unionization, but they are really designed to confuse and intimidate employees into voting against union representation.

In a 2009 study,[155] Kate Bronfenbrenner, director of research at Cornell University's School of Industrial and Labor Relations, found that nine out of ten employers utilize captive audience meetings to fight union organizing drives. Employers threaten to cut wages and benefits in 47 percent of documented cases, and to go out of business entirely in a staggering 57 percent of cases. Unions win only 43 percent of certification elections when employers run captive audience meetings (as opposed to an overall win rate of 55 percent).[156] No wonder union avoidance consultants consider it "management's most important weapon in a campaign."[157]

A fair application of the First Amendment would embrace the principle of "equal time" in mandatory presentations about the pros and cons of voting for a union in an election conducted by a government agency. For the government to grant employers a right to force employees to attend a "vote no" presentation but grant no such right to "vote yes" advocates to respond to the lies, half-truths, and threats that are presented is an obvious and shameful violation of workers' First Amendment rights.

A group of 106 leading labor scholars, led by Southern Methodist University law professor Charles Morris and Marquette University law professor Paul Secunda, have filed a rulemaking petition at the NLRB to reestablish an equal time rule (which was the NLRB standard for a brief time in the 1950s). This petition is a good start, but unions should press the matter further into the courts to establish a clear constitutional right to be free from the one-sidedness of captive audience meetings.[158] Challenging the one-sided approach to captive audience meetings at the NLRB and in the courts will serve to highlight the unfairness that workers face when trying to organize a union and could lead to more evenhanded union elections, more consistent with the purposes of the NLRA.

Labor's Second Right: The Right to Self-Defense and Mutual Aid

On a hot summer day in 1996, *a sixteen-year-old tomato picker named Edgar in Immokalee County, Florida, was beaten bloody by a straw boss when he had the nerve to take a water break.*[159] The bloodied shirt that Edgar had worn came to represent the abuse these workers faced, as organizers literally waved it at a rally to galvanize the Coalition of Immokalee Workers (CIW) to stand up against the privations of nonunion farmwork. The shirt became a symbol of their resistance.

The CIW movement eventually led to nationwide boycotts against fast-food restaurants such as Taco Bell and McDonald's, which purchased the Immokalee-grown tomatoes in bulk, at "bargain basement prices."[160] The boycotts were only lifted when those companies agreed to purchase tomatoes exclusively from growers who followed a list of rules that had been established by the Coalition, which included access to drinking water, tents for shade, health and safety committees, and a one-penny-per-pound pay increase for the workers.

The CIW campaign of rallies and boycotts was a success, and has clearly raised the working and living standards for the Immokalee workers. It should serve as a model for other labor organizations, except for the fact that, under the National Labor Relations Act, it would be illegal for a union to carry out such a campaign.

Labor's core principal and best defense is the practice of solidarity. One of the oldest slogans in the labor movement, coined by the Knights of Labor shortly after the Civil War, is "An injury to one is the concern of all." Unions are organized on this principle.

Yet our labor law has long prohibited such concerted activities, ignoring that working people have a right to self-defense when it comes to protecting and improving their working conditions. The current labor law regime makes it illegal for unions and workers to extend solidarity in the form of strikes and boycotts beyond the organizational boundaries of their immediate employer, and it punishes transgressions with crippling fines and injunctions. American labor law essentially requires union members to cross other workers' picket lines, or face punishment.

Imagine a truck driver refusing to make a delivery to a grocery store where the workers are on strike. Imagine grocery store workers refusing to stock a brand of cookies on the shelves because the cookie company shut down a unionized factory and shipped those jobs overseas. Imagine workers at an industrial laundry facility refusing to clean bed sheets that come from a hotel where the workers are locked out, or a hotel's room attendants refusing to make beds with linen that comes from a facility involved in a labor dispute.

Such solidarity activism is an essential component of trade unionism. It is carried out by unions around the world. Workers who are organized at such strategic positions in the economy would have the power to help non-union workers get organized and recognized, and they would be a strong bulwark against union-busting and offshoring.

The potential power of such solidarity actions is obvious, which is why its use is currently illegal. And unlike much of the program required to reverse anti-union judicial activism and establish labor's rights, recognizing the right to self-defense and mutual aid faces the high hurdle of reversing two amendments that Congress has made to the National Labor Relations Act to restrict workers' freedom to make common cause.

The 1947 Taft-Hartley amendments made it an Unfair Labor Practice for union members to boycott or picket a "secondary" employer, which is a company they do not work directly for but which has significant or even essential business dealings with their employer, with whom they do have a contractual dispute. The 1959 Landrum-Griffin amendments tightened those restrictions further, and even made it illegal for a union and an employer to agree to contract language that frees members to choose not to touch "hot cargo" (products of another company where there is a labor dispute).

Legislative prohibitions on solidarity activism treat workers and consumers as if they are competing interest groups (rather than two halves of the same person), and then exploit the frustration of consumers from becoming embroiled in industrial disputes over which they feel they have no obvious decision-making power. But corporations engage in secondary disputes all the time, without penalty. How many television consumers have seen entire channels blacked out, replaced with the name and number of a corporate CEO to call and complain to, simply because the cable provider did not want to pay the rate increase from the corporate owners of the blacked-out network? Cable companies have mastered the art of the secondary boycott, using their strategic position to leave television consumers in the dark since they have few alternatives to their local cable providers. Why is the use of the secondary boycott legal when employed by media companies but illegal when exercised in solidarity by workers?

Therefore, at the heart of a movement to restore the right to solidarity activism must be an equal protection argument. If corporations—which, we are told, are persons—get to enjoy an economic right that many people, in the form of unions, are denied, then that is a violation of working people's and unions' Fourteenth Amendment equal protection rights.

How to Restore This Right

One place to start in regaining labor's right to self-defense is the excessive restrictions on so-called signal picketing. Signal picketing is accomplished through demonstrations that involve hand billing and unique visual protests, such as giant inflatable rats. Signal picketing is meant to call out and embarrass unfair employers, but is not an explicit call for a boycott. Signal picketing should be protected free speech activity, but the courts have drawn on bad stereotypes of labor shake-downs, ruling that when unions engage in this sort of educational picketing, they are signaling that anyone crossing the line will face physical harm.

The twenty-first-century reality, however, is that informational picketing is as likely to be carried out by members of a worker center such as CIW, student labor activists, Jobs with Justice chapters,[161] or any other interested community activist—none of whom are union staff or even union members—than by a union covertly picketing for recognition. Furthermore, too few people in this country have grown up in union households where they were admonished to never cross a picket line, so to whom is this a signal, and what is it telling them to do? Whatever fantasies previous justices had about the physical threats implied in an informational picket are clearly relics. The current reality is that a ban on signal picketing is a clear violation of workers' First and Fourteenth Amendment rights.

The physical act of picketing is clearly a demonstration of free speech. So building upon a First Amendment affirmation of the legality of informational picketing, why is it constrained by bad law and judicial fiat when it is for union recognition? And, while courts in the post-NLRA era have ruled that the exercise of speech and economic pressure can act as constraints on commerce and therefore can be restricted, there is also a comparable amount of prior time and case law in which unions argued that the Thirteenth Amendment's protections from "involuntary servitude" justified collective worker action against the dictates of large corporations.

It is worth noting that the sponsor of the NLRA, Senator Robert Wagner, in justifying his bill, said, "We are forced to recognize the futility of pretending that there is equality of freedom when a single workman, with only his job between his family and ruin, sits down to draw a contract of employment with a representative of a tremendous organization having thousands of workers at its call."[162] Unfortunately, as James Gray Pope details,[163] Wagner rooted his law in the Commerce Clause and, once the Supreme Court upheld it, unions virtually abandoned the Thirteenth Amendment as labor law. The time is ripe for unions to return to this amendment as a justification of speech plus economic pressure.

University of Texas law professor Julius Getman writes extensively on the courts' free speech double standard.[164] Noxious hate groups such as the Ku Klux Klan and Westboro Baptist Church have seen their picketing and boycotts vigorously defended by the courts, while unions, judged instead by the impact on commerce, have had even purely political boycotts enjoined. Getman reminds readers that the International Longshoremen's Association protested the Soviet invasion of Afghanistan by refusing to load or unload cargo meant for Soviet ports. Even though there was no material gain for the union, and companies and workers in foreign lands do not fit the NLRA's intended definition of "employers" and "employees," the boycott was enjoined.[165]

But that was four decades ago, and the Supreme Court has spent the time since in an uneven expansion of the First Amendment, all on the side of business interests. Bold unions, particularly at the ports, could push the envelope with more politically motivated boycotts and push back on sanctions by arguing that the NLRB does not have jurisdiction over a dispute with a foreign government and that the workers have a free speech right to engage in the boycott. With democracy imperiled in countries like Turkey and Brazil (to name just two), and, with it, workers' rights and protections, there is no shortage of opportunities for global solidarity and free speech.

Labor's Third Right: The Right to Strike

On a cloudy afternoon in April of 2006, Roger Toussaint led a procession of union members across the Brooklyn Bridge. Toussaint, the president of Transport Workers Union Local 100 and an immigrant from Trinidad and Tobago, was walking to surrender himself to the authorities to serve a ten-day jail sentence. His crime? He led the largely black and Latino union membership in a strike against New York City's transportation authority the previous winter, in violation of New York's draconian Taylor Law.[166]

For engaging in the sixty-hour strike that shut down the city's subway and bus system, TWU Local 100 was fined $2.5 million in 2005. On top of Toussaint's jail time, the courts suspended the union's ability to collect dues money for a year, and each individual striker was fined two days' pay for every day on strike. Such draconian punishments are rare outside the world of labor law. How did this ever pass constitutional muster?

A century and a half ago, our nation was rent by a bloody civil war, centered on the issue of treating labor like property. Well over half a million Americans lost their lives in battle over perhaps our country's greatest sin: slavery and the privilege of property rights over human rights.

When the smoke cleared, the Thirteenth Amendment to the Constitution seemingly settled the matter in stark and definitive terms: "Neither slavery *nor involuntary servitude*, except as a punishment for crime whereof the party shall have been duly convicted, shall exist within the United States, or any place subject to their jurisdiction." (Emphasis added.) To this day, it remains the only section of the Constitution that expressly limits the power of individuals over each other. It is labor law explicitly codified in our nation's governing document.

The Reconstruction amendments, of which the Thirteenth was a part, were radical restatements of the concept of human freedom, but anti-labor jurists of the post-Reconstruction period reinterpreted them to fit within the common law framework of "at will" employment; freedom from involuntary servitude was, to them, merely the freedom to quit the job entirely.

Union activists following Reconstruction vociferously disagreed. "For decades," writes James Gray Pope, "workers and unions had resisted injunctions, nullified anti-strike laws, and sought legislation under the banner of the Thirteenth Amendment."[167] Leaders of the American Federation of Labor, he writes, tried in vain to have the constitutional authority of the NLRA rooted in Article XIII Section 2's positive assertion of Congress's "power to enforce this article by appropriate legislation."

As already noted, these efforts failed. As a result, labor's basic civil rights are judged according to their impact on commercial activity. Labor must assert the existence of a constitutional right to strike that transcends the current state of labor legislation.

How to Restore This Right

Public sector anti-strike legislation seems like a logical starting point for establishing that workers have a constitutional right to strike because it is where the employer (government) also makes and enforces the law; thus, the employer has the ability to compel its workers to keep working, subjecting employees who defy its order to financial penalties and jail time. The framers of the Thirteenth Amendment would likely have viewed that as "involuntary servitude."

Perhaps the best first cases are in instances where public sector employees are compelled to work without compensation. For example, case law has developed from New York's Taylor Law that says workers cannot engage in concerted actions to refuse to perform voluntary duties, such as chaperoning prom, if they had regularly volunteered prior to a contract dispute. And in Detroit, schoolteachers have been told that the district will run out of money to pay them for days they have already worked, but at the same time they will be breaking the law if they do not continue to work for no pay.[168] This command to *work for free or go to jail* is the very embodiment of involuntary servitude.

The right to strike must also include the right to return to the job when the strike is over. That was the clear intent of the National Labor Relations Act, which protected workers who engaged in concerted union activity from "discrimination in regard to hire or tenure of employment or any term or condition of employment," and further declared, "Nothing in the Act should be interpreted to interfere with or impede or diminish in any way the right to strike." And so, one important goal for restoring the right to strike must be reversing the flimsily considered 1938 Supreme Court precedent, *NLRB v. Mackay Radio*,[169] which granted employers the right to permanently replace striking workers.

For reasons that are not articulated in *Mackay*, the Court ignored the plain language of the NLRA to declare that an employer has a

right to protect and continue his business by supplying places left vacant by strikers. And he is not bound to discharge those hired to fill the places of strikers, upon the election of the latter to resume their employment in order to create places for them.

While the *Mackay* Doctrine would appear to benefit from *stare decisis*, the legal principle "to stand by things decided," the fact remains that the Court has not, in any case that cited *Mackay*, gone back and evaluated the facts and logic of the original case. As Julius Getman notes, "The Court in *Mackay* made no effort to justify its dictum. And its actual holding points in the other direction—namely, that an employer may not base reinstatement rights on participation in union activity."[170]

How is giving employment preference to workers who did not engage in strike activity not an act of discrimination against the employees who did participate in protected concerted activity? And why does it follow that retaining permanent replacement workers after the strike is over is necessary to "protect and continue his business" when there are more experienced, veteran employees ready, willing, and able to work?

Of historical note to any judicial reconsideration of *Mackay* is that employers did not exercise this right en masse until 1983. That year, the Phelps-Dodge Corporation laid out the union-busting blueprint by bargaining their employees to impasse over drastic cuts in pay, benefits, and working conditions, forcing them out on strike, and then helping the permanent replacements to decertify the union twelve months later.[171]

Many thousands of union bargaining units have been decertified using a weaponized form of the *Mackay* Doctrine since the 1980s, and I am not aware of any significant judicial evaluation of whether any case of union-busting was necessary to "protect and continue" the businesses that have exploited this law.

Mackay should be challenged as a violation of workers' First Amendment rights of free speech and assembly, Thirteenth Amendment protections against involuntary servitude, and Fourteenth Amendment guarantees of due process and equal protection. It should be challenged on the basis of legislative intent, and it should be challenged based upon the justification of the original decision as compared to its practical application by employers since 1983.

Of equal importance is returning to the broad prohibition against federal injunctions of labor strikes, pickets and boycotts in the 1932 Norris-LaGuardia Act. This requires challenging the 1970 Supreme Court decision in *Boys Market v. Retail Clerks* as a violation of workers' Thirteenth Amendment rights. In that case, the Court decided to ignore Norris-LaGuardia's sweeping ban on federal injunctions in cases where a union strikes in violation of a signed no-strike clause. This decision, charges legal scholar James B. Atleson, "while ostensibly grounded on neutral concerns for the integrity of state court jurisdiction and authority, in fact was based primarily on the Court's value choice that there is no effective substitute for an immediate halt to a strike."[172]

Many scholars agreed with the Court that the concerns that motivated the Norris-LaGuardia Act were no longer present since courts were no longer anti-union and unions were now strong and established. Moreover, standards now existed to protect against judicial abuses because the cases would involve breaches of written agreements.[173]

And sure enough, once the Supreme Court legitimized injunctions to enforce contract terms, soon courts found more kinds of strike actions to enjoin. If a contract deliberately does *not* contain a no-strike clause, courts may assume and enforce a no-strike principle if that contract includes a grievance and arbitration process. And where a contract has expired—or not yet been negotiated—courts may enjoin partial and intermittent strikes. And in this way, the labor injunction that Felix Frankfurter railed against in the early part of the twentieth century has crept back into practice as employers have no shortage of case law to cite when appealing to a judge to order a union to cease its protest.

Partial strikes, in which workers in a handful of essential job titles or categories strike while the rest of their co-workers continue to report for work, and rolling, or intermittent, strikes, in which workers may strike for one day—or even one hour—and then report back to work the next day only to briefly strike again a short time later, can be incredibly disruptive, and therefore powerful, union tactics. However, business-friendly case law made them "illegal."

The tendency of judges to place a heavy thumb on the scale for business and property when weighing the relative merits of a labor-management dispute is precisely why Congress passed the Norris-LaGuardia Act: to bar them from getting involved in the first place. As they did before the passage of Norris-LaGuardia, unions should routinely appeal, challenge, and oppose any judicial injunction against a job action as a violation of those workers' Thirteenth Amendment protections against involuntary servitude.

Labor's Fourth Right: Labor Organizing Efforts Should Be Free from Unreasonable Search and Seizure

On a fall day in 2008, the figurative autumn of the presidential administration of George W. Bush, officials at the Service Employees

International Union (SEIU) inked an organizing rights deal for employees of the global security firm G4S. These sorts of agreements are an essential tool for workers to freely and fairly choose whether to be represented by a union. This is doubly true for security workers, who are statutorily barred from seeking a union certification election with the National Labor Relations Board if they are joining a union that also represents non-guards.

The agreement was the culmination of a years-long campaign run by a global coalition of unions. Faced with a pressure campaign that transcended national boundaries, G4S zeroed in on where they had the most power to undermine its general thrust: the U.S. legal system. Specifically, the company filed a civil lawsuit against SEIU under the Racketeering Influenced and Corrupt Organizations Act (RICO).[174]

More and more organizing and counter-organizing occurs outside the context of traditional labor organizations, and outside the context of the NLRB.[175] To be successful, many unions engage in what are called "comprehensive campaigns," which may utilize legal and regulatory challenges aimed at creating liabilities for employers and interfering in complex business deals to augment worker activism.

Through statutes such as the Fair Labor Standards Act (FLSA) or Title VII of the Civil Rights Act, courts can offer workers a better chance to remedy workplace violations. Current labor law reform legislation in Congress, such as the Employee Empowerment Act and WAGE Act, seeks to expand workers' access to courts for labor violations. But however much there is an advantage to accessing the courts, this can also present a host of new problems.

Two major areas where court proceedings have been used against workers include the RICO Act to go after unions engaging in comprehensive campaigns, and a host of abusive litigation tactics against workers seeking to vindicate their workplace rights in court, particularly "strategic lawsuits against public participation" (SLAPP) suits.[176] Both sets of tactics have the intended purposes of chilling organizing activities by those with superior access to resources, and both should be pushed back against.

If workers are to have meaningful workplace rights, they cannot be subject to RICO and SLAPP suits for exercising those rights. These cases are almost always without merit, but getting them dismissed can tie up a tremendous amount of a union's money and staff attention. Indeed, the G4S RICO suit was hardly the only one darkening the skies over SEIU at the time. The global solidarity campaign did eventually put enough pressure on G4S to bring them to the table with SEIU. But the equal pressure of the RICO suit gave the company a bargaining chip to get the union to settle for a deal that protected fewer workers than the union had sought to organize (and fewer, comparably, than their foreign counterparts). As one corporate attorney told the *New York Times* about their use of RICO suits to get settlements from the union, "When they settle it normally breaks the campaign."[177]

Although the deal involved a commitment by G4S to withdraw the RICO suit, that proved to be an unnecessary concern. A federal judge moved to dismiss the meritless case just hours after it was already withdrawn.

The use of RICO suits against labor is not merely an expensive distraction; it is also "an attempt to revive a nineteenth-century conception of unions as extortionate criminal conspiracies."[178] Recognizing that organized crime had become "a highly sophisticated, diversified, and widespread activity that annually drain[ed] billions of dollars from America's economy by unlawful conduct and the illegal use of force, fraud, and corruption," Congress passed RICO with the purpose of "seek[ing] the eradication of organized crime in the United States." [179] However, starting in the 1980s, employers began using civil RICO to attack labor. The purpose of such suits is often to destroy effective comprehensive campaigns.[180]

Employer use of RICO suits when unions are trying to organize a workplace using a corporate campaign treats legitimate organizing tactics as coercive or extortionate,[181] and assigns a property value to the free speech and assembly of a civil rights organization. These suits not only expose unions and union officials to major liability, but they also link unions with criminal activities. Anti-union groups such as the National Right to Work Committee then promote these suits to further that linkage, and preserve the notion that unions are criminal organizations.

The malicious prosecution of labor is not limited to RICO suits; it is also used in SLAPP suits. The term "SLAPP suits" originated in an influential study that resulted in a book and series of papers that sought to identify a growing trend where citizens and groups were being sued for engaging in activities as diverse as circulating petitions for signatures to reporting police misconduct.[182] The purpose of the suits is to silence opponents and dissuade certain conduct.[183]

While early SLAPP suits were most common in zoning and other land use disputes, their use by employers has been growing.[184] Nicole Hallett provides an example of such suits that is becoming all too common. In response to a lawsuit by temporary guest workers that alleged involuntary servitude, wage theft, and other employment law violations, the employer filed counterclaims for "defamation/libel, invasion of privacy, tortious interference with business relations, intentional infliction of emotional distress, abuse of process, and civil conspiracy."[185] These tactics are, in many respects a modern-day continuation of employers using the courts as a weapon against workers.[186]

Workers have some limited protections in the form of the anti-SLAPP suits passed by some—but far from all—states, but Hallett proposes the creation of a labor organizing privilege that would shield communications made between workers in the context of organizing. But these do not offer robust protection against attacks from the courts because not all states have such statutes, and the protections they offer are limited.[187]

Courts recognize the need to protect privileged communications between attorneys and clients, priests and penitents, physicians and patients, between spouses, and others. By placing communications in the privileged camp, they become free from the fear of SLAPP suits and other forms of intrusion. In determining whether a communication should be privileged and therefore exempt from disclosure, the test developed by legal scholar John Wigmore is usually applied. This test requires the following:

1. The communications must originate in a confidence that they will not be disclosed.
2. This element of confidentiality must be essential to the full and satisfactory maintenance of the relation between the parties.
3. The relation must be one which in the opinion of the community ought to be sedulously fostered.
4. The injury that would inure to the relation by the disclosure of the communication must be greater than the benefit thereby gained for the correct disposal of litigation.[188]

Based on this test, some jurisdictions have recognized a privilege protecting communications with a union representative.[189] Hallett goes one step further in arguing that the Wigmore test and other societal factors show that a labor organizing privilege should be recognized. Such a privilege "would be held by the worker and would protect communications concerning organizing or collective bargaining between two or more workers, or between workers and their representatives."[190] The courts have granted broad managerial discretion to the physical workspace, but labor should push back against intrusions and after-the-fact surveillance on worker communications.

How to Restore This Right

Section 7 of the NLRA protects the right of workers to engage in "concerted activities for the purpose of collective bargaining or other mutual aid or protection," and Section 8(a)(1) categorizes employer surveillance as an unfair labor practice.[191] Unions could file Unfair Labor Practices against employers that file meritless RICO civil suits, and an activist NLRB could deem the practice to be a violation of the labor act and possibly go to court to enjoin RICO suits from interfering with workers' federally protected rights.

To have an arm of the government join with a union to get a meritless RICO suit dismissed would be powerful. Having such an ally in the proceedings could open a space for unions to argue that the twisted misuse of RICO is a violation of their First Amendment rights of free speech and assembly and of workers' Thirteenth Amendment right to be free from involuntary servitude.

Labor's Fifth Right: The Freedom From Taking Away Union Fees (or, the Right to Dues Processing)

Imagine, if you will, a situation where the federal government required a private organization to work on behalf of all people who so requested, while a state law gave individuals the right not to pay for the service. It is likely the only organization that one can imagine living under such rules is a labor organization.

This is because the NLRA has been interpreted to require a union, as the exclusive bargaining agent of workers in a bargaining unit, to represent all workers equally. However, when a state passes a "right-to-work" law, as permitted by the 1947 Taft-Hartley amendments to the NLRA, workers can choose to pay nothing for this representation. Such representation includes organizing, contract negotiation, contract administration, legal representation, and other work. Therefore, unions are in a situation where federal labor law requires them to provide a valuable and resource-heavy set of services to all workers, while state law permits workers to choose not to pay any fees. This would be akin to a law that requires Major League Baseball to admit all fans but does not require them to buy a ticket. No other type of organization in America suffers under such a rule.

Yet for decades unions have reserved their arguments against right-to-work to the legislatures and the ballot box, not the courts. But, aided by legal scholars and jurists, unions have now begun making a constitutional argument against "right to work," and though this argument has conservative roots, it should be pursued in state and federal courts. The argument essentially states that by having a federal law (the NLRA) requiring unions to represent every employee in the bargaining unit equally, while also allowing states to pass laws that require unions to do so for free, the government is unconstitutionally taking the unions' services.

The argument first arose in labor's challenge to Indiana's

controversial 2012 right-to-work law. Although the federal Seventh Circuit ruled against labor in *Sweeney v. Pence*, Judge Diane Wood (who is among the most respected Circuit Court judges, and has been shortlisted for the Supreme Court)[192] made a broad argument that right-to-work laws, by their very natures, violate the U.S. Constitution's prohibition.[193] Challenging the near six-decade acceptance of the validity of right-to-work laws, Judge Wood wrote that the majority "is either incorrect or it lays bare an unconstitutional confiscation perpetuated by our current system of labor law."[194]

Judge Wood explained persuasively that Section 14(b) of the NLRA, which has been read to permit state right-to-work laws, should be read as it was written, speaking only to "agreements requiring *membership*."[195] Agency fees, which are currently interpreted as prohibited under right-to-work laws, are paid in lieu of membership. They are equivalent to only the portion of dues that compensate for collective bargaining, contract administration, and grievance adjustment.

Judge Wood argues, rather persuasively, that such agency fees were precisely what *are* permitted under Section 14(b), because the contrary reading would require the court "to decide whether such a rule is permissible under the Takings Clause of the Fifth Amendment."[196] Judge Wood's interpretation challenges the long-accepted idea that states can pass laws that limit unions' abilities to collect full membership dues from members and partial agency fees from non-members. It challenges these laws on what she calls "the two most basic economic rights enjoyed in the United States . . . (1) that the government may not confiscate private property for public use without just compensation, and (2) that the takings power must be exercised for a public purpose, and so the government may not take the property of one private party for the sole purpose of transferring it to another private party, regardless of whether 'just' compensation is paid."[197]

How to Restore This Right

Labor has followed this cue and filed cases in state courts in Wisconsin and West Virginia, challenging those states' right-to-work laws. In one brought by the International Union of Operating Engineers, with Harvard Law professor Ben Sachs serving as counsel, the union brought forward Judge Diane Wood's argument that right-to-work laws were both preempted and an unconstitutional taking.[198] The District Court judge rejected the union's argument, expressly siding with the Circuit majorities in *Sweeney*. This case is currently on appeal to the circuit. Federal challenges have also been filed in the Fourth and Ninth Circuits, against West Virginia's and Idaho's laws.

Given that so many of these laws have only been passed in recent years, and as a part of a coordinated partisan attack on unions because they help Democrats get elected, these cases may find judges sympathetic to additional free speech and equal protection arguments incorporated into labor's judicial appeals. To buttress the legal efforts, labor should engage in a full education and public relations campaign to complement the lawsuits and expose the unfairness behind this long-standing rule. Labor opponents have long employed constitutional arguments to push right-to-work in the courts and legislatures. In her dissent, Judge Wood laid out a road map for labor to challenge such laws on constitutional grounds.

Labor's Sixth Right: The Right to Not Be Locked Out for Exercising Labor Rights

On the morning of Monday, May 9, 2016, Honeywell Aerospace employees in South Bend, Indiana, and Green Island, New York, found themselves locked out of their factories.[199] Their United Auto Workers (UAW) collective bargaining agreement with the company had expired six days earlier, and the union members had voted by a nine-to-one margin to reject the company's "last, best and final" offer. While that offer did include modest wage increases, it also called for health insurance premiums to rise by 67 percent, with deductibles increasing by $4,600 a year. It also gave management more authority to force employees to work overtime.

The union offered to continue to work under the old contract while negotiations were ongoing. But the company decided to put severe economic pressure on their unionized workforce to accept its terms. Salaried employees and temps, who had been brought in during the previous weeks to shadow the company's workers and learn their jobs, would keep the assembly line going. The locked-out union members, of course, immediately lost their income while bills continued to pile up.

The workers at Honeywell remained locked out for ten long months. Midway through the conflict, the company's spokesman said Honeywell "will resume negotiations whenever the union is ready to do so," while undermining that claim by reiterating that the company had already given the union its "last, best and final offer." In essence, the company was punishing the workers for organizing and collectively bargaining.

Labor lockouts—both full and partial—are a particularly egregious denial of the right of workers to direct the terms of their own labor. The lockout occurs when an employer, very much like Honeywell, locks out its workers as a bargaining tactic to gain concessions from them. Partial lockouts occur when an employer locks out only a portion of the workforce, and in many instances, the NLRB has permitted such tactics,[200] while severely restricting the right of unions to engage in partial strikes. Courts have long treated the lockout as the complement to the strike, with a strike constituting workers withholding their labor and a lockout constituting management withholding work. Though there is an appealing logic to this view of lockouts, it ignores the realities of labor and the goals of labor law.

Labor lockouts occur in the context of bargaining a contract between the union and the employer. Often negotiations are still underway, and the union has agreed to work under the terms of the expiring or expired contract. The employer, however, decides to lock out the entire union workforce in order to gain greater concessions. Though the NLRA's central protection states that "Employees shall have the right to self-organization, to form, join, or assist labor organizations, to bargain collectively through representatives of their own choosing, and to engage in other concerted activities for the purpose of collective bargaining or other mutual aid or protection,"[201] the

NLRB and courts have looked the other way when employers punish workers for engaging in those protected activities.

If workers have a right to form a union in order to bargain collectively, how can an employer be permitted to withhold work and compensation for engaging in collective bargaining and making negotiation demands? Furthermore, workers have a fundamental right to strike.[202] Indeed, strikes or the threat of strikes are among workers' few powerful tools in collective bargaining. However, for the right to strike to be meaningful, workers must be able to control the terms of their work stoppages. When an employer preemptively, or otherwise, locks workers out, it robs those workers of their full rights to strike.

It also robs them of a more literal "right to work." In her book *The Workplace Constitution*, University of Pennsylvania law and history professor Sophia Z. Lee documents attempts by early civil rights activists to get the due process guarantees of the Fifth Amendment and the equal protection rights of the Fourteenth to apply to the workplace.[203] These activists argued that there was a constitutional right to work in whites-only jobs for black workers, and they argued that NLRB regulation of collective bargaining provided the requisite state action to put the issue in the courts. Similar arguments should be revived against the lockout.

The act of locking out workers as a result of forming a union or engaging in collective action is incompatible with these core protections of the Act. The employer's right to lock out workers has expanded over the last several decades from a series of conservative Labor Boards and courts, and it is time for labor to start pushing back against this affront to workers' fundamental rights.[204]

How to Restore This Right

Labor should begin pushing back against the use of the lockout by challenging lockouts on their face. If an employer locks out workers for engaging in concerted activities, including organizing a union and making demands in the collective bargaining process, unions should file unfair labor practice charges, arguing that the lockout violates

Section 8(a)1 by interfering with their members' concerted activity and Section 8(a)3 by discriminatorily withholding pay from workers who are merely engaging in union activity, and when the case gets to the courts, argue that the lockout deprives workers of their due process rights under the Fifth Amendment.

Labor's Seventh Right: The Right to Your Job

Last June, Samuel was called in to his company's human resources office. As he recounted to *Forbes* magazine, he had been employed with his company for five years, and had just received his fifth annual performance review in March, a mix of his usual "Excellent" and "Very Good" ratings in every category. His manager for the previous two and a half years was out on sabbatical. Samuel had barely had any interaction with his new manager. In the meeting, Samuel was blindsided by an announcement that he was being let go, as part of a general shake-up of the firm.[205]

This is not a particularly dramatic story, except, of course, for Samuel and his family, but it is a common one. Without a union, most workers in this country labor under a judicial standard called "at will" employment. Essentially, at-will employees have the freedom to quit their job at any time, and employers have the even greater power to fire employees at any time, for a good reason, a bad reason, or no reason at all. As with so many other areas of labor and employment, the symmetry is a false one.

The alternative to at-will employment is "just cause," which is the principle that an employee cannot be fired unless it is for a good, or just, reason. Generally, this means that the infraction for which an employee is being terminated is serious enough to warrant losing her job and that the employee has been given clear feedback on her shortcomings and time and support to improve her performance.

Just-cause clauses are routinely commonly negotiated into union contracts. However, as union density has shrunk, labor's enemies are increasingly able to portray the job protections that union members have won for themselves as a special right that non-union workers—who lack it—should be jealous of. This is particularly true in the self-styled education reform movement, which has put teacher tenure in the crosshairs.

A union-led push to expand just-cause protections for all workers could give unions more mass appeal, by providing a big, visible campaign of unions pushing for universal rights that employers have sought to restrict as "special" ones.

The strange thing about the at-will doctrine is that Congress never voted on it. It is not a statute, nor is it found in the Constitution. It is entirely judge-made law. Early on in our nation's history, judges imported the at-will doctrine from English common law. This came as the Industrial Revolution was breaking up the traditional relationship between master craftsmen and their journeymen and apprentices, and it thus ensured that the new class of capitalists had no obligations to displaced workers.

Here too, unions once made arguments that the "nor involuntary servitude" clause of the Thirteenth Amendment altered the imbalance of power in the common law, but judges resisted that interpretation. The workers who fought in the Revolutionary and Civil Wars certainly didn't think they were fighting for a definition of liberty under which you can be fired at any time.

In some respects, this is the one right that could be most cleanly legislated. There is nothing stopping any state in the nation from adopting a law that simply states, "No one who works in this state may be terminated from employment by their employer except for just cause" and instantly nullify the at-will employment standard for everyone in the jurisdiction.

Call it a "Right to Your Job" law. It may be achieved by a majority vote of the state legislature, a ballot initiative, or an amendment to the state constitution. But those areas of the country where activists are successfully winning the $15 minimum wage, paid sick days, and fairness in scheduling laws should consider adding just cause to their list of initiatives. Once there has been enough public education and organizing on the issue, it may well prove to be one that, like the minimum wage, draws more progressive voters to the polls in off-cycle elections.

How to Restore This Right

If just cause for discharge laws are enacted, judicial activism on this issue will arise in implementation. While some states might choose to legislate that termination disputes be submitted to a labor or employment board of some kind, others may leave it to lawsuits or private arbitration. Preserving the right to sue, as a matter of leverage, while pushing for a body of arbitration "case law" that parallels the voluminous labor-management case law in which many lawyers and union representatives are well versed could keep many lawyers plenty busy.

Making public and popular the demand for just cause for all could open the door to litigation strategies to establish the right. The fact is that pure at-will status no longer exists. Civil rights statutes, whistleblower protection laws, and the labor act itself already limit the ability of employers to terminate protected workers for bad or no cause. Googling a phrases like "I was fired for no reason" bring a host of links providing advice and law firms advocating how to fight back. Most of that advice runs along the lines of trying to shoehorn an unexplained termination into one of the existing protections.

If the concept of just cause for all gets into the popular imagination, it's not impossible to imagine employment lawyers incorporating constitutional arguments into their wrongful termination lawsuits saying that just-cause protections should be equally applied to all workers, and that some judges will become sympathetic to their arguments. The contention would be that laboring under the implied threat of termination at any time violates an employee's Thirteenth Amendment right to be free from involuntary servitude, and that by only extending job protections to certain "protected" classes of workers, the workers who do not currently enjoy just cause protections are being denied their Fourteenth Amendment right to equal protection under the law.

Labor's Eighth Right: Freedom from Cruel and Unusual Regulation

On May 15, 2014, workers at a Staples warehouse in Georgia who were trying to organize a meeting were called in for a mandatory captive audience meeting led by one of the managers.[206] In the meeting, the manager explained how Staples cares about its associates and wanted to work directly with them. He explained that "unions come between employers and employees." And he warned, "Unions are a business that needs your money. Don't be fooled: Unions are first and foremost a business."[207]

To anyone who has listened to secret recordings of captive audience meetings or viewed confidential speeches for employers to lead an anti-union campaign, the manager's words seem strangely familiar.[208] But to many workers who are forced to listen to these speeches, they don't know that behind the speeches and literature is a vast "union avoidance" business that their employer has engaged to keep workers from exercising their rights to form a union. For over fifty-five years, the law has required employers to disclose when and whom they hire to persuade employees concerning their labor rights, but for almost as long, employers have utilized an interpretive loophole (see below) that allows union-busters to remain in the shadows.

While the "union avoidance" industry is allowed to operate in the shadows, the exact opposite is true concerning union activity. If one wants to find out how much any union staffer makes, or how much he or she was reimbursed for mileage, one need only go to the website www.unionfacts.com. The site is not an investigative news source that cleverly finds inside information on unions. Rather, it is run by an anti-union group called the Center for Union Facts (established by Richard Berman, also known as "Dr. Evil"), and has been able to create an easily searchable database and whip up outrage against unions because labor organizations are required to make massive disclosures.

Whether for good or bad, labor unions are among the most regulated organizations in the United States. The Taft-Hartley Act of 1947 began limiting union structures and requiring anti-communist affidavits from union officials. Then, in 1959, the Labor Management Reporting and Disclosure Act (LMRDA) placed strict rules on who can serve as a union official, as well as strict reporting requirements. Each year unions have to submit to the Department of Labor data on income and expenditures, salaries, and a host of other internal documents. Furthermore, following court decisions concerning agency fees, unions must disclose strict accountings of how every dollar is spent in order to determine if it is a "chargeable" or "non-chargeable" expense.

On the employer side, the LMRDA required employers to file reports with the DOL when they hire anti-union consultants—often called "union busters." The theory behind this requirement is that workers have a right to know who is speaking to them when they are receiving information from their employers, and they have a right to know how much the employer is paying for its campaign against the union. However, a huge "advice" exemption has developed wherein a consultant who does not make actual contact with the workers and only provides resources behind the scenes to run an anti-union campaign is exempt from the law. It is estimated that employers in at least 75 percent of organizing drives hire one or more consultants,[209] yet because of the massive loophole in the law, nationwide only 387 agreements were filed by employers and consultants.

A Department of Labor rule was scheduled to close this loophole, until a federal district court judge in Texas placed a nationwide injunction preventing the rule from going into effect.[210] The ninety-page decision focused exclusively on the employer's First Amendment right not to disclose its use of consultants. Though the title of the LMRDA sounds like it affects both labor and management, management has effectively been exempt from its reach.

How to Restore This Right

Labor law is constructed on the principle of a balance of power between the employer and employees. But, as in so many other areas, labor has it much harder in terms of the disclosures it is required to make. Disclosure requirements are often ineffective measures, but if they are to exist, there must be parity. Just as workers have a right to know the salaries of every person at the union, they should have a right to know the salaries of every executive and other employee at the company. And just as workers have a right to know detailed union expenditures so they can know if money that might otherwise adhere to their benefit is being responsibly spent, they have a right to know corporate expenditures.

Though the Department of Labor's recent persuader rule is currently in legal limbo, labor should continue to push for greater parity of disclosure between labor and management—a sort of equal protection, whose benefit would adhere to workers. Such disclosures would allow workers to highlight and target employer expenditures that are wasteful or against the long-term interests of the enterprise.

Labor's Ninth Right: The Right to Make Demands and Bargain Freely

In 2012, the Chicago Teachers Union (CTU) won a major strike. The teachers were motivated by a desire to prevent school closures, strengthen layoff and recall rights in the event of closures, get air conditioning in every classroom, repair crumbling buildings, and get student test scores removed from teacher evaluations. They struck, however, out of legal necessity, for more money. That's because wages are a so-called "mandatory" subject of bargaining, and the other items were deemed by lawmakers to be "permissive."

In fact, after the strike's first week, attorneys for Mayor Rahm Emanuel went to court seeking an injunction to force the teachers back to work because picketers had been talking more about air conditioning than about raises. The CTU operates under a public sector labor law, wherein employers *are* the law and craft the law to naturally be more favorable to them.

Ironically, if Republicans revive the *Friedrichs v. CTA* case, it would establish that every interaction a union has with its government employer is political speech, paving the way for unions to challenge restrictions like those in Illinois on unions' bargaining demands as violations of the First Amendment.

Still, public sector scope of bargaining is based upon a similar framework in the private sector, one that similarly distorts collective bargaining and restricts the free speech of union members. The

National Labor Relations Act's directive to employers to bargain with certified union representatives "in good faith" over "wages, hours and other terms and conditions of employment" is as broad as it is vague. There is no statutory requirement to actually reach an agreement, only to meet and respond to proposals.

Legal assistance, in the form of Unfair Labor Practice charges, only comes into play when one party refuses to meet or refuses to respond to a bargaining proposal. "Bad faith" bargaining ULPs can bring significant leverage as remedies include orders to meet more frequently, the furnishing of budgetary and other documentation to justify a bargaining position, and orders to cease, or even reverse, any changes made prior to reaching agreement or impasse.

Unfortunately, the obligation to bargain in good faith has been drastically narrowed by the Supreme Court's artificial invention of "mandatory" and "permissive" subjects of bargaining. "Permissive" subjects carry no legal obligation to bargain, and the Court has privileged "managerial decisions, which lie at the core of entrepreneurial control" in this matter.[211] As a result, an employer has no duty to bargain over a decision to subcontract, outsource, or downsize employment of union members. At best, unions can compel an employer to bargain over the impact of a decision already made. As a result, unions have little legal right to bargain to save jobs and only a little more to bargain for severance payments.

In their ambitious and groundbreaking survey of worker representation preferences, *What Workers Want*, Richard B. Freeman and Joel Rodgers concluded that workers want "more" from workplace representation: "More say in the workplace decisions that affect their lives, more employee involvement in their firms, more legal protection at the workplace, and more union representation."

But "most workers do not believe that, under current U.S. policies, they can get the additional input into workplace decisions that they want."[212]

My interpretation of these findings is that workers want co-determination.

Teachers at charter schools vote to form unions to gain a say in

textbook purchases, advanced placement offerings, student discipline, and extracurricular activities. Nurses organize to gain a voice in
staffing ratios, patient treatment regimens, how patients are billed and
when they are discharged. Autoworkers bemoan the fact that their
employers design and produce cars that leave them, as auto *consumers*, unenthusiastic.

Above all, workers want the ability to veto or amend management's
decisions to downsize, subcontract, automate or shift work overseas.
One of the most powerful taunts that employers make in union-busting campaigns is "The union can't save your job." It is perverse that the
law restricts unions from being what workers want them to be, and
that pro-business commentators then sneer at the low levels of new
union win rates.

How to Restore This Right

The place to begin expanding the scope of bargaining is the public
sector, where a combination of statute and judicial interference has created a third category of undemocratic bargaining subjects: those that
cannot even be proposed. In New Jersey, teachers' unions are prohibited from proposing contract language to reduce class sizes (which is
only one of the most important issues to teachers), and all unions are
prohibited from patterning proposals on what other unions in the state
have won. Wisconsin infamously reduced the scope of bargaining so
severely that unions are legally prohibited from proposing anything
other than a wage increase that does not exceed the rate of inflation.

A government employer using the force of law to restrict its employees' rights of free speech to advocate for the working conditions they
desire, and to use the force of law to dictate working conditions to its
employees—particularly in Wisconsin, where hard-fought work rules
and compensation were instantly revoked—is vulnerable to constitutional challenges based upon the First, Thirteenth, and Fourteenth
Amendments.

For the private sector, ultimately the *NLRB v. Wooster Division of
Borg-Warner* precedent must be overturned. In this case, the Court

ruled that the employer could not refuse to bargain over pay and benefits (now deemed "mandatory" subjects) until the union agreed to stage a ratification vote in the manner the employer demanded (a "permissive" subject, if ever there was one). While the initial thrust of Court opinion had a laudable goal, the NLRB and the Court could simply have declared the employer's demands regarding union governance to be a violation of Section 8(a)2's prohibition on employer dominance of unions, and the refusal to deal with pay and benefits, in and of itself, to be "bad faith" bargaining.

Once judges begin tinkering with what demands are fair and which are foul, then the very process of collective bargaining becomes warped, in the words of legal scholar James B. Atleson, by "the *assumption* that certain rights are necessarily vested exclusively in management or are based upon an economic *value judgment* about the necessary locus of certain power."[213] These obvious class biases favor management and hamper industrial democracy.

While there is some truth to Atleson's observation that "a party needing Board assistance to compel bargaining over a particular matter is hardly in a position to achieve notable bargaining success,"[214] written as it was in 1983, it misses two key points. First, the value of ULPs as a point of leverage in comprehensive organizing campaigns is a more recent tool for unions, one of particular value in contract fights where the employer's ultimate goal is to break the union. Second, the first union members who do seek to have a voice in matters at the "core of entrepreneurial control" (marketing, quality control, environmental impact, etc.) will see employers strongly resist, to the point of necessitating legal assistance to break the logjam.

Labor's Tenth Right: Powers Not Exercised by Unions Are Reserved to Workers Who Act in Concert

Like many non-union white-collar workers, Jacob Lewis was getting screwed. A technical writer for a health care software company called Epic Systems,[215] Lewis was a salaried employee who worked long hours with no overtime compensation. He did some research and talked with his fellow technical writers, who decided that they were being improperly misclassified as exempt from overtime laws.

A little while earlier, on April 2, 2014, Epic Systems sent an email to its workers that included an arbitration agreement that required workers to bring their employment claims through arbitration while waiving their rights to bring a class action case. Such arbitration agreements have become widespread following a pair of Supreme Court decisions in 2011 and 2013 that effectively held that they were permissible in most instances.

Lewis, however, brought his overtime claim as a class action in court, rather than proceeding individually in arbitration. The company sought to have Lewis's case dismissed because the agreement required him to proceed solely through arbitration. However, the Seventh Circuit Court of Appeals, in a decision written by Judge Diane Wood, held that the National Labor Relations Act prohibited such class action waivers because such legal actions are among the Section 7 rights protected by labor law. In doing so, the Seventh Circuit doubled down on the NLRB's important precedent in *D.R. Horton* that first held that collective and class court actions are substantive rights protected by labor law.[216]

Labor law in the United States is unique among the nation's laws because it protects collective rather than individual rights. The individual worker is protected only insofar as he or she is part of a group that acts for mutual aid or protection. Though the collective rights model has at times proven problematic in application, or has been significantly misunderstood by judges, it also contains significant unique advantages.

Class action waivers have wreaked havoc on consumer and employer rights, and until recent decisions that viewed them in light of rights protected by the NLRA, it looked as if there was no stopping them.[217] Class actions, which protect the rights of groups, have long been considered to be merely procedural rights, even though they are often the only means for many to receive meaningful relief. However, through the lens of collective labor law, the Seventh Circuit found that the right to a class action is a substantive right that cannot be abridged in the workplace. If it stands, this decision now protects workers who want to bring all manner of workplace actions, whether or not there are class action waivers in place.

If the NLRA can be used to strike down class action waivers in the employment context, workers should try to extend the law's protections to the myriad other areas where they are pushed into isolation in the workplace.

Already, there have been some very good free speech cases arising from workers' use of Facebook to complain about employment practices that affect them and their co-workers.[218] Crucially, a worker's social media advocacy must apply to an issue that affects more than just herself in order to be protected concerted activity. More crucially, a worker must know that she has recourse to the NLRB even if she is not organized into a union.

The NLRB attempted to enforce a rule that would have mandated all covered workplaces to post a sign about employees' rights under the labor act, alongside minimum wage and other relevant laws. That action was enjoined by conservative circuit court decisions, and the NLRB declined to appeal to the Supreme Court in January of 2014. The next Democratic-majority NLRB should revive the effort.

How to Restore This Right

Potentially, a more effective education campaign is within the labor movement's power. There are many Netroots-style digital organizers and social justice organizations skilled and creative in the use of social media. A few relatively small financial grants could fund a significant campaign of memes and popular education aimed at teaching young workers that there is power—and protection—in working in concert with your fellow workers.

The campaign of judicial activism that we advocate will require an exponential increase in the number of unfair labor practices filed at the NLRB. Unorganized workers at non-union firms experience hair-raising abuse on a daily basis. Availing themselves of the workers' law will open up interesting opportunities to expand all workers' rights.

Conclusion

From the beginning of our nation's history, the earliest union efforts were treated by conservative jurists as criminal conspiracies. They interfered with employers' property and contract rights and with Congress's responsibility to regulate interstate commerce. As detailed in University of Texas law professor William Forbath's *Law and the Shaping of the American Labor Movement*, unions spent the nineteenth and early twentieth century decrying "judge-made law" and seeking, essentially, to get the government and courts out of labor disputes.[219]

For a brief time this worked. The Norris-LaGuardia Act of 1932 sought to prevent the federal courts from enjoining or interfering in union protest activity, and many states passed similar laws to keep their courts and police out of the fray. The NLRA made it the official policy of the United States to encourage the practice of collective bargaining. The Act established a federal agency, the NLRB, that would certify the existence of a union at a workplace and sanction employers who refused to deal with a bona fide union.

Much of the thrust of midcentury labor law was to encourage a private system of jurisprudence: contract negotiations, arbitration, and the occasional industrial warfare of strikes, boycotts (and later, lockouts). Though unions point proudly at the legislative and regulatory successes they have achieved since the nineteenth century, the courts retain a vestigial bias against legislating and litigating our rights and benefits. The courts pretty quickly waved away legal job protections for striking workers, and they have granted employers wide "free speech" latitude to conduct campaigns of terror to break their employees' resolve to form unions and have removed large categories of workers from protection under the Act.

In 1984, labor law scholar James Gray Pope began calling attention to what he termed a "black hole" in First Amendment jurisprudence.[220] The courts had long provided different levels of protection to various types of speech, wherein political speech received the greatest protection, commercial speech received a medium level of protection, and obscene speech or "fighting words" received no protection. However, in this "hierarchy of First Amendment values"[221] (as the Supreme Court termed it), there existed a black hole, wherein speech that would normally receive intermediate protection because it is commercial or maximum protection because it is political "may be sucked into the black hole when spoken by labor unions or workers."[222]

The courts' interpretation of the Constitution has changed a great deal since 1984, when Pope first described the ladder straddling a black hole. The Commerce Clause of the Constitution, which serves as the grounding for the nation's labor law, has been diminished, and the First Amendment has been unevenly expanded for largely anti-regulatory purposes. However, the black hole still exists for labor.

Labor organizations and workers have generally not been treated kindly by the courts. However, there are certain fundamental rights that adhere to workers and the organizations they choose to represent them that should be challenged at the courts.

There remains some value connecting labor rights to the Commerce Clause. The "Findings and Policies" section of the 1935 National Labor Relations Act was written with this telling paragraph (emphasis added):

> The *inequality of bargaining power* between employees who do not possess full freedom of association or actual liberty of contract and employers who are organized in the corporate or other forms of ownership association substantially burdens and affects the flow of commerce, and *tends to aggravate recurrent business depressions, by depressing wage rates and the purchasing power of wage earners in industry* and by preventing the stabilization of competitive wage rates and working conditions within and between industries.

Today, there is a growing recognition that the massive and nearly unprecedented inequality in our country and the economic recessions that occur more frequently and hit with greater severity is a direct result of the decline of union membership. As a result, we see more courts willing to restore and defend workers' rights. This trend will obviously be blunted by at least four years of right-wing judicial appointments, but it is the long-haul trend that we must aim for.

Likewise, we see a lesson in the activist policymaking of the NLRB, under the direction of General Counsel Richard F. Griffin Jr. In recent years, the National Labor Relations Board has taken some actions to help better balance the unequal bargaining position of unions. For example, it has expanded the joint employer obligations of franchises, expanded organizing rights for graduate employees and temporary workers, curbed employers' unmitigated right to permanently replace strikers and expanded "make whole" remedies for illegally fired activists.

Most of these welcome decisions were swiftly reversed by Trump's NLRB. Republicans came into office with aggressive plans to upend the rules. Labor advocates should spend the next four years forming our NLRB agenda and demand that the next president move with great haste.

Part of the Labor's Bill of Rights agenda involves pressing the NLRB for more rule changes, and then raising constitutional arguments in court when the employers inevitably appeal. Obama's NLRB, of late, appeared very open to some of the changes we advocate. The next Democratic NLRB should be keenly aware of what a limited window of time for action it will have.

Other parts of Labor's Bill of Rights will necessarily require unions and workers breaking unjust labor laws. Such actions may be a matter of life or death for unions in the coming years. The NLRB is statutorily obligated to prosecute unions that violate the NLRA. It does not seem crazy to us that a future, sympathetic NLRB might note in court filings its legal obligations and take the position that the unions have raised some valid constitutional questions that merit judicial consideration.

None of this should be viewed as relying on the courts and the federal government to be the labor movement's savior.[223] It is more a matter of recognizing political moments and adjusting our strategies.

Aside from a consensus among Roosevelt's advisers that stronger unions could redistribute wealth and prevent economic depressions, the other major factor that contributed to the passage of the

1935 Wagner Act was, obviously, the massive and growing strike wave. Not much will change in the realm of labor rights and power absent a crisis.

Unions have been playing defense for so long, we tend to accept the rigged rules of the system as a given, as largely unchangeable. But a look at the body of labor law with fresh eyes reveals much of the worst of the restrictions on union activity to be plainly unconstitutional. There is a sound legal basis to challenge a number of unequal and unjust aspects of labor law that restrict workers' speech and activism as violations of workers' First Amendment rights to free speech and assembly, Thirteenth Amendment rights to be free from involuntary servitude, including employer-dictated terms of employment and unbalanced bargaining power, and the Fifth and Fourteenth Amendment rights of equal protection under the law to have the same freedoms of speech and economic pressure that corporations enjoy.

This is, obviously, a long-term strategy made longer-term by the inability to achieve more progressive judicial appointment making. And, like the strike wave that accompanied the passage of the original NLRA in 1935, change is not likely to occur absent a rising tide of protest.

The original Wagner Act was drafted and passed in a relatively brief amount of time in part because it reflected long-standing and consistent rights-based demands that unions had been advancing for decades prior to that point. It is time for unions to return to rights-based rhetoric and strategy. Labor needs a new Bill of Rights.

Notes

1. Ruth Milkman and Kim Voss, eds. *Rebuilding Labor: Organizing and Organizers in the New Union Movement* (Ithaca, NY: Cornell ILR Press, 2004), 29.

2. Julius B.Getman, *Restoring the Power of Unions: It Takes a Movement* (New Haven: Yale University Press, 2010).

3. With only a little bit of creative accounting. Steve Early notes in *The Civil Wars in U.S. Labor: Birth of a New Workers' Movement or Death Throes of the Old?* (Chicago: Haymarket Books, 2011) that the union counted 342,864 represented workers who did not pay dues to get the eye-popping number (288).

4. The proportion of private sector non-farm and non-construction wage and salary workers who were union members in 1955 was 39.2 percent. Union density, which measures the percentage of workers across the public and private sector who are covered by a union contract (but don't necessarily pay dues), wasn't measured until later. See William T. Dickens and Jonathan S. Leonard, "Accounting for the Decline in Union Membership, 1950–1980," *Industrial and Labor Relations Review* 38/3.

5. Joe Burns, *Reviving the Strike: How Working People Can Regain Power and Transform America* (New York: IG Publishing, 2011), 87..

6. Stanley Aronowitz, *The Death and Life of American Labor: Toward a New Workers' Movement* (New York: Verso, 2014).

7. Lewis was playing fast and loose with the word *president.* He, the president of the Mineworkers, wanted workers to join the union, and he stretched Section 7 as far as it would go as an implicit endorsement from U.S. President Roosevelt. See: Melvyn Dubofsky,*The State and Labor in Modern America*, (Chapel Hill, NC: University of North Carolina Press, 1994), 113.

8.   Dana Goldstein, "Democrats Are United on Teacher Strikes. But They're in a 'Gladiator Fight' Over Education," *New York Times*, January 18, 2019, https://www.nytimes.com/2019/01/18/us/la-teacher-strike-lausd.html; Dan Merica, Kyung Lah, and Alberto Moya, "Democrats see energy behind teachers strikes as a force in 2020," CNN. May 28, 2019, https://www.cnn.com/2019/05/28/politics/2020-democrats-teachers-unions/index.html; Kimberly Hefling, "2020 Democrats court teachers galvanized by protest movement," *Politico*. May 14, 2019. https://www.politico.com/states/california/story/2019/05/14/2020-democrats-court-teachers-galvanized-by-protest-movement-1014757.

9.   Dylan Matthews, " 'Unions for all': The new plan to save the American labor movement," *Vox*. September 2, 2019, https://www.vox.com/policy-and-politics/2019/9/2/20838782/unions-for-all-seiu-sectoral-bargaining-labor-unions.

10. Iian Killgren, "How Beto O'Rourke would help workers," *Politico*, August 22, 2019, https://www.politico.com/story/2019/08/22/beto-orourke-workers-1676332.

11. Dave Jamieson, "White House Contender Jay Inslee Rolls Out a Plan to Restore Unions, Boost Wages." *Huffington Post,* July 26, 2019, https://www.huffpost.com/entry/jay-inslee-union-wage-plan_n_5d39fe96e4b0419fd339f4ab.

12. For a fairly engaging account of this period, I recommend *Our Own Time: A History of American Labor and the Working Day* by David Roediger and Philip S. Foner (New York: Verso, 1989).

13. The fortunes of the Amalgamated Association of Iron and Steel Workers is documented by David Montgomery in his classic *The Fall of the House of Labor: The Workplace, the State, and American Labor Activism, 1865–1925* (New Haven: Yale University Press, 1988).

14. Charles J. Morris, *The Blue Eagle At Work: Reclaiming Democratic Rights in the American Workplace* (Ithaca, NY: Cornell University Press, 2005).

15. Philip Taft, *The AF of L from the Death of Gompers to the Merge.* (New York: Harper & Brothers, 1959), 98.

16. Melvyn Dubofsky and Warren Van Tyne, *John L. Lewis: A Biography* (New York: Quadrangle, 1977), 181–221.

17. Art Preis wrote a pretty comprehensive history of the CIO's organizing campaigns, and of how the AFL responded: *Labor's Giant Step: The First Twenty Years of the CIO: 193–55* (New York: Pathfinder, 1972).

18. How unions were forever changed by the War Labor Board experience is the subject of Nelson Lichtenstein's essential *Labor's War at Home: The CIO in World War II* (Cambridge: Cambridge University Press, 1982).

19. A note for pedants: Congress passed a labor law for railroad workers a few years before passing the NLRA in 1935. To this day those workers are covered by a slightly different labor board and body of labor law, although in the case of racial discrimination both sets of labor laws wound up adhering to the same principles of fair representation.

20. Herbert Hill, *Black Labor and the American Legal System: Race, Work, and the Law* (Madison: University of Wisconsin Press, 1985).

21. Sophia Z. Lee, *The Workplace Constitution: From the New Deal to the New Right* (Cambridge: Cambridge University Press, 2014).

22. Again, Sophia Z. Lee's *The Workplace Constitution: From the New Deal to the New Right* is an invaluable read on this subject.

23. Epigraph: Nelson Lichtenstein, *The Most Dangerous Man in Detroit: Walter Reuther and the Fate of American Labor* (New York: Basic Books, 1995), 149.

24. Ibid., 271–98.

25. Ibid., 229.

26. Ibid., 230.

27. Ibid., 245–55.

28. Nelson Lichtenstein, *Labor's War at Home: The CIO in World War II* (Cambridge: Cambridge University Press, 1982), 67–81.

29. Lichtenstein, *The Most Dangerous Man in Detroit,* 282.

30. James B. Atleson, *Values and Assumptions in American Labor Law* (Amherst: University of Massachusetts Press, 1983), 111–135.

31. Ibid., 123.

32. James B. Atleson, "The Circle of Boys Market: A Comment on Judicial Inventiveness," *Berkeley Journal of Employment & Labor Law* 7 (1985): 88, http://scholarship.law.berkeley.edu/cgi/viewcontent.cgi?article=1103&context=bjell.

33. Richard B.Freeman and Joel Rodgers. *What Workers Want* (Ithaca, NY: Cornell University Press, 1999), 154–55.

34. A trusteeship is a constitutional procedure in which a parent union can temporarily suspend the autonomy of a local in order to reorganize it. Traditionally, these have been reserved for cases of impropriety or corruption. During the era discussed in this chapter, trusteeships were also utilized to enforce mandates to commit resources to organizing.

35. Stephen Lerner, "An Immodest Proposal: Remodeling the House of Labor," *New Labor Forum,* July 2003, Vol.12, 9–30. http://qcpages.qc.cuny.edu/newlaborforum/old/html/12_2article9.html.

36. See http://democracyjournal.org/magazine/29/fortress-unionism/.

37. This earlier period and its influence on union thought is masterfully explored in William E. Forbath's *Law and the Shaping of the American Labor Movement* (Cambridge, MA: Harvard University Press, 1991).

38. James Gray Pope, "The Thirteenth Amendment Versus the Commerce Clause: Labor and the Shaping of American Constitutional Law, 1921–1957," *Columbia Law Review* 102/1 (January 2002): 14, https://www.jstor.org/stable/pdf/1123631.pdf?seq=1#page_scan_tab_contents.

39. Shaun Richman, "Could a New NLRB Case Limit Bosses' Best Anti-Union Tool, the Captive Audience Meeting?," *In These Times*, February 3, 2016, http://inthesetimes.com/working/entry/18820/captive-audience-meeting-nlrb-boss-union.

40. Labor Relations Institute, Inc., "Anti Union Campaign Tips—How Many Meetings?," http://lrionline.com/anti-union-campaign-tips-how-many/.

41. *Labor Board v. Mackay Radio & Telegraph Co.*, 304 U.S. 333 (1938), https://supreme.justia.com/cases/federal/us/304/333/case.html.

42. *NLRB v. Erie Resistor Corp.*, 373 U.S. 221, 53 LRRM 2121 (1963).

43. Getman, *The Supreme Court On Unions.*

44. Rosenbum, Jonathan D. *Copper Crucible: How the Arizona Miners' Strike of 1983 Recast Labor-Management Relations in America* (Ithaca, NY: Cornell ILR Press, 1998).

45. Shaun Richman, " When the Hell Did the NLRB Become More Activist Than Labor?," *In These Times*, July 12, 2016, http://inthesetimes.com/working/entry/19288/how_the_hell_did_the_nlrb_become_more_activist_than_labor.

46. *NLRB v. Erie Resistor Corp.* (1963).

47. Charles R. Morris, *The Blue Eagle at Work: Reclaiming Democratic Rights in the American Workplace* (Ithaca, NY: Cornell ILR Press, 2005).

48. "Debate: How Should Unions Deal with Free Riders?" *Labor Notes*, May 4, 2018. https://www.labornotes.org/exclusiverep.

49. Anne Zacharias-Walsh, *Our Unions, Our Selves: The Rise of Feminist Labor Unions in Japan* (Ithaca, NY: Cornell ILR Press, 2016).

50. A once-common phrase that was used to describe how some socialists responded to the rivalry of the Industrial Workers of the World and the traditional craft unions of the 1910s and 20s. As James P. Cannon described them in a 1955 essay: "The left-wing socialists were ardent sympathizers of the IWW, and quite a few of them were members. The same was true in large measure of the more militant trade unionists in the AFL. 'Two-card men' were fairly numerous—those who belonged to the AFL unions for bread and butter reasons and carried the 'red card of the IWW for the sake of principle" https://www.marxists.org/archive/cannon/works/1955/iww.htm.

51. Annual work stoppages involving 1,000 or more workers, 1947–2018, Bureau of Labor Statistics, https://www.bls.gov/web/wkstp/annual-listing.htm.

52. Bureau of Labor Statistics. Work Stoppages Summary, February 8, 2019, https://www.bls.gov/news.release/wkstp.nr0.htm.

53. Eric Dirnbach, "The FMCS Must Be Happy: The U.S. Private Sector Strike Rate Is Declining," *Medium*. August 15, 2018, https://medium.com/@ericdirnbach/the-fmcs-must-be-happy-the-u-s-private-sector-strike-rate-is-declining-4058e4b69ed5.

54. Eric Blanc, "The State of the Strike," *Jacobin*, March 4, 2019, https://www.jacobinmag.com/2018/03/west-virginia-strike-teachers-capitol-shutdown.

55. Jeremy Brecher, *Strike!* (Boston: South End Press, 1972).

56. This topic is well covered in David Roediger's *Seizing Freedom* (New York: Verso, 2015) as well as in pages 29–48 of Erik Loomis's *A History of America in Ten Strikes* (New York: New Press, 2018).

57. On both "the general strike of the slaves" and "revolutionary time," I cannot recommend Reodiger's recent *Seizing Freedom* more highly.

58. Brecher, Jeremy. *Strike!* (Boston: (Boston: South End Press, 1972), 1–25.

59. David Roediger and Philip S. Foner, *Our Own Time: A History of American Labor and the Working Day* (New York: Verso, 1989), 123–44.

60. David Montgomery, *The Fall of the House of Labor* (Cambridge: Cambridge University Press, 1987), 36–44.

61. Phulip S. Foner, *History of the Labor Movement in the United States,* vol. 2: *From the Founding of the American Federation of Labor to the Emergence of American Imperialism* (New York: International Publishers, 1955), 213.

62. Brecher, *Strike!*, 63–64.

63. Ibid., 64–66.

64. Stanley Buder, *Pullman: An Experiment in Industrial Order and Community Planning, 1880–1930* (Oxford: Oxford University Press, 1970), 147–67.

65. Nick Salvatore, *Eugene Debs: Citizen and Socialist* (Chicago: University of Illinois Press, 1982), 127–46.

66. Brecher, *Strike!*, 101–43.

67. Philip S. Foner, *History of the Labor Movement in the United States,* vol. 7: *Labor and World War I 191–1918* (New York: International Publishers, 1987), 174–76.

68. Brecher, *Strike!*, 103.

69. Philip S. Foner, *History of the Labor Movement in the United States,* vol. 8: *Postwar Struggles 1918–1920* (New York: International Publishers, 1988), 63–79.

70. Ibid., 92–101.

71. James R. Barrett, *William Z. Foster and the Tragedy of American Radicalism* (Chicago: University of Illinois Press, 1999), 71–82.

72. Brecher, *Strike!*, 121–22.

73. Barrett, *William Z. Foster and the Tragedy of American Radicalism*, 83–101.

74. Danielson, Leilah. *American Gandhi: A. J. Muste and the History of Radicalism in the Twentieth Century* (Philadelphia: University of Pennsylvania Press, 2014), 97–125.

75. Barrett, *William Z. Foster and the Tragedy of American Radicalism*, 118–47.

76. Ahmed White provides a useful example of how vital old TUEL cadre were during the darkest hours of the CIO's steel organizing campaign in *The Last Great Strike: Little Steel, the CIO and the Struggle for Labor Rights in New Deal America* (Berkeley: University of California Press, 2014), 85–116.

77. Dubofsky, Melvyn. *The State and Labor in Modern America* (Chapel Hill: University of North Carolina Press, 1994), 112–13.

78. Preis, Art. *Labor's Giant Step: Twenty Years of the CIO* (New York: Pathfinder Press, 1972), 19–24.

79. Brecher, *Strike!*, 150–58.

80. Preis, *Labor's Giant Step: Twenty Years of the CIO*, 24–31.

81. Erik Loomis, *A History of America in Ten Strikes* (New York: New Press, 2018), 121–29.

82. Dana Frank, *Women Strikers Occupy Chain Store, Win Big: The 1937 Woolworth's Sit-Down* (Chicago: Haymarket Books, 2012).

83. Lichtenstein, *The Most Dangerous Man in Detroit: Walter Reuther and the Fate of American Labor*, 220–47.

84. Brecher, *Strike!*, 228.

85. Bureau of Labor Statistics, "Annual work stoppages involving 1,000 or more workers, 1947–2018," https://www.bls.gov/web/wkstp/annual-listing.htm.

86. Joshua B. Freeman, *Working-Class New York* (New York: New Press, 2000), 201–14.

87. David Selden, *The Teacher Rebellion* (Washington, DC: Howard University Press, 1985), 23–64.

88. Jon Shelton, *Teacher Strike! Public Education and the Making of a New American Political Order* (Chicago: University of Illinois Press, 2017), 26–55.

89. Brecher, *Strike!*, 271–74.

90. Ibid., 279–81.

91. Erik Loomis, *A History of America in Ten Strikes* (New York: New Press, 2018), 168–74.

92. Robert M Schwartz, "One-Day Strikes: A Word to the Wise," *Labor Notes*. October 2, 2013, https://www.labornotes.org/2013/10/one-day-strikes-word-wise.

93. Lichtenstein, *The Most Dangerous Man in Detroit: Walter Reuther and the Fate of American Labor,* 136–38.

94. *Labor Board v. Fansteel Metallurgical Corp.,* 306 U.S. 240 (1939).

95. David Roediger and Philip S. Foner, *Our Own Time: A History of American Labor and the Working Day.* (New York: Verso, 1989), 7.

96. Joe Burns, *Reviving the Strike: How Working People Can Regain Power and Transform America* (New York: IG Publishers, 2011), 20.

97. Joe Burns, *Strike Back: Using the Militant Tactics of Labor's Past to Reignite Public Sector Unionism Today.* (New York: IG Publishers, 2014).

98. Bill Fletcher Jr. and Shaun Richman, "What the Revival of Socialism in America Means for the Labor Movement," *In These Times*, October 9, 2017, https://inthesetimes.com/working/entry/20587/labor-movement-workers-socialism-united-states.

99. Stanley Aronowitz, *The Death and Life of American Labor: Toward a New Workers' Movement* (New York: Verso, 2014), 100–102.

100. Vincent, "Amazon employees protest sale of facial recognition software to police," *The Verge*. June 22, 2018. https://www.theverge.com/2018/6/22/17492106/amazon-ice-facial-recognition-internal-letter-protest.

101. Noah Feldman, "The Google Walkout Is a New Kind of Worker Activism," *Bloomberg*, November 2, 2018, https://www.bloomberg.com/opinion/articles/2018-11-02/google-walkout-isn-t-a-traditional-union-workers-strike.

102. Daisuke Wakabayashi, "Google Ends Forced Arbitration for All Employee Disputes," *New York Times*, February 21, 2019, https://www.nytimes.com/2019/02/21/technology/google-forced-arbitration.html.

103. Daisuke Wakabayashi, "Google's Shadow Work Force: Temps Who Outnumber Full-Time Employees," *New York Times*, May 28, 2019, https://www.nytimes.com/2019/05/28/technology/google-temp-workers.html.

104. Melvyn Dubofsky, *We Shall Be All: A History of the Industrial Workers of the World*, abridged ed. (Chicago: University of Illinois Press, 2000), 92.

105. Martin Sprouse, *Sabotage in the American Workplace: Anecdotes of Dissatisfaction, Mischief and Revenge* (San Francisco, CA: Pressure Drop Press, 1992), 123.

106. Ibid., 90.

107. Ibid., 54.

108. Ibid., 7.

109. Samantha Winslow, "Marriott Hotel Strikers Set a New Industry Standard," *Labor Notes*, December 20, 2018. https://labornotes. org/2018/12/marriott-hotel-strikers-set-new-industry-standard.

110. American Federation of Teachers, "Joining Voices: Inclusive Strategies for Labor's Renewal," submitted to the AFL-CIO in December 2004, https://archive.org/details/JoiningVoices.

111. Richard B. Freeman, "Do Workers Still Want Unions? More Than Ever," Economic Policy Institute, May 16, 2007, https://www.epi.org/publication/bp182/.

112. For how it happened in our universe, see Melvyn Dubofsky and Warren Van Tine, *John L. Lewis: A Biography* (New York: Quadrangle, 1977), 272–77.

113. Again, Ahmed White's history of the CIO's steel organizing campaign, *The Last Great Strike,* is essential on this topic.

114. Elizabeth Anderson, *Private Government: How Employers Rule Our Lives (and Why We Don't Talk about it)* (Princeton: Princeton University Press, 2017), 35.

115. William E. Forbath, *Law and the Shaping of the American Labor Movement* (Cambridge, MA: Harvard University Press, 1989), 85–88.

116. Loomis, *A History of America in Ten Strikes,* 123.

117. Lane Windham, *Knocking on Labor's Door: Union Organizing in the 1970's and the Roots of a New Economic Divide* (Chapel Hill, NC: University of North Carolina Press, 2017).

118. Shaun Richman, "Ideology vs. 'Rule or Ruin' Politics in the Downfall of the Communists in the NYC Hotel and Restaurant Employees Union, 1934–1952. *American Communist History* (2012), 11. 10.1080/14743892.2012.750083.

119. David Trainor, "Not Too Big, Not Too Small—Michaels Is Just Right," *Forbes*, August 7, 2018, https://www.forbes.com/sites/greatspecula tions/2018/08/07/not-too-big-not-too-small-michaels-is-just-right/#7edc5b7e26ca.

120. *Burwell v. Hobby Lobby*, 573 U.S. (2014).

121. Bureau of Labor Statistics, "Employee Tenure Summary," Economic News Release, September 20, 2018, https://www.bls.gov/news.release/tenure.nr0.htm.

122. This federally chartered corporation was designed by the Retirement Income Security Act of 1974 to support and encourage defined benefit pensions in the private sector. Of late, employers have used its backstop provision to dump their pension obligations altogether. See Lydia DePillis, "It just became easier for employers to dump retirees' pensions," *CNN Business*, March 20, 2019, https://www.cnn.com/2019/03/20/economy/lump-sum-pensions-retirement/index.html.

123. David Webber, *The Rise of the Working Class Shareholder* (Cambridge, MA: Harvard University Press, 2018).

124. Ibid., 30–48.

125. Ibid., 248–49.

126. Dubovsky and Van Tine, *John L. Lewis: A Biography,* 220–21.

127. James A. Gross has a pretty detailed history of this game in *Rights Not Interests: Resolving Value Clashes Under the National Labor Relations Act* (Ithaca, NY: Cornell University Press, 2017).

128. James Gray Pope, "The Thirteenth Amendment versus the Commerce Clause: Labor and the Shaping of American Constitutional Law, 1921– 1957," *Columbia Law Review* 102/1 (January 2002): 14, https://www. jstor.org/stable/pdf/1123631.pdf?seq=1#page_scan_tab_contents.

129. Sophie Quinton, "Why Janitors Get Noncompete Agreements, Too," *Pew Charitable Trusts,* May 17, 2017. https://www.pewtrusts.org/en/ research-and-analysis/blogs/stateline/2017/05/17/why-janitors-get-noncompete-agreements-too.

130. Moishe Z. Marvit, "Stop Calling It an Arbitration Agreement— Employers Are Forcing Workers to Give Up Their Rights," *In These Times,* May 23, 2018, http://inthesetimes.com/working/entry/21161/ arbitration-agreeement-supreme-court-neil-gorsuch-epic-systems-workers.

131. Nelson Lichtenstein, *Labor's War at Home: The CIO in World War II* (Cambridge: Cambridge University Press, 1982), 118.

132. Stanley Aronowitz, *From the Ashes of the Old: American Labor and America's Future* (New York: Houghton Mifflin, 1998), 172.

133. *Leedom v. Kyne,* 358 U.S. 184 (1958).

134. Frank Swoboda, "Labor Wants to End FedEx's Railway Act Protection," *Washington Post,* October 2, 1996, https://www. washingtonpost.com/archive/business/1996/10/02/labor-wants-to-end-fedexs-railway-act-protection/6b55a503-8df1-449b-8522-c9ab124471e1/?noredirect=on&utm_term=.de5cf39d967c.

135. Clifford Krauss, "House Passes Bill to Ban Replacement of Strikers," *New York Times,* June 16, 1993, https://www.nytimes.com/1993/06/16/ us/house-passes-bill-to-ban-replacement-of-strikers.html.

136. César Chávez Workplace Fairness Act, H.R. 5, 103rd Congress (1993– 1994), https://www.congress.gov/bill/103rd-congress/house-bill/5.

137. For the umpteenth time, go read James B. Atleson's *Values and Assumptions in American Labor Law* (Amherst, MA: University of Massachusetts Press, 1983); or Julius B. Getman's *The Supreme Court on Labor: Why Labor Law is Failing American Workers* (Ithaca, NY: Cornell ILR Press, 2016).

138. Sheldon Friedman and Richard W. Hurd, Rudolph A. Oswald, Ronald

L. Seeber. *Restoring the Promise of American Labor Law* (Ithaca, NY: Cornell ILR Press, 1994), 258–59.

139. *NLRB v. Babcock & Wilcox Co.,* 351 U.S. 105 (1956).

140. *Lechmere, Inc. v. NLRB,* 502 U.S. 527 (1992).

141. *Labor Board v. Electrical Workers,* 346 U.S. 464 (1953).

142. *NLRB v. Yeshiva Univ.,* 444 U.S. 672 (1980).

143. *Leedom v. Kyne,* 358 U.S. 184 (1958).

144. Michael O'Brien, "Obama in 2007: 'I'll walk on that picket line' if bargaining rights threatened," *The Hill,* February 25, 2011, https://thehill.com/blogs/blog-briefing-room/news/146091-obama-in-2007-ill-walk-on-that-picket-line-if-bargaining-rights-threatened.

145. Dubovsky and Van Tine, *John L. Lewis: A Biography,* 289.

146. Moshe Marvit, "Labor Opponents Already Have the Next 'Friedrichs' SCOTUS Case Ready to Go Under Trump," *In These Times,* January 4, 2017, http://inthesetimes.com/working/entry/19776/will_trumps_supreme_court_reverse_fair_share_fees_unions_foes_hope_so.

147. "House Resolution 785," 115th U.S. Congress, 2017, https://www.congress.gov/bill/115th-congress/house-bill/785.

148. U.S. Department of Labor, Bureau of Labor Statistics, "Union Members Survey," January 26, 2017, http://www.bls.gov/news.release/union2.nr0.htm.

149. Jake Rosenfield, *What Unions No Longer Do* (Cambridge, MA: Harvard University Press, 2014).

150. Pope, "The Thirteenth Amendment versus the Commerce Clause," 14.

151. *Labor Board v. Electrical Workers* 346 U.S. 464 (1953); see also James B. Atleson, *Values and Assumptions in American Labor Law* (Amherst: University of Massachusetts Press, 1983), 84–85.

152. Atleson, *Values and Assumptions in American Labor Law,* 84–85.

153. Gil A. Abramson and Emily J. Glendinning, "When Employee Disloyalty Makes Otherwise Protected Conduct Unprotected: The NLRB's Decisions Under Jefferson Standard Get Mixed Reception in Appellate Courts," American Bar, 2009, http://apps.americanbar.org/labor/dlcomm/mw/papers/2009/papers/mw-d.pdf.

154. Recently, the courts' tilt in favor of the rights of employers was in sharp relief when a Texas federal judge placed a nationwide injunction blocking the Department of Labor's new rule that would require employers and union-busters to register their activities so that workers would know who was speaking to them. The judge based his injunction on the First Amendment rights of the employers and union-busters. In the course of a ninety-page order, he did not mention once the First Amendment rights of workers, those this rule was intended to protect. See Moshe Marvit, "Judge's Ruling Re-Opens a Major Loophole that Allows Union

Busters to Remain in the Shadows," *In These Times*, July 5, 2016, http://inthesetimes.com/working/entry/19263/new_ruling_re_opens_a_major_loophole_that_allows_union_busters_to_remain_in.

155. Kate Bronfenbrenner, "No Holds Barred: The Intensification of Employer Opposition to Organizing," Economic Policy Institute, Briefing Paper #235, May 20, 2009, http://www.epi.org/publication/bp235/.

156. Ibid.

157. Labor Relations Institute, Inc., "Anti Union Campaign Tips—How Many Meetings?," http://lrionline.com/anti-union-campaign-tips-how-many/.

158. To do so, unions that have recently lost a certification election in which employers utilized captive audience meetings should file to have the results of those elections overturned. Unlike Morris and Secunda's rulemaking petition, the NLRB would have to respond to the unions' request. The NLRB has, in recent years, shown a willingness to revert to old rules that better protect workers' rights. (This kind of appeal is more likely to be successful under a Democratic NLRB, but the arguments should be raised now.)

   This major area will proceed to the courts, no matter which way the NLRB rules. Challenging the one-sided approach to captive audience speeches will serve to highlight the unfairness that workers face when trying to organize a union. Too few know the struggles that workers face when they attempt to exercise their labor rights. Win or lose in individual court cases, these sorts of cases will have the salutary effect of showing the world the lopsided rules that apply to workers.

159. Lois K. Solomon, "Tomato Pickers Persuade Big Food Companies to Sign on to Human-Rights Movement," *Sun-Sentinel*, December 31, 2015, http://www.sun-sentinel.com/news/florida/fl-tomato-pickers-20151231-story.html.

160. Ibid.

161. Mark Vorpahl, "What Can We Learn from 25 Years of Jobs with Justice?," *Labor Notes*, September 3, 2013, http://www.labornotes.org/blogs/2013/09/what-can-we-learn-25-years-jobs-justice.

162. Jean-Christian Vinel, *The Employee: A Political History* (Philadelphia: University of Pennsylvania Press, 2013), 53.

163. Pope, "The Thirteenth Amendment versus the Commerce Clause."

164. Julius G. Getman, *The Supreme Court on Unions: Why Labor Law Is Failing American Workers* (Ithaca, NY: Cornell University Press, 2016), 89–109.

165. Ibid., 97.

166. Thomas J. Lueck, "Transit Leader Marches to Jail to Start Serving

10-Day Term," *New York Times*, April 25, 2006, http://www.nytimes.com/2006/04/25/nyregion/25union.html.

167. Pope, "The Thirteenth Amendment versus the Commerce Clause," 14.

168. Lori Higgins, "Detroit Union: No need for teachers to return to school Tuesday," *Detroit Free Press*, May 3, 2016.

169. *Labor Board v. Mackay Radio & Telegraph Co.*, 304 U.S. 333 (1938), https://supreme.justia.com/cases/federal/us/304/333/case.html.

170. Getman, *The Supreme Court on Unions*, 65.

171. Jonathan D. Rosenblum, *Copper Crucible: How the Arizona Miners' Strike of 1983 Recast Labor-Management Relations in America* (Ithaca, NY: Cornell University Press, 1998).

172. James B. Atleson, "The Circle of Boys Market: A Comment on Judicial Inventiveness," *Berkeley Journal of Employment & Labor Law* 7 (1985), http://scholarship.law.berkeley.edu/cgi/viewcontent.cgi?article=1103&context=bjell, 88.

173. Ibid.

174. Author's phone interview with Stephen Lerner, August 16, 2016.

175. See, for example, Benjamin I. Sachs, "Employment Law as Labor Law," *Cardozo Law Review* 29 (2008), 2685, 2687.

176. "Comprehensive campaign is a term used to define a union pressure tactic using a broad variety of strategies designed to impact the particular employer's business, including its dealings with customers, suppliers, shareholders, lenders and regulatory agencies and its standing with the public." Douglas E. Ray, William R. Corbett, and Christopher David Ruiz Cameron, *Labor-Management Relations: Strikes, Lockouts and Boycotts* (Eagan, MN: Clark Boardman Callaghan, 2016).

177. Adam Liptak, "A Corporate View of Mafia Tactics: Protesting, Lobbying and Citing Upton Sinclair," *New York Times*, February 8, 2008, http://www.nytimes.com/2008/02/05/us/05bar.html.

178. Benjamin Levin, "Criminal Labor Law," *Berkeley Journal of Employment & Labor Law* 37 (2016): 43.

179. *Beck v. Prupis*, 529 U.S. 494, 496, 120 S. Ct. 1608, 1611 (2000).

180. James J. Brudney, "Collateral Conflict: Employer Claims of Rico Extortion Against Union Comprehensive Campaigns," *Southern California Law Review* 83 (2010), 731, 756.

181. Levin, "Criminal Labor Law," 43, 70.

182. See, for example, George W. Pring and Penelope Canan, *SLAPPS: Getting Sued for Speaking Out* (Philadelphia: Temple University Press, 1996); George W. Pring and Penelope Canan, "Striking Back at the Dreaded SLAPP," *National Law Journal* 15 (October 12, 1992): 13; Penelope Canan et al., "Using Law Ideologically: The Conflict Between Economic and Political Liberty," *Journal of Law and Politics* 8 (Spring 1992): 539;

Penelope Canan et al., "The Chilling Risk of SLAPPs: Legal Risk and Attitudes Toward Political Involvement," *Research in Politics and Society* 6 (1992); Penelope Canan et al., "Political Claims, Legal Derailment, and the Context of Disputes," *Law and Society Review* 24 (1990):923; George W. Pring, "SLAPPs: Strategic Lawsuits Against Public Participation," *Pace Environmental Law Review* 7 (1989): 3; Penelope Canan, "The SLAPP from a Sociological Perspective," *Pace Environmental Law Review* 7 (1989): 23; Penelope Canan and George W. Pring, "Strategic Lawsuits Against Public Participation," *Columbia Journal of Law and Social Problems* 35 (1988): 506; Penelope Canan and George W. Pring, "Studying Strategic Lawsuits Against Public Participation: Mixing Quantitative and Qualitative Approaches," *Law and Society Review* 22 (1988): 385; George W. Pring, "Intimidation Suits Against Citizens: A Risk for Public-Policy Advocates," *National Law Journal* 7 (July 22, 1985): 16.

183. In one article, Pring and Canan present a non-comprehensive list of the types of activities that are resulting in SLAPP suits:
    - Circulating a petition for signatures;
    - Voicing criticism at a school board meeting;
    - Testifying at a zoning hearing against a new real estate development;
    - Sending a letter to public officials;
    - Reporting police misconduct;
    - Filing a complaint with a government consumer, civil rights, or labor relations office;
    - Reporting violations of law to health authorities;
    - Lobbying for reform legislation;
    - Filing administrative agency appeals;
    - Engaging in peaceful, legal demonstrations;
    - Being a named party in a non-monetary, public-interest lawsuit; and
    - Just going to a public meeting and signing the attendance sheet.

    George W. Pring and Penelope Canan, "Strategic Lawsuits against Public Participation: ('Slapps'): An Introduction for Bench, Bar and Bystanders," *Bridgeport Law Review* 12 (1992): 937, 938.

184. Nicole Hallett, "From the Picket Line to the Courtroom: A Labor Organizing Privilege to Protect Workers," *N.Y.U. Review of Law & Societal Change* 39 (2015): 475, 490.

185. Ibid., 481.

186. Ibid., 482.

187. Ibid., 494.

188. Edward J. Imwinkelried, *The New Wigmore: A Treatise on Evidence* §3.2.3 (New York: Aspen Publishers, 2017).

189. See, for example, *City of Newburgh v. Newman*, 421 N.Y.S.2d 673 (App. Div. 1979); *Seelig v. Shepherd*, 578 N.Y.S.2d 965 (Sup. Ct. 1991); *Peterson v. State*, 280 P.3d 559 (Alaska 2012). See also Michael D. Moberly, "Extending A Qualified Evidentiary Privilege to Confidential Communications between Employees and Their Union Representatives," *Nevada Law Journal* 5 (2005): 508.

190. Hallett, "From the Picket Line to the Courtroom," 480.

191. 29 U.S.C. §§157–158; see also *Local Joint Executive Bd. of Las Vegas v. NLRB*, 515 F.3d 942, 944 (9th Cir. 2008).

192. Kristina Moore, "Nominee Analysis: Judge Diane Wood," *SCOTUSblog*, May 20, 2009. http://www.scotusblog.com/2009/05/nominee-analysis-judge-diane-wood/.

193. The argument was first articulated in the unions' state court appeal in an amicus brief by Indiana University Law Professor Kenneth Dau-Schmidt, who pointed out that American labor law is built upon a principle of exclusive representation, and since the NLRB does not currently confer on minority unions bargaining rights, unions must seek a certified majority of workers. Once they do, Section 9(a) of the Act requires that the union "fairly represent" all members of the bargaining unit, without regard to their membership. This duty of fair representation essentially means that the union must represent all workers equally and spend equivalent resources on all members. Dau-Schmidt argued that federal labor law explicitly "allows unions to negotiate union security agreements to recoup the costs of the representation services they are required to provide both members and nonmembers." Without allowing these union security agreements, unions are left without a means to fund their representational activities. And any law that prohibits unions from negotiating such agreements violates the Indiana constitution.

194. *Sweeney v. Pence*, 767 F.3d 654, 671 (7th Cir. 2014) (J. Wood dissenting).

195. National Labor Relations Act, *29 U.S.C. § 164(b)*.

196. *Sweeney v. Pence*, 767 F.3d, at 683.

197. Ibid.

198. *IUOE Local 370 v. Wasden*, WL 6211272 (D. ID, 2016).

199. Steven Greenhouse, "Honeywell workers say lockout aims to destroy union: 'It's corporate greed,' " *The Guardian*, October 4, 2016, https://www.theguardian.com/us-news/2016/oct/04/honeywell-union-lockout-united-auto-workers.

200. See, for example, *General Portland*, 283 NLRB 826 (1987); and *Bali Blinds Midwest*, 292 NLRB 243 (1988).

201. National Labor Relations Act, 29 U.S.C. §157.

202. See, for example, "Right to strike preserved," 29 U.S.C. §163.

203. Sophia Z. Lee, *The Workplace Constitution: From the New Deal to the New Right* (Cambridge: Cambridge University Press, 2014).

204. Moshe Marvit, "Is It Time for the Courts to End Labor Lockouts?," *The Century Foundation*, June 30, 2016, https://tcf.org/content/report/time-courts-end-labor-lockouts/.

205. Liz Ryan, "My Performance Review Was Outstanding—and Then I Got Fired," *Forbes*, June 7, 2016, http://www.forbes.com/sites/lizryan/2016/06/07/my-performance-review-was-outstanding-and-then-i-got-fired/#3acf64bc746a.

206. Organize GA, "XPO Calls Police on Union Organizers," *Soundcloud,* 2016, https://soundcloud.com/organizega.

207. Dave Jamieson, "This Is What It's Like to Sit Through an Anti-Union Meeting At Work," *Huffington Post,* September 3, 2014, http://www.huffingtonpost.com/2014/09/03/captive-audience-meetings-anti-union_n_5754330.html.

208. "The Captive Audience Meeting," IBEW District 4, https://wcb.archive.org/web/20141229215156/http://www.ibew.org/4thdistrict/captive_audience_meeting.htm.

209. Kate Bronfenbrenner, "No Holds Barred: The Intensification of Employer Opposition to Organizing," Economic Policy Institute, 2009.

210. Marvit, "Judge's Ruling Re-Opens a Major Loophole that Allows Union Busters to Remain in the Shadows."

211. *Fiberboard Paper Products vs. NLRB*, 379 U.S. 203 (1964).

212. Richard B. Freeman and Joel Rodgers, *What Workers Want* (Ithaca, NY: Cornell University Press, 1999), 154–55.

213. Atleson, *Values and Assumptions in American Labor Law,* 123.

214. Ibid., 119.

215. "*Lewis v. Epic Systems Corp.*: Seventh Circuit Invalidates Action Waivers in Employment Arbitration Agreements," *Harvard Law Review* 1032 (2017): 130, https://harvardlawreview.org/2017/01/lewis-v-epic-systems-corp/.

216. "D. R. Inc. and Michael Cuda," 357 NLRB No. 184 (2012).

217. Jessica Silver-Greenberg and Robert Gebeloff, "Arbitration Everywhere, Stacking the Deck of Justice," *New York Times,* October 31, 2015, https://www.nytimes.com/2015/11/01/business/dealbook/arbitration-everywhere-stacking-the-deck-of-justice.html.

218. Adriana Gardella, "Here's Why Employees Can Trash Their Bosses on Social Media," *Forbes*, May 21, 2015, http://www.forbes.com/sites/adrianagardella/2015/05/21/can-your-employees-trash-you-on-social-media/#5e43b78536b6.

219. William Forbath, *Law and the Shaping of the American Labor Movement* (Cambridge, MA: Harvard University Press, 1991).

220. James G. Pope, "The Three-Systems Ladder of First Amendment Values: Two Rungs and a Black Hole," *Hastings Constitutional Law Quarterly* 11 (1984): 189.

221. *Carey v. Brown*, 447 U.S. 455, 467 (1980).

222. Pope, "The Three-Systems Ladder," 196–97.

223. Labor has a progressive lawyering tradition that needs to be reinvigorated. We are reminded of the story of the UE (United Electrical Workers) labor lawyer Arthur Kinoy, who in 1948 found himself representing a union that faced intense redbaiting by Congress. It became so intense that Congressman Fred Hartley's subcommittee would travel around the country and come to cities and towns where UE had scheduled a union vote in order to hold anti-communist hearings and subpoena union leaders. UE was constantly on the defensive, harassed by the full weight of the House of Representatives, the company, and the media, which would run salacious stories about alleged communists in the union. In response, Kinoy and others at UE decided to sue the House Subcommittee and companies on behalf of the union and workers, alleging that they had conspired to violate the fundamental rights of working people to form unions and elect leadership of their own choosing. They resurrected a civil rights law passed after the Civil War to get them into federal court. Although the case was swiftly dismissed, it provided the workers a chance to take the offensive and to ground their arguments in fundamental rights. Kinoy wrote that "at certain moments, bringing a lawsuit can be a form of political expression for people in struggle." Labor's argument was not just a moral victory, but it helped to lay the groundwork for the resurrection of the Civil Rights Act of 1868, which the Supreme Court validated fifteen years later. This law has now become the means that all persons can sue the government for violations of their civil rights, from police brutality to unlawful firing in public employment. Without these early crazy lawsuits, the Constitution would still be an enumerated list of rights without remedies. The quote from Kinoy is from his autobiography, *Rights on Trial: The Odyssey of a People's Lawyer* (Cambridge, MA: Harvard University Press, 1983).

Index